PROGRESS COMPROMISED

LOUISIANA STATE UNIVERSITY PRESS
BATON ROUGE

PROGRES

COMPROMISED

Social Movements and the Individual
in African American Postmodern Fiction

JOHN L. GLENN

Published by Louisiana State University Press
Copyright © 2018 by Louisiana State University Press
All rights reserved
Manufactured in the United States of America
First printing

DESIGNER: Michelle A. Neustrom
TYPEFACES: Whitman, text; Gotham, display
PRINTER AND BINDER: Sheridan Books, Inc.

LIBRARY OF CONGRESS CATALOGING-IN-PUBLICATION DATA
Names: Glenn, John, 1981– author.
Title: Progress compromised : social movements and the individual in African
    American postmodern fiction / John L. Glenn.
Description: Baton Rouge : Louisiana State University Press, 2019. | Includes
    bibliographical references and index.
Identifiers: LCCN 2018017801 | ISBN 978-0-8071-6992-6 (cloth : alk. paper) |
    ISBN 978-0-8071-6994-0 (pdf) | ISBN 978-0-8071-6993-3 (epub)
Subjects: LCSH: American fiction—African American authors—History and
    criticism. | American fiction—20th century—History and criticism. |
    African Americans in literature. | Race discrimination in literature.
Classification: LCC PS374.N4 G496 2019 | DDC 813.009/896073—dc23
LC record available at https.//lccn.loc gov/2018017801

To my parents,
from whom I continue to glean an insatiable work ethic.

CONTENTS

ACKNOWLEDGMENTS

Even if I had documented every single encounter that inspired me throughout the development of this book, I would still find this section lacking. Nonetheless, I want to begin by thanking my earliest academic mentors. Thank you to Prof. Melvin Nevett, who made literature something dynamic and enjoyable in undergrad; to Prof. Anthonia Adadevoh for immersing me in the humanities and cultural studies; to Prof. Constance Pedoto, who challenged my writing and encouraged me to take it on the road to my first academic conference at Florida State University in 2001; to Dr. Ellen Wright-Vance and Dr. Erin Mullally, whose classes opened my eyes to the rigors of critical reading; and to Prof. Paul Mahaffey, who taught African American literature in a way that is still unfolding for me years later.

I also want to express my gratitude to those who provided feedback on this project and helped me understand the potential in writing about African American literature and postmodernism. Prof. Mark Reid, Prof. Faye Harrison, Prof. Debra Walker King, and Prof. Tace Hedrick brought indispensable intellect and experience in their readings of this manuscript in its early stages. I'm very grateful to Mark because at the time he served as an example of what a long and distinguished career in this field could look like. Several times, Mark not only demonstrated the hospitality of a seasoned academic but also of a good friend, which was a welcome reprieve from the politics of graduate school. I recall similar collegiality with Tace, whose independent-study sessions clarified for me the big picture surrounding textual analysis and critical theory. I also want to thank my University of Florida BGSO and BOE colleagues.

Over the years, there have been discussions with friends, students, critics, and other guiding lights who have paved the way for the completion of this book; namely, Dr. Sean Madison, Dr. Larry Johnson, Prof. Alex Alessandri, Dr. Brittany Roberts, Prof. Rudy Jean-Bart, and many others in the English, ESL, and Journalism Department at Broward College, South Campus. I especially appreciate my current colleagues at Atlanta Metropolitan State College, with whom I have discussed my research on black postmodern cultural politics and social movements: Dr. Stephanie Ricks, Prof. Shawn Mitchell, and Prof. LaShelle Turner-Gaston. I also extend special thanks to James Long and the other editors and staff at Louisiana State University Press for their patience, for approving this project, and for shepherding it to completion.

I thank my intelligent and discerning family for holding me accountable to my academic efforts through insightful questions, blunt critiques, and turns-of-phrases, which require one's full wits. God in his wisdom created our rousing bunch, and I thank Him that the Holy Spirit leads us down paths that guide us back to one another. I send love and appreciation to my father and mother, Jimmy and Mary Glenn; to my siblings, Jimmy, Rena, Ronnie, David, and Christina; and to my nieces and nephews, Alicia, Jordan, Anjel, Mike, Matthew, Faith, Lael, and their respective little ones. I could not have endured the many revisions of this project without drawing also on the love and strength of cousins, aunts, uncles, friends, and family. I extend my gratitude to my late Aunt Dorothy (and fondly recall her encouragement), and to Aunt Lorraine, Aunt Joann, and Ms. McCain who saw the best in me and spoke great things into being.

My beloved wife, Rachel, in her boundless intelligence, helped round out this project by reading it and recommending I tweak key components. Rachel made this project her own, bearing my academic burdens in addition to her own professional responsibilities. And completing this project in a timely manner would not have been possible without her dedication. My amazing daughter, Audrey, opened her heart to me throughout this endeavor with a broad smile that both energized and helped sustain my intellectual labor. My in-laws, Paul and Chantale André, whose love and support remains ironclad, and Patricia and Timi Fadiran—whose kindness, sense of humor, and poise speak volumes—are exemplars of diligence and commitment. I say thank you for allowing me to reflect your light. This work belongs to us all.

PROGRESS COMPROMISED

INTRODUCTION

Toni Cade Bambara's *The Salt Eaters* is a novel about politics, cultural tradition, and healing. In it, Bambara lays out alternatives to familiar social norms, and these alternatives, largely spiritual and social, play out in the fictional southern town of Claybourne. Throughout the novel, Velma Henry—a mother, civil rights activist, and employee at Transchemical (an infamous chemical plant outside the town)—seeks wholeness. Following a failed suicide attempt, Velma finds herself listless and psychologically wounded. When the novel opens, we see a local healer by the name of Minnie Ransom guiding her through a kind of holistic restoration. In one flashback, Velma participates in a protest march that leaves her sullied by a frenzied crowd and vexed by one of the venal organizers. At the end of the march, a charismatic civil rights leader pulls up in a limo: "He looked a bit like King, had a delivery similar to Malcolm's, dressed like Stokely, had glasses like Rap, but she'd never heard him say anything useful or offensive" (35). This experience leads Velma to reject the insulated male leadership of Claybourne's activist community (the Brotherhood) and to encourage the women's counterpart, Women for Action, to branch off and go their separate way. Velma's actions represent an ideological struggle, in that she resists the hemmed-in nature of group politics and vies for agency away from the confines of patriarchal interests.

Tensions surrounding the Transchemical Company are also part of Velma's predicament, as some believe the plant threatens to destroy the town with radioactive waste or to contaminate the local infirmary. However, Transchemical has provided employment opportunities to generations of black workers and—despite its suspect practices and the fact that some movement activists are "collecting information about conditions at the plant" (71)—Velma works there as a computer programmer. It appears that her inaction against the company makes her complicit in a system that uses its foothold on black employment to obscure environmental and political mischief. Still, Velma's main concern in the midst of her recovery is that she regain control of a splintering reality: "Something crucial had been missing from the political/ economic/ social/ cultural/ aesthetic/ military/ psychosocial/ psychological/ psychosexual mix" (259). Near the end of the novel, Velma grapples with the futility of trying to make the harried conditions of her town amenable to her fragile mind and accepts her decenteredness—cut off from "the best of her people's traditions" and "anesthetized by dazzling performances with somebody else's aesthetic . . ." (258). The aesthetic referred to has to do with a new reality unfolding before Velma, who cannot tame a reality in which the stress of her endeavors nearly brings about her demise.

Velma sees the status quo of striving, self-sacrifice, and job pressures coming apart at the seams. Drawn out though it may be, her recovery process very much represents an alternative to the *modern* paradigm she has followed. Velma no longer wants to make sense out of an insane world; instead, she decides to retool the strivings of her foremothers and forefathers. No longer trying to beat back social fragmentation, Velma embraces her brokenness, laughs at her entire ordeal, and, at the end of the novel, stands to her feet without the aid of Minnie Ransom. Ultimately, Bambara's narrative provides a fascinating perspective on a set of community issues surrounding 1960s social movements. She situates the struggle for black civil rights in a particular kind of configuration. Depicting the polarizing nature of in-group politics and the impact of mainstream organizations, *The Salt Eaters* pinpoints an important trope in African American literature.

In the late twentieth century, African American novelists, while scrutinizing race relations, opted for a full-on observation of the complexities of historical experience and postmodernism. Inasmuch as writers like Bambara engage issues of social and political uncertainty, they also reflect on the critical vacillation around ideas about history within theories of postmodernism. In light of the terrain I think African American postmodern fiction aims to retrospectively cover, I examine the ways in which writers have explored the cultural and societal tensions that took shape and hardened in the context of black social movements during the 1950s and 1960s.

Laying claim to commentary on the profound shifts in black culture that helped set in motion postmodern conditions, black writers have teased out discourses on social movements and their respective impacts. They have given particular attention to the era of racial integration, the civil rights movement, black nationalism, and the post–civil rights era. My project claims that writers have delved into the upheavals amid movements to extract knowledge and strategies for negotiating late-twentieth- and twenty-first-century challenges. To determine what these challenges are, I ask questions about some of the observations writers have made: Why does so much thematic content revolve around movement politics? Why the focus on burdensome intraracial baggage or on the need to maneuver through inequitable systems? Lastly, why has a consideration of hegemonic forces taken center stage? The answers to these questions emerge out of a postmodernism that problematizes essentialist habits of being and exploitative structures.

In *Progress Compromised,* my primary purpose is to shed light on the existential assault on the black individual, via the pressure imposed by constraining group narratives and norms (family or community-derived) and the threat of institutional (industry, college, social entity, or city) exploitation in mainstream spaces. I explore a critical moment in African American literature in which writers are concerned with the series of vulnerabilities and exploitations that plague blacks who have been bequeathed the spoils of opportunity through historic rights struggles. These constraints, which are part and parcel of black social relations in the latter part of the twentieth century and in recent years, have created a condition in which we see two features: the constraining nature of black group practices and the threat of black individuals having their ambitions co-opted by mainstream forces. In linking fictionalized experiences to watershed moments in American history, black novelists have crafted a discourse on postmodern black cultural politics that interrogates the cultural, ideological, and socioeconomic upheavals that characterize social movements. This approach represents an attempt to make a unique angle on postmodern culture accessible.

One feature of African American postmodern fiction is that it militates against the kind of social arrangements that are detrimental to the individual. Writers imagine that their protagonists become keenly self-aware in the ways they negotiate society. For the purposes of this study, the discourse I chart across African American literature conveys several points about how characters disrupt the predicament of group constraints and mainstream exploitation. First, the theme of adopting an interrogative posture, which helps to unravel long-held cultural notions of progress, appears and informs our understanding of postmodern cultural politics. As men and women seized new work opportunities in the late twentieth century and maneuvered through cities and industries, it became necessary to reassess conventional ideologies (that combat alienation and social disorientation) and to ponder how it is that African Americans have made and will continue making progress. This reassessment is postmodern in that it invites fragmentation and uncertainty and creates a context in which mere opportunity for economic mobility can be sacrificed for the coveted prize of agency.

The postmodern questioning and reflection by those both mindful of the legacy of rights movements and enduring the mental anguish from their own blood-and-sweat equity also stand out in this discourse. Wading through an aura of black struggle to find individual purpose is a difficult project, particularly for activists, and it requires a capacity to reframe organized struggle. In this context, a postmodern reframing is about questioning one's trauma and self-sacrifice and imagining activism outside a hierarchical context.

There is a postmodern penchant for resisting consensus in group contexts. Communicating across class boundaries in African American communities sometimes involves the impulse to impose depthlessness on the lower stratum and to prescribe certain cultural norms. The postmodern cultural ethos depicted provides the means for individuals to do the culture work of demystifying class stratification—by not only acknowledging the flexibility inherent in adopting any class-based identity but also by illuminating the problematic outlook of upper-class black organizations. Lastly, writers have honed in on the self-renewal that comes through postmodern introspection. In the midst of multiple perspectives, convictions, and truths about family and purpose, feelings of fracture and decenteredness set in—and those who strike out on journeys to find themselves end up dislocated geographically and socially. Among similar conditions like fragmentation and alienation, dislocation too is an assault on the self. Highlighting attributes of postmodernism in *Toward a Postmodern Literature*, Ihab Hassan suggests that postmodern social phenomena create ideologies around the unmaking of the self. This imposition upon the self must be embraced, considering that a fraught atmosphere, which both necessitates social change and is influenced by it, is the link between an adaptable notion of selfhood and the postmodern. To this end, postmodern mores embrace the alienating influence of myriad cultural epistemologies and use them to catalyze a sense of renewal in following one's own precarious convictions and paths.

As evidenced in this postmodern discourse, new formations in African American literature have followed from writers highlighting the discursive nature of cultural experience, and there has been closer inspection of the material reality that underpins it. Studying the portrayal of the aura around black social movements, I attempt to show that the upheavals of the 1950s and 1960s not only resulted in access to more opportunities for African Americans but also in more subtle challenges in terms of race and society. In the following texts—Colson Whitehead's *The Intuitionist*, Alice Walker's *Meridian*, John Oliver Killens's *The Cotillion*, and Toni Morrison's *Tar Baby*—each author either takes as his or her backdrop a given social movement or makes reference to the impact of some cause célèbre, which can be linked to the peak or aftermath of a particular movement. These novels appear out of order in this book in relation to their publication date because I am more concerned with the chronology of the subsequent social-movement eras around which they frame their works. My sense is that these works provide a rich and untapped discourse because they feature, in some way, the tension between in-group friction and dominant oppression. Bringing, as it does, marginal perspectives to the forefront of literary and cultural studies, my research signals an expansion in the lexicon around black postmodernism.

Ultimately, the novels I cover prioritize individual autonomy as the key to developing a progressive politics. I critique works that portray ambitious protagonists in their negotiation of group politics and the maneuvers they make in society—usually in workplaces, educational systems, and institutional structures. I include the aforementioned texts because the characters within them not only pursue self-knowledge but also struggle for autonomy in the systems upon which they depend for stability and meaning. Even though a celebrated postmodern text like Ishmael Reed's *Mumbo Jumbo* traffics in a number of cultural ideologies, I exclude it because it does not situate male and female protagonists who must negotiate practical cultural frameworks in society. Rather, I focus on novels that feature the strivings of men and women attempting to climb the socioeconomic ladder while weighed down with certain cultural baggage and challenged by strong group practices and mainstream power.

African American Literary Contention and Individual Autonomy

A brief overview of the academic context in which I situate my claims (debates over the historical import of the African American literary tradition and the cultural and political influence of academic work) will underscore the stakes in traversing this literary terrain. In his treatment of African American literature as a historical entity under the tensions of Jim Crow–era racism, Kenneth Warren views it as lacking coherence in the post–civil rights era: "African American literature took shape in the context of this challenge to the enforcement and justification of racial subordination and exploitation represented by Jim Crow. Accordingly, it will be my argument here that with the legal demise of Jim Crow, the coherence of African American literature has . . . eroded as well" (2).

The tensions of the Jim Crow era reverberate across these works and hold far-reaching and broad implications. As writers endeavor to critique and delineate an era that spurred some of the most historically significant rights movements in America and inspired resistance around the globe, the impact of the nonviolent direct action taking place between *Plessy v. Ferguson* and the Voting Rights Act of 1965 becomes impossible to fix in a single era. Gene Andrew Jarrett writes that "African American writers across a *longue durée* persisted, through success and failure, in making an artistic and political impact on social attitudes and practices precisely because they recognized that Jim Crow, narrowly or broadly defined, was not the only kind of racism that afflicted the world" ("What Is Jim Crow?" 390). This long view of historical concerns more adequately accounts for the extensive process involved in writing a literature with an eye toward not only penning social reform but also grinding out masterworks and stretching convention with postmodern narratives.

While Warren identifies an overarching white commitment during Jim Crow to dehumanize, disenfranchise, and terrorize as the impetus for blacks to produce a literature, the novelists in this study respond to other stimuli. Warren relies heavily on the historical moment of Jim Crow and elides other oppressions that emerged before and after the passage of civil rights legislation that were certainly malicious enough (that is, police brutality, redlining, government surveillance, global colonial hegemony) to occasion a response and prompt blacks again "to consider their literature [and culture] as a corporate enterprise" (18). Warren is content to view the creative, literary, and critical resistance of the Jim Crow era as a one-off in black writing and, in effect, black intellectual thought.

Even as Warren argues in *What Was African American Literature?* that weighty demands were especially placed on black literary practice during the late nineteenth and early twentieth centuries, he does not entertain the demands placed upon black literary practice in the late twentieth century and the contemporary era. The widespread calls that went out during Jim Crow to create a literature that could accommodate "indexical assessments of racial progress and instrumental responses to systematized second-class citizenship" still echo today. Perhaps the sense of urgency lingers in the minds of the many black writers who see themselves as equal parts social reformer and artist. While I think Warren's critique—which suggests the social reformer ethos can be problematic for writers—has merit, I also believe that this ethos has stubbornly persisted among black writers and critics along with the desire to convince the public that blacks could produce a viable literature. Warren offers abolition, reconstruction, and desegregation as the necessary broader conditions for "treating African American literature as literature" and solidifying its progressive politics during Jim Crow. However, he glosses over the extant, psychic conditions needed to animate and support attempts to prove black artistic ability—even today. At a time when black writers endeavoring within African American literature have pursued and obtained commercial success, the "necessary *psychic* conditions" undergirding their writing have fortified the black literary field. If the vast scourge of Jim Crow spurred the development of black literature, then, too, the current political gesturing toward white supremacy, the presumption of black menace (currently fueling the state-sanctioned killing of black bodies), and the perpetuation of mass incarceration, which characterize contemporary times, provide enough of a coordinated assault on black communities to sustain the driving impulses behind African American literature.

In his study, Warren does not show much regard for the fact that the group construct, which was the cultural dominant of Jim Crow, comprised only a single angle from which critics and writers could interpret black life. And though this construct may have precipitated the establishment of something called African American literature, there is no reason why a vibrant academic discipline and market commodity must end as a result of a long, fraught transition from group definitions. The waning of a group demarcation and the emergence of new frameworks are grappled with in Charles Johnson's essay "The End of the Black American Narrative." According to Johnson, "It simply is no longer the case that the essence of black American life is racial victimization and disenfranchisement, a curse and a condemnation, a destiny based on color in which the meaning of one's life is thinghood, created even before one is born." Just as black people today "defy easy categorization," the same can be said of black writing, which is continually evolving in form and content. Johnson's more progressive reading of the temporal shifts surrounding the discipline of African American literature is due to his hope that a new black American narrative potentially could arrive at more varied and direct perceptions "of the specific phenomenon before us" instead of relying on trite interpretations of black experiences. Johnson sees little value in what he describes as narratives about racial victimization, even though those works will continue to have a seat at the table. Interestingly, Johnson offers a caveat that Warren seems unwilling to entertain: "It is always wise, I believe, to see all our propositions (and stories) as provisional, partial, incomplete, and subject to revision on the basis of new evidence, which we can be sure is just around the corner."

While Warren suggests early on that "the turn to diasporic, transatlantic, global, and other frames indicates a dim awareness" that a distinct African American literature has eroded, I believe increasing interdisciplinary study suggests that claims to write African American literature today are more nuanced than "take[ing] what was (even under the Jim Crow conditions that lent it plausibility) a problematic assumption of race-group interest" or "asserting black identity and black solidarity . . ." (110). Of course, some writers have a hankering for protest and identity politics, but more are re-visioning history and exploring the vernacular notions, idioms, and social facts that mark black American experience. Further, black literature having been disabused of its "collective undertaking" ethos does not sound its death knell. Instead, the discipline now seems free to derive its cultural and political relevance from socioeconomic forces, public policy, and decentralized social movements.

Since its publication, many critics have weighed in on *What Was African American Literature?* Some have read it as reductive in its historicizing of black literature while others have found Warren's focus on politics as obscuring the importance of literary form. My goal is not to reject Warren's study of African American literature as a historical entity whole-cloth but to offer a critique, which shows that African American literature actually has engaged, consistently and coherently, in a critique of the newly integrated, sociocultural terrain that unfolded *during* and *following* several black social movements. Inhabiting new worlds in the midst of Jim Crow and afterwards, black writers began reckoning with the costs and benefits, strides, and missteps of the struggle for civil rights. These concerns cropped up in the work of writers like Ernest Gaines, Toni Morrison, Alice Walker, and others. As someone who participated in the direct action that chafed against Jim Crow and whose work appears in this study, Walker captures a sense of this cultural reckoning: "In *Meridian,* I started out being really concerned about some of the things people did to each other in the sixties, in the name of change, in the name of revolution. I wanted to see what qualities we were giving up in exchange for other qualities. Somehow part of it really understands the questions, not just understands the answers" ("I Know What the Earth Says" 231). Walker's unease about the lasting implications of black social movements, which runs through her novel, brings into focus the concerns of Warren's critics. Walker was remarking on a complicated and messy cultural nexus, which Marlon Ross suggests helped shape African American literary production. As Ross puts it, since Jim Crow segregation, black literature has been in the business of "inhabiting and yet challenging American literary structures and ideologies based in an ongoing distinct cultural experience of and in the United States" (397). Xiomara Santamarina rightly discerns that this distinct cultural experience and the literature linked to it have been invested in holding on to racial particularity precisely because there is so much "uncertainty about the form and content of equality" (400) in our current moment. If this uncertainty has reached such a fever pitch since the demise of Jim Crow that writers are rendering and contextualizing its intricacies within postmodern fiction, then African American literature is still hard at work interpreting the ghastly social ills wrought by not only segregation but also the vast apparatus of present-day hostilities aimed at African Americans.

Moreover, the texts in this study militate against some of the expedient narratives about progress that have emerged during the early part of the twenty-first century (the Obama era) concerning black political clout. In particular, *Meridian* posits a cynical view regarding the belief that a rising political tide across black communities lifts all boats (particularly for those outside the political class). *The Cotillion* rejects the idea that what happens to be socioeconomically advantageous for middle-class blacks somehow redounds to the benefit of poor, urban blacks. Today, along with scrutiny in the realm of cultural production—under which tenuous narratives about progress collapse—the work of racial justice continues. And public efforts in the form of contemporary activism (Black Lives Matter) and other traditional civil rights advocacy have prompted more reflective thinking about race.

Late-twentieth-century African American literature portrays a crisis of individual autonomy in American social relations. I use the term *progress compromised* in my title to highlight the tangle of exploitations, fragmentations, and vulnerabilities confronting black individuals in communal and societal contexts as a result of the seismic impact of social movements. I am concerned with why this sociocultural reality gets portrayed in a pattern in which group traditions tend to confine individuals while mainstream institutions work to exploit them. I am also interested in the inclinations of characters inhabiting this predicament to jettison their ideological and cultural hang-ups for the purpose of maneuvering through this assault on individual autonomy. While there are numerous factors that explain the mainstream exploitation writers explore, one factor behind in-group dissonance is that generations bequeathed the legacy of social movements have experienced "weakened ties" (*Race, Modernity, Post-modernity* 14) to racial tradition because sociological changes have made it difficult to maintain group-based, cultural norms. Since the late 1960s, African American literature has depicted protagonists navigating black cultural spaces and meeting hostility at mainstream sites. In doing so, the literary field has clarified the crosscurrents and tensions between both. Still, the cultural terrain remains particularly vexed because the political requirements of the time meant that black reform efforts had the effect of setting a uniform agenda. Even as political shifts in the United States were taking shape, this group-based agenda planted seeds that would invariably constrain the autonomy of future generations of black individuals.

Weighing in on the impediments to critical dialogue within black communities, Adolph Reed, in *Stirrings in the Jug: Black Politics in the Post-Segregation Era*, looks at the misdirected nature of past black political practices. Reed critiques civil rights leaders' integrationist demand and their alliance with corporate liberals while at the same time chiding nationalists for not being adamant enough about their aim of establishing economic and political control in black communities. Reed does ascribe to both movements the expansion of a sizable political base. However, because of their "effectively reinscribed hierarchy" (65–69) and insistence on a monolithic ideology, he also attributes to them the decline of robust, black opposition to systemic injustice. Broadly speaking, this observation identifies the targets of critique in each of the novels discussed in this book.

Just as American politics has historically foundered when it came to the interests of marginalized groups, black politics has always relied on collective struggle against de jure and de facto injustice.[1] Hanes Walton observed that for years the U.S. Congress had operated under a biased standard against African Americans, which said "that the individual-level of constitutional relief was better than the group-based model, even though African Americans had suffered in the American political system as a group" (54). In his discussion of liberalism and race, David Cochran remarks on an interesting dynamic in black communities. As he points out, "[a]utonomy depends upon a cultural context in which an individual's internal choices make sense" (110). Cochran goes on to argue the point: "Black Americans participate in a distinct cultural tradition that provides an ongoing dialogue about the content of a good life, about the nature of a good person, about worthy values and norms of behavior, about justice and human dignity, about the proper relationship of individual members to their families and communities, and so on" (110). In this sense, the ethic under which blacks have made collective strides is a telling contour of black cultural politics. And it is the consciousness that emerged out of resistance that made black participation in American democracy substantive; the failure to grasp this notion threatens to hamper black autonomy today. Indeed, it creates a situation in which blacks feel compelled to pursue collective gains but not to assert their personal sense of self-determination.

In the mid-twentieth century, American politics underwent a crisis as a result of countercultural resistance, economic volatility, and political shifts. Nowhere did this crisis register more acutely than in marginalized, minority communities. As a result, the 1960s witnessed an uptick in public policy geared toward addressing civil rights issues. However, by 1970, President Johnson's War on Poverty had ended and economic stagnation was setting in. At this point, American politics lacked consensus, which the nation's still uncertain course regarding race relations illustrated. Writing about consensus in political affairs, Jean François Lyotard observed that "invention is always born of dissension" (xxv). To Lyotard's point, the growing discontentment with disparity actually bolstered 1970s counterculture.[2] While at the federal level backlash surfaced from politicians cynical about social spending, at the local level New Left radicals challenged liberalism through the empowerment of the poor and disenfranchised.

Moreover, black grassroots movements challenging discrimination cultivated a critical mass, which was willing to voice concerns and act on them. In this context, resistance began at home—perhaps by way of what bell hooks calls an oppositional gaze—then spread abroad toward the corridors of power. hooks's oppositional gaze, which involves critiquing the prevailing oppressive paradigms, has historically been a fragmenting endeavor. The prevalence of fragmentation in contemporary life, I think, illuminates the need for individuals to cultivate the capacity to make progress within societal arrangements that diminish black life chances. In *Postmodernism and Its Critics*, John McGowan argues that "the individual is a functionary of power" and that the desires emanating from the seats of power cannot be conceived apart from "human agents" (254).[3] Perry Anderson writes in *The Origins of Postmodernity* that "any hegemony, as Raymond

Williams insisted, was a 'dominant' rather than a total system, one virtually ensuring—because of its selective definitions of reality—the coexistence of 'residual' and 'emergent' forms resistant to it" (64). Opening up new forms of resistance and transgressive spaces through which to grapple with and navigate this reality has been the province of African American literature and is part and parcel of achieving individual autonomy in this moment.

Black Postmodernism and Historical Insight

Debates over how best to describe African American postmodernism have compelled cultural theorists to centralize black social reality. Critics have argued that if nothing else postmodernism is certainly inflected by black cultural production, artistic autonomy, a politics of difference, and an expanding black critical presence.[4] However, because several theories residualize and marginalize the experiences of people of color, African American postmodernism approaches black experiences in contexts that frame the world distinctly from other paradigms. Therefore, critics often seek out those contexts as they emerge in black literature. For instance, there has been much assessment of print culture and its limited capacity for racial representation, and critics have privileged not only analyses of fragmented subjectivity and psychic decenteredness but also the foregrounding of numerous black cultural paradigms.[5]

African American postmodernism, in framing its own epistemologies, is not only informing widely read theories but also mapping its wider concern for historical reality. Wahneema Lubiano directs the attention of critics toward serious reflection on a key issue: the "insist[ence] on the representation of history in the present moment" (157). A number of studies seem to share Lubiano's concern about how history is viewed in postmodernism, but to varying extents. Fredric Jameson's well-known theory of postmodernism describes one feature of present-day aesthetics as a loss of historicity, in which we can no longer look to history as a meaningful tool to explain the present. Jameson offers us a degraded historicism, which holds out little hope that society will appreciate historical context in the twenty-first century. History becomes a casualty of the "breakdown of the signifying chain" and is reduced in language to "a series of pure and unrelated presents in time" (x–27). Linda Hutcheon sees postmodern cultural production as both historical and critical due to its interaction with discourses of the past. She applies her historiographic metafiction concept to narratives that problematize history "by stressing the [discursive] contexts in which the fiction is being produced—by both writer and reader" (40).[6]

While these accounts tend to see postmodernism as chiefly oppositional to previous cultural and aesthetic formations, some critics have characterized prominent interpretations of postmodernism as ahistorical. In Cornel West's view, "the postmodernism debate has remained inscribed within narrow disciplinary boundaries, insulated artistic practices, and vague formulations of men and women of letters. The time has come for this debate to be moved more forthrightly into social theory and historiography" ("Black Culture and Postmodernism" 392). This emphasis on historical reference across the critical board can be advanced in African American postmodernism. Still, without careful consideration of larger historical influence, black postmodernism cannot succeed in its intent to nourish generative perspectives and enrich critical theory.

Cautioning against the elevation of African American postmodernism as a critical space empty of thorny notions about difference, Lubiano explains it this way: "It seems to me more useful to think of African American postmodernism as a way to negotiate particular material circumstances in order to attempt some constructions of justice. . . . It theorizes ways that prevent engagement with differences from concretizing into intellectually and politically static categories" (157–58). Because Lubiano wants to draw attention to the contexts in which "African American texts write themselves" (153), she pinpoints the texture of black postmodernism and elevates sideline perspectives into theories of postmodernism. For Lubiano, *static constructions*—tools used in postmodernism to generalize about cultural difference—largely ignore the ways African Americans have conceptualized the disadvantages they have faced in society. Lubiano argues that African American postmodernism continues "working over the conflicted ground of discourse genealogies" so as to not only resist the dominant discourse but also to theorize the complexities of black participation in the American body politic, mainly in the late twentieth century.

To fully resist the construction of black culture as other, Madhu Dubey, in *Signs and Cities: Black Literary Postmodernism*, suggests that postmodern cultural studies should give attention to the racialized, structural, and systemic issues plaguing African Americans. The discipline might accomplish this by considering the uneven development of black communities (9); by looking to what we know of the operative class politics in society (*Framing the Margins* 12); and by positing concrete and translatable experiences, not abstraction, as a basis for black postmodern cultural politics ("Postmodern Blackness" 29). These ideas concern themselves with the much-neglected social realities that serve to distinguish black postmodernism from the narrow constructions offered by leading theories. Among the many areas glossed over is the need to consider socioeconomic challenges through the prism of African American postmodern fiction, which operationalizes historical experience. We might stretch the limits of criticism, too, by discerning lessons from historically seminal movements whose insights hold relevance for current situations. To arrive at this point, critics will need to question broad conceptions of postmodernism that flatten out social and cultural particularity.

In order to inoculate black postmodernism against a degraded historicism, it is essential to avoid preemptively limiting the scope of postmodern fiction. The key is to utilize its explanatory power, pairing it with social science, literary theory, philosophical discourses, and political science, among other disciplines. Then we can determine the ways in which history has been recently conceptualized. Many of the generalizations in postmodernism bypass cultural difference even though minorities often live out a relationship to capitalism's ebbs and flows that is distinct from nonminority Americans. If we take seriously, instead, the interdisciplinary nature of black postmodern fiction, then interrogations of history can be linked to Afro-diasporic paradigms, globalizing theories, womanism, and feminism.

In *Feminism/Postmodernism*, Nancy Fraser and Linda Nicholson's notion of postmodern feminism comments on the analysis of history in a way that bears significance for what the novelists in this study achieve. In their argument, "the postmodern critique need forswear neither large historical narratives nor analyses of societal macrostructures" but must critique sexism's embedded history in society (34). Against the backdrop of eras that have been complicated and reassessed, men and women characters embody this critical approach in their willingness to critique, dispense with, and destabilize the gendered traditions (and agendas) against which they struggle. In this way, writers call into question the stultifying structures in society, which often escape critique.

A more extensive turn toward spotlighting lived experience could elicit more reflection on the historical contestations of minorities opposing raced and gendered perspectives. Yet even as critics observe political and cultural struggles, they must analyze the perspectives and discourses that grow out of these moments. In this way, writers can eschew a cursory glance and thoroughly examine cultural vantage points. Gaining a broader sense of local or global black struggles requires understanding the influence of social movements on group perspectives. In one sense, social movements have taken center stage in African American postmodernism: they have emerged in the reassertion of history as a means of critical inquiry in black postmodern fiction.

As critics search for reference points that facilitate a deeper cultural understanding, in my view the challenge is to encourage the introduction of new critical positions for postmodernism. Problems can arise if critics fall back to the familiar discourses and usual presuppositions. Those working in a seemingly hermetic Euro-American framework are often given the space to conceive of ideas with little attention to subaltern experiences. In this context, historical campaigns like racial integration and black nationalism, which disrupted repressive conditions for African Americans, are given short shrift. My sense is that the insight we may glean from *past* engagements is very much relevant in today's postmodern cultural production.

African American postmodernism, where it intersects with literary and cultural studies, has worked to explore past social movements. In light of this effort, history can neither become a despised entity nor a phenomenon divorced from social context. Moreover, African American postmodernism in invigorating the historical actuality of black experiences has begun interrogating its own assumptions about black history. Writers and critics can underwrite this effort by opening up new points of departure into discussions about the ways in which historically shaped black cultural difference plays out in fiction and in reality. Our purpose must be to fully mine notions of the sociocultural real in black postmodern fiction (*Signs and Cities* 11–13) and thereby resist becoming someone's postmodern other.

While I am concerned with the fate of history (its conceptualization) in postmodernism, I am not so much interested in periodization. Though

I, at times, refer to the aftermath of pivotal rights movements throughout the book as a kind of postmodern moment in America, my main concern is with a particular zeitgeist that I view as necessitating postmodern ways of being. In addition, the *postmodern moments* I identify in African American fiction are distinct as actualizations of postmodern subjectivity. In aesthetic terms, postmodernism is an intellectual construct, which can exist alongside other constructs like late modernity, post-Marxism, and countermodernity.[7] My goal is to draw from the wealth of ideas and sets of assumptions attached to the term, both as a historical marker and as cultural and aesthetic phenomena. I believe postmodernism should serve a more expansive role, in that many incidents in black history approximate something like the uncertainty and ruptures associated with it.[8] Throughout the book, I operationalize African American postmodernism as a critical space for exploring ideas about cultural difference and social maneuverability.

To flesh out the various tensions that I highlight in postmodern African American fiction, I look at the shifts that constitute attempts to resist, reframe, and navigate group-oriented constraints and institutional hegemony. My own formulation of such shifts is that they signal a complexity around social relations, which was shaped by the struggle for black civil rights, and point to individual choices that have been compromised by sociocultural uncertainty in the aftermath. To account for the social status quo of the late twentieth century, critics have sought to revise outmoded narratives that imply unimpeded cultural advancement and draw attention to the stubborn reality of compromised life chances and draconian power structures.

Another feature of the literature I cover signals an unsettling moment in which male and female protagonists, in narratives written during the post–civil rights era, find it nearly impossible to conceive of upwardly mobile trajectories with aplomb. Sent scrambling for opportunities that do not hold out much promise for inner stability and cultural grounding, this generation has become increasingly aware of socioeconomic alienation that is not overtly tied to race. This is a telling theme that rethinks access as something less like the culmination of collective struggle and more like an opening salvo in a precarious battle for mobility. Lastly, a key postmodern current throughout the book is a critique of politics that marginalize the functions of individuals in social or organizational contexts. Forms of repression, which subvert individuals on behalf of larger interests, are targeted by these novelists because the persistent nature of this subversion disturbs the cultural interworking of marginalized communities. Overall, postmodern African American fiction has turned on notions of individual agency, a reframing of social and cultural obligations, and the navigation of in-group and institutional oppression.

African American literature unfolds around these and other features through conspicuous sociocultural tangles, which not only unsettle characters but are often left unsettled as well. This is because in fiction the postmodern does not bring about the transcendence of various dilemmas but facilitates the wherewithal to negotiate them. Writers typically weave in multiple moments of transformation in which there is either a tamping down or a rethinking of one's expectations of the larger society. Critics ought to hone in on these thematic elements, which amount to a vibrant, postmodern black cultural politics.

African American Critical and Cultural Paradigms

Among the critics[9] whose work attempts to situate black postmodernism in the world of literary and cultural theory, W. Lawrence Hogue has foregrounded its efforts to push against the mid-twentieth-century American political apparatus. In discussing the capacity of black postmodern writing to serve the cultural and ideological needs of African Americans, Hogue points out the ability of 1960s social movements to create extra-textual discursive formations in which black novelists could not only flesh out uninvestigated experiences but also stretch the genre's established conventions. Ultimately, he suggests in *Discourse and the Other* that movements spurred "discourses [that] allowed new myths about, or representations of, the American and Afro-American historical past to emerge" (60). Dubey explores the political-economic crisis in urban spaces and black communities that has registered across African American literature and cultural studies. Dubey is concerned with the extent to which the modern print tradition can claim to represent a knowable racial community at a time when truth-claims of literature (and other cultural forms) are being critiqued. While the premise of this study probes elsewhere, Dubey's sense that African American literature "form[s] a vital resource for debates about postmodernism" that is "conspicuously missing" (2) in the postmodernism fray has informed my work. However, this study diverges in its focus on identifying and interrogating tropes about black social movements and analyzing portrayals of fraught social mobility. I am concerned with black literature's efforts to adequately portray social realities in light of technological mediations and disruptions. My aim is to broaden the intellectual climate around postmodernism by using African American fiction as an indispensable discourse on postmodern uncertainties, constraints, and compromised societal conditions.

If I extend Hogue's sense of the postmodern defamiliarization done to established literary and critical conventions by cultural difference, then I can locate a similar defamiliarization process in black cultural production, which was reshaped by black social movements that unleashed cultural strivings and angst across black art. Bernard Bell has said about reinvigorating black cultural discourse that "[i]t would be unreasonable, however, to throw out the baby that is the relentless struggle of African Americans for freedom, justice, equality, and unity as subjects and agents of change . . ." (14). In light of this idea, the novelists I discuss write from the perspective of past crisis points in American history to think critically about some of the misgivings and assumptions of the black freedom struggle. Because I take contestation to be central to cultural production, I examine the recognition of textured, sociopolitical oppressions and compromises in the context of postmodern fiction.

Among myriad challenges, black communities have to resist longstanding gender and sexism dynamics, particularly those that reigned in the context of social movements. Subsuming black women's autonomy within patriarchy poses a threat to African American progress. hooks addresses this issue in her concept of radical black subjectivity,[10] which moves identity formation beyond essentialist notions of male dominance to individual process. hooks favors "identity that is not informed by a narrow cultural nationalism masking continued fascination with the power of the white hegemonic other" (20). When we move beyond essentialism to view identity as a process, black men and women can share co-creative space in conversations about black experiences, which are not framed by group politics. Through hooks's perspective, black men in particular can move away from outmoded notions of male leadership toward arrangements that foster greater agency for men and women.

Novels written by African American women in the late twentieth century have explored gender, sexism, and cultural heritage to generate discussion in the public sphere. Barbara Christian has remarked that this literary endeavor clarifies "that an understanding of [black women's] reality and imagination is essential to the process of change that the entire society must undergo in order to transform itself" (*Black Feminist Criticism* 185). As it concerns transformation, black women have opened new conceptual windows by emphasizing the erotic and other cultural tensions. Writing about black women's sexuality, Patricia Hill Collins has remarked that the erotic is a key site for resistance and self-definition. This particular conception reads sexuality as a site where systems of oppression intersect. According to Collins, "Just as harnessing the power of the erotic is important for domination, reclaiming and self-defining that same eroticism may constitute one path toward Black women's empowerment" (128). This type of cultural and political project is consistent with turns toward similar forms of agency which are not premised on respectability politics and refuse to be sublimated into racialized narratives of an essentialist black collectivity.

Within black postmodernism, gender and sexuality serve as analytical categories, particularly to provide more fluid notions of identity and to critique narratives about racial authenticity. Not many years after Kobena Mercer suggested that "the presence of new social actors and new political subjects—women, black people, lesbian and gay communities, youth . . ." (260) represented a plurality of voices and conflicts, Kendall Thomas's "Ain't Nothin' Like the Real Thing" argued that gay and lesbian blacks should advocate for black sexual freedom as a component of antiracist resistance. Thomas's idea calls for a "reworking of the terms of the identity debate from questions of ideology and consciousness to material matters of bodies, life, and death . . ." (63). Specifically, Thomas shows how heteronormative illogic, which demanded that some black activists choose between black and gay identity, required sole loyalty to the black freedom struggle. Lastly, Thomas calls into question rigid and collective notions of identity, which, although they once seemed to assure liberation, are, in this moment, burdensome. Perhaps Mae Henderson and E. Patrick Johnson's sense of the need for complex subjectivities best sums up the current moment: "Monolithic identity formations, like monologic perspectives, cannot survive the crisis of (post)modernity. In today's cultural marketplace, the imperatives of race and sexuality must give way to messier but more progressive stratagems of contestation and survival" (6). Their assertion seems to place an onus on subjectivities that gain legitimacy as uncertainty and indeterminacy saturate current experience.

Suffice it to say, African American criticism and cultural studies have been sites of ideological and conceptual struggle. Throughout the twentieth century and into the twenty-first century, these traditions have been consistently debated. As a result, black writers have blurred critical/aesthetic lines by creating a discourse on postmodernism within their fiction. When writers create new paradigms, they not only throw criticism off-center but also they force critics to read literary constructions in ways that complicate traditional interpretive practices. In this fictional space, black writers have sparked a reconsideration of disciplinary boundaries, in terms of the capacity of both critics and writers to richly theorize about postmodern black cultural politics.

In chapter 1, "Unraveling Cultural Notions: Black Progress in Colson Whitehead's *The Intuitionist*," I explore the ways in which Whitehead's protagonist, Lila Mae Watson, as well as her counterparts are exploited by unscrupulous, industry power brokers and burdened by fidelity to a group narrative resting on ambition and a determination to rise through the ranks in mainstream bureaucracies. In particular, Lila Mae gets embroiled in a controversy that compels her to process the vulnerability that comes with her role as the first black female elevator inspector. I examine the era of integration rendered in the novel, under which issues of tokenism, worker angst, and the threat of co-opting the agency of black workers unfold. In light of Whitehead's portrayal of the postmodern cognitive practices acquired by Lila Mae and James Fulton, a visionary elevator theorist, this chapter also considers the particular challenges conscious individuals pose to power brokers. Lila Mae and her male counterparts struggle to rethink and reframe their notions of what progress actually means for African Americans newly integrated into civil service and industry.

Chapter 2, "Restless Questioning: Anguish and the Ethos of Black Struggle in Alice Walker's *Meridian*," looks at Walker's exploration of political and academic arrangements that serve to stifle the drive of black activists and intellectuals. Exploring how the novel's main character, Meridian Hill, copes with the psychological distress gripping activists who participate in the civil rights movement (and who bear the psychic weight of the black freedom struggle), I highlight the persistent inner trauma. Meridian and Truman Held, a second protagonist, become increasingly aware of ulterior, top-down agendas shrouding their commitment to direct action. However, Meridian learns to embrace her own ambivalence about her life's purpose, revealing the ways in which the divide between movement activists and political figureheads forces her to seek out a more personal politics. Lastly, I explore the tensions around friendship and mobility alongside issues of family and relationships. Meridian's restless questioning of the freedom struggle represents a fascinating postmodern move—one that is vital in a contemporary culture coming to grips with social apathy.

Chapter 3, "Resisting Consensus: Class-Driven Politics in John Oliver Killens's *The Cotillion*," analyzes Killens's portrayal of class stratification among black communities and social organizations. I investigate the operative class politics among the Femmes Fatales, a high-society black women's organization, and the ways in which two protagonists—Yoruba Lovejoy and Ben Ali Lumumba—work to disrupt the club's biases. The backdrop of late-1960s black nationalism (and its cultural flourishing) acts as a counterpoint to rigid notions of black identity because it evinces the sociopolitical overlap and cultural slippage across black experiences. Exploring layers of class division, the novel installs a postmodern posture of resisting consensus and inserts dissent as an option preferable to social conformity. Lastly, I make the case that Killens portrays this dichotomy expertly because he wants to resist the modern and convenient fix of locating common ground upon which the black bourgeoisie, nationalists, and working-class blacks can meet.

Lastly, chapter 4, "Self-Renewal through Introspection: Endless Journeys, Endless Becoming in Toni Morrison's *Tar Baby*," examines Morrison's attempt to highlight the personal capital ascribed to different truths, convictions, and ways of knowing across communities and generations. This chapter also explores the journey toward racial consciousness taken by Jadine Childs, who is on the cusp of fame and fortune as a Sorbonne-educated, black fashion model and artist. I critique Jadine's tenuous relationship with her family and her struggle to find the inner resolve to follow her own path. In the novel, each character's journey becomes unending in the sense that the characters—set adrift in the throes of a postmodern uncertainty—are always in the process of becoming (or groping toward a fresh perspective). Jadine's journey converges with William "Son" Green in a burgeoning, rocky relationship. Son is a fugitive trying to work out his relationship to modern society and its compulsory systems of control. In the post–civil rights era, the two must contend with horizons of prospects and reified worldviews. Jadine wants to achieve self-renewal by wading through the deluge of opinions and perspectives and coming to terms with her own convictions. Son, however, gets mentally wrapped up in the sway of conformist pressure and finds it difficult to move beyond a sense of alienation.

Progress Compromised is my attempt to explore the discourse on postmodern black cultural politics circulating within late-twentieth-century African American literature. In doing so, I discuss African American fiction that deploys resistance to both cultural repression and societal constraints. The novels in this study, produced from the early 1970s to the late 1990s, thematize the effect of particular historical moments on black individuals and their respective communities. Nonetheless, these writers explore phenomena that can be read in relation to other cultural and aesthetic iterations of postmodernism. While postmodern cultural politics is a subject of interest for many critics, I read this subject from a nuanced historical and literary perspective, which will allow scholars and intellectuals to grasp the more recent social circumstances that require strategic and reconditioned habits of being.

1

UNRAVELING CULTURAL NOTIONS
Black Progress in Colson Whitehead's *The Intuitionist*

The Intuitionist functions as a racial allegory in that it offers a commentary on the interminable progress of race relations by critiquing the group constraints and mainstream politics that throttle black ambition. Marginalized because of her race and gender in this mid-twentieth-century setting, Lila Mae Watson epitomizes a sense of vulnerability that is only complicated by access to economic corridors previously shut off to blacks. In addition, there is her internal motivation to attain success, which is wrapped up in group cultural tradition. Pompey, Lila Mae's coworker, is also bent on surviving the whims of bureaucracy and workplace politics as best he can though his ideas about progress are not neatly aligned with a narrative of uplift. Colson Whitehead works to situate the impact of racial integration upon black individuals who work in an environment where technological innovation and practices serve to disrupt age-old paradigms. Through Lila Mae, Pompey, and others, *The Intuitionist* lays bare the tensions around issues of tokenism, identity formation, and the threat of co-optation facing black workers seeking access to the levers of mobility and power. The novel also sheds light on the sociocultural predicaments that are underscored in *Meridian, The Cotillion,* and *Tar Baby.*

Here the postmodern has to do with the unraveling of cultural notions of progress and Whitehead's concern with cognitive shifts made by black men and women navigating city departments, industry politics, and corporations. Lila Mae, the first black female elevator inspector, adopts an interrogative posture that allows her to rethink the longstanding ideologies about progress and striving that have been seeded into the consciousness of blacks. To do so, she has to test the viability of her commitment to hard work and her faith in the cherished ideas that propelled her from the South into higher education and then into a noteworthy career. Whitehead challenges readers to rethink ambition through a postmodern lens that acknowledges the decenteredness and social fragmentation that begins to saturate America as it moves through the growing pains of racial integration. Another figure, James Fulton, a deceased elevator theorist, writes a text that contains musings on elevators of the future and initiates an epistemological challenge to the intellectual status quo in the world of elevation. Whitehead installs the political origin of elevation early on by referencing the U.S. vice-president's address during the 1853 World's Fair, where Elisha Graves Otis unveils the first safety elevator. The vice-president blithely remarks, "We are living in a period of most wonderful transition, which tends rapidly to accomplish that great end to which all history points— the realization of the unity of mankind" (80). Fulton exists to combat the kind of malignant indifference articulated at the fair, which glosses over the struggles of those who are marginalized in society. Through Fulton, Whitehead also critiques the sight-based practices that abound in the elevator industry, and, by extension, Western theoretical discourse, with abstract sense perception, which gets marginalized and othered by city and corporate gatekeepers. The new cultural formations that Fulton and Lila Mae champion are built on difference and have the potential to serve as catalysts for greater equality of opportunity and broader perspective. Ultimately, *The Intuitionist* unravels cultural notions by scrutinizing black cultural and ideological assumptions about what social progress means for black individuals.

The novel's significant postmodern elements extend to its formal features. Working in the tradition of detective/speculative fiction, Whitehead anchors rival camps, the Intuitionists and the Empiricists. He engages in a kind of border crossing between the two throughout the text. Whitehead's goal is not to preserve either but to illuminate both the fractious nature of each group and the political vortex of in which they operate. As a nonlinear narrative, *The Intuitionist* traffics in flashbacks, tangential scenes of history and theory, and reticence around character backstory—but the formal crux of the novel lies in its tone. While the tone vacillates from subdued to cerebral to menacing and humorous, it informs Whitehead's lines of argument around race and progress. The scenes littered with esoteric knowledge and elevator jargon loop back into a larger sense of cultural and societal unraveling. Even as the society Whitehead fashions is on the cusp of the reinvigorating the innovation that birthed the city, the contradictions undergirding the intellectualization of elevation are revealed tonally. Elevation and integration, for that matter, are seen as the tangled, messy undertakings they are, which not only rest on the sordid commingling of industry and bureaucracy but also the deflated, crumpled, and patched hopes of ordinary individuals.

To understand the vacillating tone in *The Intuitionist*, one can read it as illuminating the critical humor Whitehead uses to satirize specialization in escalators/elevators, higher education, and the genre of detective fiction. Taken together, this commentary comes to mirror the overarching cultural countercurrent that runs through the text. In the novel, Chuck Gould, a Jewish *escalator* expert and Lila Mae's only friend in the Department of Elevator Inspectors, labors in a context where elevator experts reign. Whitehead inserts Chuck's specialty as a humorous and trivial site of contestation. While Chuck acknowledges the "undeniable macho cachet and preferential treatment within the Guild" (21), he sees himself as gifted with the "unique personality to specialize in escalators, the lowliest conveyance on the totem pole." Discerning opportunity within the field, he also reasons that "there's a nationwide lack of escalator professors in the Institutes, so . . . he's a shoo-in for a teaching job." Dreaming that he will one day become a tenured professor of escalators, Chuck types away on his monograph about escalators and department stores and tells himself that, when he finally makes it, "he'll throw in the Intuitionist counterarguments where necessary." Whitehead offers the absurdity of Chuck's situation to the reader to draw attention to the vying for access and space by other discredited knowledges in the novel. Ironically, Otis introduced the escalator at the World's Fair of 1900. However, it garnered less fanfare and was displayed as a machine that facilitated leisurely shopping as opposed to the hardnosed corporate work ethic that the elevator represented. The escalator nuisance serves as an example of what Hutcheon describes as a contradiction "marking the site of the struggle of the emergence of something new" (3). Lastly, the escalator/elevator debate unfolds when Chuck crosses rhetorical swords with an internal affairs agent named Arbergast, who is searching for Lila Mae. Arbergast scolds him by asking, "Why don't you just start your own guild instead of trying to weasel in with the elevator boys?" (108). Chuck's response exposes the political nature of the question: "If the higher-ups would recognize that escalators are just as important for speedy conveyance as elevators, there wouldn't be such headaches all the time." Chuck's futile and humorous struggle for recognition is what frames Whitehead's postmodern view on dominant discourses that exclude other perspectives and voices.

As it concerns Whitehead's representation of the way higher education can constrict discourse, his tone is both satirical and critical. In a flash-back, Whitehead places Lila Mae in a sophomore seminar on theoretical elevators at the Institute of Vertical Transport. Professor McKean, a war veteran who lost his arm presumably in World War II, teaches the class in the basement of an auditorium. While the few students attending the class are either converts to Fulton's Intuitionism or "well-meaning liberals," Frederick Gorse, a staunch Empiricist, "signed up for the seminar to understand, and thus better arm himself against, the apostate rabble who were making so much noise in the community" (100). Gorse is committed to thwarting theoretical pluralism and bolstering Empiricist thought. In contrast, Lila Mae is rapt with the idea of "pierc[ing] the veil of this world and discover[ing] the elevator world." Near the end of the seminar, Professor McKean broaches a satirical discussion about "the Dilemma of the Phantom Passenger." The Phantom Passenger is a thought experiment posed in Fulton's *Theoretical Elevators,* which asks what happens to an elevator that is summoned by a passenger-to-be who departs after pressing the call button. Lila Mae responds by saying, "Fulton is trying to trick the reader. An elevator doesn't exist without its freight. If there's no one to get on, the elevator remains in quiescence. The elevator and the passenger need each other" (101–2). If Lila Mae's response figuratively acts as a kind of appeal to an improbable sense of racial unity, then Gorse's frustrated rejoinder—"Just because you can't see it doesn't mean it's not there!"— seems to absurdly imply that the elevator (white capitalist and suprema-cist dominance) is self-sufficient and does not require the freight (labor or patronage) by racial others for its maintenance. Whitehead uses Gorse's attempt to disappear the passenger from the equation to critique the desire to whitewash and render incomprehensible the contribution of racial others to American modernity. Challenging Gorse's simplistic view, Professor McKean unpins the left sleeve of his jacket where his arm is missing: "'That's the funny thing,' Professor McKean said, smiling now. 'My arm is gone, but sometimes it's there.' He looked down at his empty sleeve. He flicked at the sleeve with his remaining hand and they watched the fabric sway." Professor McKean's dramatic gesture calls attention to the relentless countercultural impulses (embedded in Fulton's text, and by extension, African American cultural production) that exist as a substrate within modernity, and that refuse to be eclipsed by prevailing theories.

Just as *The Intuitionist* features Fulton's notions about future elevators to lampoon academic theory, it also uses the trope of the *detective with superior deductive reasoning* to satirize the conventions of detective fiction. This trope becomes apparent in Lila Mae's conversation with Ben Urich, a journalist for *Lift* magazine, who has written an article about Fulton's missing manuscript, known as the black box. In a scene that would typically showcase a detective's mental prowess, Lila Mae's fixation on Fulton's genius compromises her ability to ascertain the larger entities at work in the search for the black box. Absent from this scene is the magic of piecing together the multiple strands of corruption, backdoor deals, and sabotage. Instead, when Urich points Lila Mae to some of Fulton's missing journals, which she is seeing for the first time, she reminisces about the "giddy days of her conversion" to Intuitionism. It is not until Urich implicates Reed, Lever, and Chancre in the sordid search that, "after too long pondering the minutiae, [Lila Mae] looks up from Fulton's notes" (206). Then he asks Lila Mae, "'Until Fanny Briggs anyway. Who do you think really needs the black box?' She stares at him, the pages in her small hand bending to the floor. 'I can see you're genuinely taken aback,' Ben Urich says. He reaches into his pocket and withdraws a shiny dime. 'Arbo and United—they're the real players here. I see I've upset you. Why don't you have a seat?'" (207).

As Urich parses the wider conspiracy at play, Lila Mae begins to grasp its manifold dimensions. This arrival at an understanding certainly departs from the kind of detective-type sussing out of clues in a comic like *Daredevil*, to which Whitehead alludes not only with a character named Ben Urich but also with Lila Mae's keen senses and ability to diagnose an elevator's malfunctions in her mind's eye. Unlike Daredevil's detective sense,

Whitehead relegates Lila Mae's Intuitionist skills to the technical and philosophical realm. The same inspector that possesses a sixth sense when it comes to assessing the functionality of elevators and who wills herself intellectually in tune with Fulton's theories cannot so fluently decipher the intentions of the cronies and con artists that populate the novel.

Ironically, this scene with Urich and Lila Mae, which serves to clarify plotlines for the reader, has a humorous tone. Throughout their conversation, Urich is tossing his dime in the air, failing to catch it, and scrambling around on the floor to recover it. He also invents a tall tale to convince Lila Mae that he defended himself heroically when he was ambushed by Jim and John, two industry thugs from Arbo (a leading elevator manufacturer) sent to quash his article. Then, as their brief meeting gets interrupted by Jim and John, Whitehead describes Urich's attempt to defend the intrusion as hopelessly ill-fated: "Ben Urich takes his lumps. Ben Urich always takes his lumps" (212). Even though Lila Mae ultimately escapes John's clutches by darting into a dance club, Whitehead forfeits the moment that could have been triumphant for his inspector protagonist. Flouting the tropes of detective fiction, Whitehead neither allows this scene to be neatly tied off nor suggests a linear resolution.

Gene Andrew Jarrett's *Deans and Truants: Race and Realism in African American Literature* provides a disciplinary backdrop for African American novels like *The Intuitionist* in its interrogation of sociocultural change. Jarrett makes the case that deans—those who believe black writers should exclusively address the inequities of black life through realism—view writers that do not primarily emphasize race as truant. Regarding a shift in aesthetic tradition since the early twentieth century, he argues that the efforts of authors "to interrogate racial hierarchy and celebrate inclusive Americanism, yet remain attentive to the history of race and racism in the United States, implies a more sophisticated way of thinking about the connection of racial history to the canons or traditions of African American literature" (186). Jarrett's argument calls to mind the tensions in black postmodernist work, which, as of late, finds some if its compelling implications in Afrofuturism.

Because the term *Afrofuturism*, at times, gets activated to mean all things black and future, it requires some contextualization, particularly as it concerns black literature and technoculture. One well-known attempt to explore what constitutes Afrofuturism is Mark Dery's 1994 essay "Black to the Future," which describes it as "African-American signification that appropriates images of technology and a prosthetically enhanced future . . ." (180). In his essay, Dery solicited insight on the cultural politics of the evolving genre from Samuel Delany. Delany acknowledged that his own writing has "situated material that encourages the reader's engagement with some of the political questions that the disenfranchised people in this country" must contend with (188). Then he insisted that, if speculative fiction was to have aesthetic or political force, it must inhabit a marginal position: "I don't want to see it operating from anyone's center: black nationalism's, feminism's, gay rights', pro-technology movements', ecology movements', or any other center" (189). It is almost impossible not to grasp the postmodern sensibility in Delany's words—which seems to describe the model Whitehead offers in *The Intuitionist* half a decade later. Likewise, Delany's commentary reveals the strength of Afrofuturism, which lies in its decentered significations on race and oppression in a world of both technological and societal machinations. Afrofuturism constitutes a cultural and aesthetic means of getting at the insidious power relations that are maintained by technologically savvy agencies. Such agencies tend to marginalize minoritized others who gain, at best, trial access to the corridors of power but are not afforded, as Delany puts it, "equitable input."

In her essay "Future Texts," Alondra Nelson delves into the twenty-first century rhetoric around race and technoculture that underscores the marginalization of black thought in this arena. Nelson is critical of mainstream discourses, which offer a paradigm of future technology that attempts to disappear race and ignore identity altogether. And when those discourses diverge from this perspective, they embrace a framework premised on the capacity of future technology to decenter the self in computer-mediated ways—and thereby render racial oppression moot. Nelson particularly takes aim at the notion of a "digital divide" among blacks and whites, in which "Blackness gets constructed as always oppositional to technologically driven chronicles of progress" (1). In *Dark Matter: A Century of Speculative Fiction from the African Diaspora*, Sheree Thomas exposes this obfuscation using the dark matter metaphor to describe the overlooked cultural contributions blacks have made to both technoculture and speculative fiction.

Perhaps more than any other focus within her essay, Nelson asserts that black intellectual thought had long ago posited tools by which to analyze futurism (namely Du Bois's notion of double consciousness in which the psyche and the self are in flux). So it makes sense that Nelson is able to conceptualize Afrofuturism as a phenomenon "grounded in the histories of black communities, rather than seeking to sever all connections to them" (9). In this context, Afrofuturism signals an interesting tone in black literary studies. The tone is derived from several discourses—slave narratives, protest literature, nationalist rhetoric—which have used literature to defend black humanity and demand racial equality. Throughout the twentieth century these trends furnished the vernacular-based idioms that propelled African American literature. More recently, postmodern culture has ushered in concerns about technoculture and race. Bridging these elements, Afrofuturism imagines the complicated implications of technological change for race relations and vice-versa.

Situating Colson Whitehead's Work

While black science-fiction writers Samuel Delany, Octavia Butler, and Tananarive Due are often referenced in discussions about Afrofutrism, I believe particular works by postmodernist writers like Toni Cade Bambara, Ishmael Reed, and Colson Whitehead could be described as Afrofuturist. Each of these writers has thematized around the influence of the industrial sector and remained "attentive to the history of race and racism in the United States" (*Deans and Truants* 186). Whitehead is unique among the particular writers (Walker, Killens, and Morrison) I explore in this study because of his Afrofuturist sensibility. His aesthetic operates in several ways: it explodes notions of a singular kind of blackness, transforms the ways readers see society, features (technological) futurist elements or unsustainable mechanized practices, and illustrates the discursive quality of literature. For instance, *The Intuitionist* heralds the coming of a futuristic elevator with heretofore unseen malleability. At the same time, the elevator industry itself overruns with special interests working to manipulate the novel's protagonists.

Because Whitehead's fiction is concerned with race and history, it hints at futuristic environs, and these settings offer insight into past social crises. Investigating an insidious racial order, Whitehead has opted for a focused approach to understanding the motivating force behind the will to advance in society and the snares that await. His fictional project is about evaluating a set of cultural assumptions. But it can only be practical, in literature and otherwise, if it can portray the means not only to "interrogate racial hierarchy" but also to maneuver through it. While Whitehead's work and current black fiction may not engage race with the protest zeal of earlier literary and social movements, it supplies a useful take on the burdens borne by ordinary individuals making their way in the aftermath of these movements.[1] If this shift allows for a more comprehensive representation of black American life, then considering the tensions blacks encounter in everyday social exchanges can serve as a significant starting point. In fact, the more open the canon becomes, the more critical attention should lean toward the cognitive shifts African Americans have had to make since the mid-twentieth century.

In an interview with Linda Selzer, Whitehead states, "Every advancement has its benefits and its price. My outlook on the world prohibits me from cheerleading the latest thing—I always have to find the weakness. The hidden cost. So—the Intuitionists, despite their philosophy, have to be a bit corrupt as a group because they are human beings" (396). Because Whitehead's skepticism drives him, he does not take even the appearance of virtue in his novels at face value. He acknowledges that, as a result of integration, a culture of pride emerged that ignored some of the criticism of the gains from that era. As Whitehead suggests in the interview, at the crux of *The Intuitionist* rests his suspicion of events and changes, historic or otherwise, which purport to be a net positive for ordinary individuals.

Whitehead's novels make a number of critical moves, giving his oeuvre the task of "explicating racial authenticity, cultural memory, and cross-cultural interpenetration" (New 242). For Bernard Bell, Whitehead and his contemporaries "experiment with the conventions of legend, tale, and fable" (82). His work has also been read as postmodernist in Brian Norman's *Neo-segregation Narratives: Jim Crow in Post–Civil Rights American Literature* and Dubey's *Signs and Cities: Black Literary Postmodernism* because of its capacity to play with time and to exploit assumptions about the historic past and future. Fritz Gysin's "From Modernism to Postmodernism: Black Literature at the Crossroads" describes Whitehead's aesthetic as "a postmodern brand of historiographic metafiction" (149). Thus, his literature has a manifold quality to it.

With the publication of *The Intuitionist*, which incorporates futuristic ideas about technology, Whitehead entered the broad arena of speculative fiction. On the one hand, this genre has not been known for elevating much diversity. On the other hand, perhaps because of this, it is ripe for new themes and voices. In it, Whitehead has been able to apply racial concerns to issues of technology, politics, and industry. Isiah Lavender and Frankie Bailey have written about the intersection of cultural politics and speculative fiction in Whitehead's work.[2] Taken together, these elements give *The Intuitionist* in particular a strong Afrofuturist bent, through which a commentary on race emerges.

Whitehead's second novel, *John Henry Days*, suggests that one of his concerns has not been merely recasting the past. William Ramsey in "An End of Southern History" writes that the southern setting in *John Henry Days* "undermines the whole project of traditional historical explanation" (780). Similarly, in "City Memory, City History," Tamar Katz remarks that *The Colossus*, though set in an urban environment, "generates a perpetually vanishing past and unlike *The Intuitionist* doesn't imagine a city in any substantial way organized around racial lines or by divisions in politics, class, or ethnicity" (811, 822). I focus on *The Intuitionist* because it not only portrays an identifiable historical moment (the era of racial integration) but also does not shy away from a confrontation with the burdens his protagonists face in work contexts and in working through long-held cultural narratives. Some narratives have to do with religious tradition and heritage. The most complex, however, center on what it means to make progress as a black American. While Whitehead's work has taken its place in black literary studies, not enough attention has gone toward identifying critical subtexts in *The Intuitionist*, specifically around the auxiliary role blacks are compelled to play as workers in corrupt organizations.

* * *

One main trope in *The Intuitionist* supports its racial allegory: the notion of "interminable progress." The concept emerges during a confrontation between Pompey and Lila Mae in which Lila Mae accuses him of sabotaging her career. As soon as Lila Mae ends the conversation, "A thin old gentleman with a wooden cane, on his interminable progress up the street stops to wave at him, and Pompey returns the greeting" (195). The insertion of the old gentleman is significant because he represents a bygone era of communal solidarity; the last positive remnants of the neighborhood are embodied in the saunter of an elderly man. The "interminable progress," he exemplifies, though slow and steady, cannot serve as an adequate hedge against the encroaching forces of drugs, crime, and socioeconomic deprivation, which Pompey cites for Lila Mae as deleterious to his neighborhood. In this scene, Whitehead conveys the message that, while progress as blacks have known it has been slow, but steady, and wearisome, it also has been a cultural bulwark against hopelessness. Yet embedded in the old man's amble is Whitehead's point that new definitions of progress, which can revitalize and energize it as a cultural force in black communities will need to emerge—budding in a new era in which previous ideas about progress have become unsustainable. The notion of achingly slow progress rests neatly in black traditions of freedom songs and spirituals, which champion steadiness while acknowledging the setbacks of racial animus that threaten hope but fail to extinguish it entirely.

Perhaps this interminable progress is most evident in the atmosphere of group constraints and institutional exploitations in *The Intuitionist,* wherein Whitehead highlights black workers' self-conscious pursuit of socioeconomic mobility. Lila Mae hails from a tradition of resilient black women invested in the promise of racial progress, namely Harriet Beechum, a prominent black actress mentioned in the text; Fanny Briggs, an enslaved African who teaches herself to read; and Lila Mae's vigilant third-grade teacher, Ms. Parker. Lila Mae builds upon a foundation of strength, curiosity, and, at times, riskiness. This foundation is a counterweight to her affinity for the "unsettling void" that attracted her to elevators in the first place. In *From Modernism to Postmodernism: Concepts and Strategies of Postmodern American Fiction*, Gerhard Hoffmann says of the notion of the void that the "ineffable takes the form of a mystery, a 'paradoxical verity'" (630), and this holds true for Lila Mae. Yet her sense of a void evolves throughout the text and is probably best epitomized in her favorite line from Fulton's writings: "*There is another world beyond this one*" (63).[3]

The legacy from which Lila Mae draws propels her to become a top elevator inspector. But it also compromises her capacity to the meet the unspoken demands of a society in transition. Harriet Beechum, Fanny Briggs, and Ms. Parker all converge on Lila Mae's shoulders to create the "strong black woman" ethos to which she is beholden. Not only do these figures represent dynamism and the capacity to work one's way up to great accomplishments, but also they provide for her a core narrative, which suggests that motivation and effort are essential elements of a successful career. After Lila Mae has achieved noteworthy feats, they exemplify what is possible for her as she challenges herself through education and meaningful work. Her decision to attend the Institute for Vertical Transport (IVT), study elevation, and subsequently begin a career in a male-dominated field is less about putting a chink in the armor of patriarchy than it is about filling a personal, through group-derived, void. This void is at the root of Lila Mae's feelings of self-consciousness, which urge her to work tirelessly and endure hardship to achieve her goals. For example, Lila Mae studied hard and "lived in the janitor's closet because the Institute for Vertical Transport did not have living space for colored students" (43).

One of the reasons this cultural narrative of diligence becomes a burden is because Lila Mae embraces the idea that her capacity to endure will enable her to overcome any systemic obstacles. Her ability to survive IVT by "not mix[ing] much with the other students, who were in turn thankful that she had spared them the burden of false conciliation" (44) suggests that staying above the fray is a legitimate approach to surviving mainstream spaces. The unwitting problem with this is that Lila Mae does not account for either the corrosive effect of this kind of social alienation, which others her intelligence, or the ways in which it could render her vulnerable to nefarious forces in her career. Lila Mae cannot experiment with connections across racial lines not only because of white hostility but also because the stories of the women she idolizes exist in a vacuum for her. Because Lila Mae's cultural narrative does not equip her with the means to externalize her feelings, she can only entertain the idea of a clear path from education to career and is left ill-prepared to deal with the jagged detours and complications that emerge outside of her comfort zone. Tucked into Lila Mae's narrative is also the desire to gain back the cultural credibility lost by leaving the South and abandoning some of the social norms she once embraced (religion, class, gender roles). Really, Lila Mae follows a group ideology that feeds her inner life and offers her a romanticized, mental mooring to return to in order to cope with the city. This proves to be more of a curse than a blessing because, if one's answer to systemic institutional problems is to blindly push forward through hard work and a sense of purpose, then one gains little ability to combat the sidelong animosity and ulterior motives that may be at play in a work environment. In fact, one is left to assume naively that any such duplicity can be mitigated by procedures that exist for that purpose, and that the system will unequivocally support its workers. Ultimately, Lila Mae is blinkered by the logic of uplifting the race through individual sacrifice and achievement.

The mainstream exploitation that befalls Lila Mae stems from an evolving zeitgeist around technology. As a devout member of the Intuitionist camp of inspectors and touting an accuracy rating of 100 percent, Lila Mae is laser-focused on executing her duties. However, disdain for her perfectionism is in part what gets her embroiled in controversy. Much of the drama clouds around the Elevator Guild's (the inspector's association that oversees the department) election year. Two candidates vie for guild chair, Frank Chancre (Empiricist) and, hopeful, Oliver Lever (Intuitionist). Blamed for the inexplicable Number Eleven elevator crash at the Fanny Briggs Memorial Building, Lila Mae becomes a scapegoat for the guild officials, rank-and-file Intuitionists believe this incident will discredit their camp and hurt their candidate's chances.

The next phase of exploitation that comes down the pike toward Lila Mae is particularly insidious because of its convoluted, political nature. The entire elevator sector is searching frantically for Fulton's black box. The result of an intense study of elevation, the black box is believed by many insiders and special interests to contain a blueprint for technologically unparalleled elevators of the future. Meanwhile, Lila Mae cannot figure out how or why she was swept up into the opposite pole of the controversy, the elevator crash. Because of obfuscation at the department, Lila Mae also cannot pinpoint who might be directing the animus toward her. In short order, her home is burglarized, and then she is given a room at the company residence, Intuitionist House, by Lever's secretary and campaign manager, Mr. Reed, who assures Lila Mae that her name will be cleared from suspicion. But, at this point, Lila Mae is not content to leave her fate to anyone, not even her fellow Intuitionists.

In the novel, access to any substantive power follows a racialized logic. Whitehead highlights the ability of both the Department of Elevator Inspectors and various industrial entities to conceal agendas, rendering Lila Mae, Pompey, and their industrial peer Raymond Natchez Coombs as something less than stakeholders in the organizations for which they work. In addition, veiled or covert attempts to curtail their mobility are significant because they speak to the perceived threat of black and minority workers who must be kept at bay, away from power. The most maddening feature of this type of ill-treatment is that it entangles workers and ultimately denies them the mechanisms to work outside the system to make any recourse possible. In effect, the threat of exploitation in mainstream entities becomes imminent because black workers are figuratively walled inside the bureaucracy, placing them in situations where they are both undermined and surveilled by virtually every interest group in the elevator sector. In this context, The Intuitionist opens up a dialogue with readers that is as relevant to shifts in the opportunities available to African Americans as it is to the historical worker oppression (divide and conquer) blacks have endured.

When Lila Mae confronts Pompey about the Number Eleven elevator incident, we gain a window into Pompey's own conundrum regarding group logic and his mainstream vulnerability. Lila Mae accuses Pompey of being involved in the incident, but he denies playing any role in targeting her. Still, Whitehead suggests that he despises Lila Mae for possessing some of the same conformist values as he did when he became an elevator inspector. Even before Lila Mae's tenure, a vicious rumor about Pompey circulated within the department. The rumor depicts blacks as obsequious opportunists groveling for promotions. The story suggests that Holt, the former guild chair, once summoned Pompey upstairs for a conference: "He [Pompey] expected confidences; Holt told him he was going to kick him in the ass. Pompey laughed (this executive humor was going to take a little getting used to) and went along with the joke, even after Holt told him to bend over. Which he did. Pompey continued to chortle until Holt kicked him in the left ass cheek with the arrowhead of one of his burgundy wing-tips. . . . The next day a small memo appeared on Pompey's desk informing him of his promotion to Inspector Second Grade" (25).[4]

The rumor about Pompey indicates the degree to which the department conspicuously freights workers of color with the burden of being political hires. This dynamic challenges black workers themselves with accepting the validity of each other's employment. For example, before their confrontation, Lila Mae thinks Pompey himself sabotaged the elevator and suspects that he "would have jumped at the chance, white foamy saliva smeared across his cheeks. Didn't he say something to that effect when they were in O'Connor's, just after the crash when Lila Mae crouched against the wall like a thief? She's finally got what's been coming to her" (83). Interestingly, Lila Mae does not give a convincing reason why Pompey would stoop so low, other than what she perceives as job-related resentment and Pompey's self-loathing of his own blackness.

Pompey's reflection on his own rise to elevator inspector sheds some light on how thoroughly the department exploited his vulnerabilities in that position. Even though, for Lila Mae, Pompey's rant obscures his own anguish, Whitehead presents it to readers as central in understanding his politics. As Pompey puts it, "You come along, strutting like you own the place. Like they don't own you. But they do. If not Chancre, then Lever. I was the first one in the Department. I was the first colored elevator inspector in history. In history! And you will never, ever know what hell they put me through. You think you have it bad? You have no idea. And it was because I did it first that you're here now. All my life I wanted to be an elevator inspector. That's all I wanted to be. And I got it. I was the first colored man to get a Department badge" (195). One gathers that, as a Negro firster, Pompey has had to sublimate his anger toward racist co-workers, and that he still harbors bitter memories that continue to plague him. Pompey has also endured so much degradation that he compromises his own integrity. After correcting the rumor, he admits taking bribes from Frank Chancre (current Empiricist president of the Elevator Guild) and his mob-boss friend, Johnny Shush. Pompey is tasked with helping some of Shush's buildings pass inspection.

As suggested in the passage, the notion of owning/ownership is an important one, particularly for Lila Mae. For the most part, Pompey seems to have come to terms with the bleakness of any legitimate future opportunities he might have had. Hemmed in economically, Pompey cedes his autonomy for kickbacks from corrupt brass and for some semblance of economic control in his personal life. Pompey has endured for years the ethical dilemma in which Lila Mae finds herself. Robbed of his agency because of his zeal to get a "Department badge," he plans to "go to work on Monday like I always do and see what happens" (195). While Pompey has devoted his life to what appeared to be a progressive track (tokenism), his integration into the department has only paved the way for Lila Mae to make compromised choices and to occupy an untenable position—one winnowing her meager sense of agency down to department bidding.

Lila Mae's observations when she first enters Pompey's neighborhood to confront him draw attention to one source of group- and community-based pressure. They live only two blocks away but in different situations: "On her street she [Lila Mae] is anonymous; the Caribbean immigrants share a code, a broad and secret choreography she is excluded from. But these [Pompey's neighbors] are American colored" (190). Lila Mae's neighbors greet each other, wear extravagant hats, and look out for each other's children, keeping their less-sanitized behavior indoors. In contrast, the bad habits of Pompey's neighbors spill out into the community.

When Lila Mae calls Pompey out for violating the inspector's oath, he unapologetically tells her that he needed the money to move his family out of a rapidly deteriorating neighborhood. Pompey delivers a diatribe about the socioeconomic conditions he faces: "I was raised in this neighborhood. It's changed. . . . A few years from now, it won't be reefer [sold] but some other poison. My kids won't be here when that happens. I need money to take them [his wife and two sons] out of here" (194). The burden that Pompey bears can be encapsulated in the idea that, as the black community goes, so does the black individual. The problem is not that Pompey does not want to leave his community behind. The problem is that his choices are tethered to group experience. Even though these conditions may be the result of outside discrimination and disparity around employment, he does not have the means to escape them. The pressure he feels as an individual to make a decision that is in his family's best interest is linked to the community (or group) conditions that surround him. Presumably, Pompey grew up in this neighborhood at a time when the social norms were such that racial hostility ensured blacks would ban together for safety and stability. Attaining mobility, in spite of racial hostility, was the order of the day, but now the community seems to be hollowing itself out. Pompey cannot entertain the idea of enduring the current cultural reality.

Lila Mae may take a certain amount of comfort in her living conditions, but it is fleeting at best. Lila Mae too surrenders considerable autonomy to become an elevator inspector—and following the crash, her future in this role becomes tenuous at best. The industry robs her of the basic security needed to show up to work and do her job. Still, none of this adds up to the hard fact that her ambition has been subverted by the industry in ways she had not anticipated. Simply put, Lila Mae cannot own her accomplishments anymore. The sacrifices she made to earn a perfect inspection record do not pay off; rather, they make her a target of incessant corruption. Still, Lila Mae neither realizes that Pompey's bitterness has implications for what the job will do to her nor sees herself as a cog in the machine of unseen, competing interests. Unaware that the department has coerced her into searching for the black box, she sees Pompey as "a small man on a dirty stoop in an endless city" and continues her investigation.

Whitehead's insertion of Raymond Coombs, a strong-arm industrial consultant for Arbo, into the black-box commotion highlights the race consciousness he espouses, his corporate status, and his role as trickster. Surreptitiously installed as a butler at Intuitionist House, Coombs curries favor with Lila Mae through faux southern hospitality. Lila Mae could use a friend, he determines, and his feigned concern makes him appear an ally. Later, Coombs claims to be Fulton's nephew, tells of Fulton's passing for white, and affirms that the black box does exist. His story is that he wants to reclaim the box for all black Americans. In the face of Coombs's gratuitous race pride, Lila Mae grows skeptical of Fulton's motivations. She wonders: "did he remain silent, smile politely at their darkie jokes. Tell a few of his own" (139). Cautioning Lila Mae's cynicism while playing on her sensitivities to Fulton's work, Coombs speaks of hearing the brass "talk about his invention, they always saying it's the future. It's the future of the cities. But it's our future, not theirs. It's ours. And we need to take it back. What he made, this elevator, colored people made that. It's ours. And I'm going to show that we ain't nothing. Show them downstairs and the rest of them that we are alive" (140). Revealing his motivations, Coombs says: "I wanted to give them a warning, I guess. Of what I'm gonna do to them. . . . I wanted to get back at them. For what they did to my uncle that messed up his head. For what they did to you [Lila Mae]" (168). Coombs's zeal seems genuine to Lila Mae because it resonates with the ambition that has animated not only her search for the black box but also her purpose for becoming an elevator inspector.

Though much of Coombs rhetoric is couched in dissimulation, he is seizing upon cultural notions brought about by racial integration, which resulted in an ethos that encouraged blacks to see themselves as a collectivity invested in the same goals around advancement and the acknowledgement of contributions made by blacks to the modern American experience. While Coombs seems to be devoid of any real allegiance to a cultural narrative, that is not the case. Lila Mae soon learns that, while he has no interest in paving the way for other blacks to enter the corporate world, he is invested in maintaining his privilege and Arbo's bottom line. Yet, Coombs is a complicated figure. The novel suggests that, while he embraces a middle-class politics of black elitism, the head shot of Martin Luther King that adorns his wall suggests that he is—at least by default—concerned with the state of black America as a whole. When Lila Mae observes another photograph, of his family, Coombs identifies his wife by her occupational pedigree as a registered nurse, indicating his careerism. If anything, what distinguishes Coombs from Lila Mae and Pompey is that he has no reservations about embracing both an elitist cultural identity and a corporate structure that wields him as a weapon to defend their material interests.

Coombs exploits Lila Mae's preference for staying as neutral as possible in the scramble for the black box. Earlier, she offers Coombs a sort of truce: "I just want to clear my name—and for you to get what belongs to you" (169). Here she frames her budding relationship with Coombs as similar to her social contract with the city. If Lila Mae can keep "the city vertical and intact, and the city will leave her alone. And now look at her: she let the city down last Friday, was remiss in her duties, and look at the metropolis's retribution" (170). Lila Mae believes her neutral "exchange of services" perspective has failed because the contract to which she alludes required that the city (elevator corporations, the department, and the Intuitionist camp) operate with the same disinterestedness. Yet these stand-ins for the city act in their own interests, which leaves these entities capable of rendering Coombs and Lila Mae as objects acted upon, rather than as actors with agency.

Ultimately, Urich reveals to Lila Mae that Coombs is a corporate spy, and Lila Mae decides to confront him at Arbo headquarters. Acting as what W. Lawrence Hogue in *Race, Modernity, Postmodernity* describes as a postmodern subject, Coombs occupies "many subjective positions" and is a "phenomenon of African American urban reality" (152). This feature of Coombs's persona is what enables him to cleverly navigate corporate bureaucracy. Coombs lends his fidelity to the enterprise end of things, not the political. He spies on Pompey and takes sides against the guild. In addition, he sabotages Chancre's verticality demonstration at Funicular Follies, the guild's annual celebration.

Though he works for Arbo, Coombs knows that surviving corporate power is about playing multiple advantageous roles and watching his own flank. Coombs's own agenda is tenuous and rests on a "certain latitude" granted him by his employers. He has managed to snag a sliver of agency as a special projects executive. To Coombs's own detriment and benefit, he gives himself over to corporate cronyism for the enjoyment of a titular executive post. Just as the creative destruction of the elevator industry will serve his corporate handler well in boom time, the incessant process will eventually backfire, leaving Coombs on the wrong end of the bust. On the one hand, Whitehead gives readers an example of what it would look like to willingly embrace the extremes of group consensus and mainstream co-optation. On the other hand, the novel implies that this choice is unsustainable, and, worse, it subverts individual consciousness. The crucial point is that undermining this kind of group/mainstream bind requires more nuanced assumptions and practices than those to which Coombs subscribes.

When Lila Mae questions Coombs about his knowledge of Fulton's race in his office, he responds, "No one cares where he came from" (250). Coombs rebuffs what he reads as the unproductive distraction blacks impose upon themselves when seeking the acknowledgement of black achievement from whites. As Coombs explains, "[T]he rank and file in the industry won't believe, and those who know care more about his last inventions. His color doesn't matter once it gets to that level. The level of commerce. They can put Fulton into one of those colored history calendars if they want—it doesn't change the fact that there's money to be made from his invention." The hopelessness of such ventures is figured in the granite menagerie located outside Arbo headquarters. Replete with stone animals, the menagerie symbolizes the corporate status quo, which involves putting on display (or othering) tokens and firsters for repetitive glances while the industry profits from their labor and intellectual property. Lila Mae's refusal to add another piece (the company emblem, Arbo Excelsior) to the menagerie outside indicates a previously unseen understanding of her larger predicament.

When Lila Mae encounters Coombs at Arbo, he "wears a crisp white oxford shirt punished by gold suspenders—corporate creation as opposed to the coarse fabrics of the man's former disguise. Those struggling working-man stitches" (248). His voice has morphed from southern drawl to northern finishing-school diction: "He no longer speaks like a colored man from the South. Like Natchez. Nor is his face the same as it was, in this fluorescent light, in this circulated air" (249). Coombs describes for Lila Mae the onus behind her fixation on the black box and says it makes her predictable: "Let one colored in and you're integrated. Let two in, you got a race war as they try to kiss up to whitey" (249). This snide remarks runs counter to Lila Mae's own ideas about her motivations. She has been intent on following her passion and unable to revise her ideas about what constitutes progress for blacks. We get the sense that, as an inspector, Lila Mae has given short shrift to racial concerns because she believed that putting forth her best effort on the job and navigating her way around race would protect her from its troublesome orbit. While Coombs's dissimulation gains him a modicum of mobility in a corrupt system, Lila Mae's overt diligence plays right into the wiles of the political and industrial elite.

Whitehead's Integration Metropolis

Whitehead, in *The Intuitionist*, explores the socioeconomic tensions of racial integration as the elevator bureaucracy and industry collide. In doing so, he fleshes out a discourse critical of the shifting social tides that were part and parcel of integration. The black characters—Lila Mae, Pompey, Fulton, and Coombs—all find themselves cobbling together just enough agency to survive the less than savory schemes that surround them. Lila Mae and the others grasp the unstable nature of equal access. Though Whitehead has his characters become self-aware and employ tactics to avoid being mired in career-tarnishing corruption, they cannot escape some level of compromise. Nor do institutional protections intervene to fulfill their egalitarian purposes. Instead, integration unmoors an avalanche of duplicity and misdeeds, which serve as a collective backlash against inclusion. With the inextricable links between labor and unchecked power structures exposed, the key in overcoming these conditions lies in mounting an effective resistance. Whitehead suggests that everyday workers—with the same machinations as well-heeled brass—must fend off hegemonic domination.[5]

In *The Intuitionist*, integration is threatened by leaders and interest groups embedded in the elevator industry. Whereas many industries tended to view integration as an encroaching political phenomenon, for African Americans the effort signified access to employment and opportunity. Nonetheless, the bureaucratic and political ploys of the elevator industry work to eclipse this historic milestone. An early scene captures the tension. When Lila Mae is called back to headquarters to discuss the Fanny Briggs crash, she fixates on a billboard. Lila Mae believes that ordinary citizens view the billboard, which features an elevator ad, as a "dim affirmation of modernity, happy progress to be taken for granted and subconsciously cherished" (14). This passage serves as a clear description of the environment Whitehead creates—one that portrays society slow-walking inclusion in the early stages of integration. The presence of token blacks in positions previously held by whites strikes a chord that reverberates throughout the text. The move toward the inclusion of African Americans is also reflected in an expansive phrase from the novel: "summoning them into tumultuous modernity" (158). Even though this line describes the impact that the elevator had upon the American city, when read in relation to the novel's integration backdrop, the phrase stresses that elevation (or equality) helps to offset the failings of modern society.

Whitehead's integration metropolis should be contextualized within the history of the northern city and black subjectivity. Writing about twentieth-century migration out of the agrarian South in "*Who Set You Flowin'?" The African-American Migration Narrative*, Farah Jasmine Griffin discusses the desire of many African Americans to create a new self in the North because "for many, the sites of the ancestor are stifling and provincial and as such they inhibit . . . progress" (8). In *The City in African American Literature,* Yoshinobu Hakutani and Robert Butler remark that, though "never hesitant to criticize the negative aspects of American city life, [twentieth century black literature] has only rarely suggested that pastoral alternatives to the city exist for black people" (10). Stressing the unique development of "black urban consciousness" in the city, the writers cite Amiri Baraka's essay "Black Literature in the Afro-American Nation," which argues that, "if the cities represent higher levels of perception and sophistication for us in America, they must be the focal point of yet more advanced levels of struggle."[6]

One level of struggle in the novel is that integration efforts are hijacked and used as a foil for ideological disputes in the elevator industry. Whitehead creates controversy around two groups, the Empiricists and the Intuitionists, not for the sake of privileging one faction over another but to have readers question their respective allegiances. Whitehead sets Empiricism at odds with Intuitionism, showing how the former allies with Western modernity and the latter with postmodern difference. Empiricists vilify Intuitionist inspectors, calling them witch doctors. Intuitionists decry Empiricists as overreliant on sight perception. For instance, in a press conference following the Fanny Briggs crash, Chancre poses the rhetorical question: "Why hold truck with the uppity and newfangled when Empiricism has always been the steering light of reason? Just like it was in our fathers' day, and our fathers' fathers'. Today's incident is just the kind of unfortunate mishap that can happen when you kowtow to the latest fashions from overseas" (27). Chancre deliberately historicizes Empiricism and seems to render Intuitionism as a Eurocentric, postmodern paradigm deserving outsider status.

Later in the novel, Lila Mae offers a critique of Empiricism: "They [elevator companies] have already bought off many of the street men— building owners lay cash on inspectors in exchange for fastidious blindness to defect. Their sacred Empiricism has no meaning when it can be bought" (240). Nonetheless, for Whitehead, privileging either framework ignores the cronyism among those that make the products and those that service them. Significantly, the presence of African Americans in the industry only expands the supply from which power brokers can pluck inspectors for their foul purposes.

Empiricism in the novel is conspicuously premised on logic and reason. When an Empiricist services an elevator, he or she does so literally by-the-book and based upon prior experience. However, as the name suggests, Intuitionists utilize their intuition when servicing elevators, which includes sensory experience and extrasensory methods. For example, Lila Mae literally "leans against the dorsal wall of the elevator and listens" as the "elevator's vibrations are resolving themselves in her mind . . ." (5–6). Whitehead uses the racialization and gendering of Intuitionism to critique what he sees as an always already compromised empirical "light of reason."

Whitehead draws attention to the status of Intuitionism through its most prominent practitioner, Lila Mae. The logic behind scapegoating her for the elevator crash stems from what Chuck describes as "innovation and regression." One side of this dichotomy is backlash from executives as a result of the entrance of women and minorities into the Elevator Guild. During a press conference, the mayor and the guild chair promise to launch a full investigation, yet they sidestep any accusations of foul play and dismiss racial animus as a factor. They claim a neutral focus "on the facts at hand, such as the inspection records" (23). Slipping undetected into O'Connor's bar, which is frequented by elevator inspectors, Lila Mae comprehends that "she's a lost tourist among heavy vowels, the crude maps of ancestral homelands, and the family crests of near-exterminated clans. Her position is precarious everywhere she goes in this city, for that matter, but she's trained to keep invisible in its ubiquity . . ." (23). One random comment that seems to echo her thoughts comes from the bar: "Everything known is now different" (24). The language here speaks to what Cornel West calls homogeneous communalism[7] and brings Chuck's ruminations full circle. The challenge to breaking this kind of status quo exclusion lies in the power of cultural difference, in terms of both race and intellectual legitimacy. However, even as difference challenges prescribed authority, it also represents an opportunistic moment for leaders who self-servingly tout diversity while simultaneously stoking fear about change.

Whitehead encapsulates the conundrum hamstringing black inclusion: "Habits clamp down on the ankle and resist all entreaties, no matter how logical. As it is in politics, the only victor in the end was ugly compromise" (16). The notion of an ugly compromise between black people, companies, and public policy is the sword dangling above the heads of newly integrated workers. While the doors to inspector positions like the one Lila Mae walks through are pried open by activism and protracted movements, Whitehead pinpoints the ways this compromised and tainted access is felt in the psyche of firsters. It is significant that in African American literature some of the most prominent characters (Sethe, Bigger Thomas) have embodied the deep ambiguities and rifts germane to particular eras in American history. One of the most significant constructions in this text is the black-firster identity, which Whitehead mines for its overt and subtle conflict. If ugly compromise is the unfortunate but obvious resolution to the anxieties around integration, then it is borne by black individuals equipped with the moxie to persevere while the guiding lights needed to navigate the prickly terrain of inclusion are in short supply.

Swept up in a web of duplicity, backroom deals, and political corruption, Lila Mae must confront the existential crisis of an embroiled inspector by making subtle compromises. Whitehead interrogates this dilemma by emphasizing Lila Mae's cultural consciousness and ambitious pursuits. He does this not only through the friction of her token status but also by placing her at odds with the elevator industry writ large. In the scene where Lila Mae goes home to contemplate the crash, she finds Jim and John, two industry cronies from Arbo, searching her apartment for Fulton's missing papers. Whitehead muses on racial integration through Jim's and John's observations, which betray an anxiety about the city's changing racial landscape. In one of *The Intuitionist*'s most interesting passages, John reveals his views about the circularity of life. He muses that "there must be patterns, experience is recursive, and if the pattern has not announced itself yet, it will, eloquent and emphatic in a mild-mannered sort of way" (28). To square this moment with other points throughout his life, John requires a new perspective that the lens through which he has viewed life has not given him. Jim and John represent the white mythical norm despite their criminality, a norm being winnowed away in the racial sea-change John philosophizes about.

As they methodically search Lila Mae's apartment, they busy themselves with an appraisal of her drab, identical suits. Pondering her sense of regularity, Jim and John confront their status as average individuals, "invisible everymen, the true citizens. Lila Mae counts few people in this world as friends. Jim and John are the rest. Dusty brown clumps of hair, prow jaws, complexions quick to blood" (29). Whitehead inscribes into John's philosophical position awareness of the crises in American industry and the way in which its veneer unravels, belying the idea that the rugged individualism of the majority alone ushered in modernity. In one instance, John peers through a window out over Lila Mae's neighborhood. From this vantage, Whitehead posits a fluid understanding of the tensions between speculators and immigrant communities that have shaped Lila Mae's surroundings. Acknowledging the influx of African Americans during the Great Migration and the flight of Polish and Russian immigrants (the latter maintains stores in the neighborhood), Whitehead exposes the hand of speculators in framing the meaning of the neighborhood for each group: "The neighborhood is changing again. Its meaning blurs at the edges as white people return, obeying the city's rules of teeming density and insidious rents. Only the real estate agents, who understand that meaning is elastic, know the borders of the neighborhood for sure, modulating their sales pitches to reassure their clients that they are not moving into the colored neighborhood, but into the farther reaches of the adjacent white neighborhood" (30). In describing a speculator's skill at shaping the meaning of a community to outsiders, the novel reveals an understanding of minority living conditions. This speaks to the wider socioeconomic implications of integration. In fact, Jim's and John's conversation explores the complexities of inclusion, which frames integration as a mixed bag of opportunity and exploitation.

In *The Intuitionist,* just as Lila Mae earns the coveted status of elevator inspector via integration, she also inherits the thorny industry practices that go along with it. Not long after the burglary, when Lila Mae is at Intuitionist House, she reflects on her diminishment in the face of the fallout (tabloid articles, rumors) surrounding her career. She muses on her small living quarters: "She thinks of her room at the Bertram Arms. It's a miracle she lives there, how accustomed she is to this small world. 'How small her expectations are'" (63). Her sense of smallness sits opposite to the capacity of those in power to exploit her. When Mr. Reed visits to tell her she has been set up because of the chaos over Fulton's black box, he ponders Chancre's motives for a preemptive strike, for involving someone in the outer circle away from high-profile orchestrations.

Mr. Reed speaks of Lila Mae's value to the Intuitionists in a way that paints her in a contradictory light, as fall-girl, token, and asset. Despite his linking Lila Mae's employment to the Intuitionists' liberal policies, he thinks it does not follow that the department implicates her in the elevator crash because of her race, gender, or perfect inspection record. His subsequent statement however reveals his disingenuousness: "You'd be surprised how many people have taken an interest in your career, Miss Lila Mae. The first colored woman to become an elevator inspector. That's quite an accomplishment. We're glad to have you in our camp. . . . We take care of our own" (64). Even though Mr. Reed promises absolution for Lila Mae after he sorts things out, Whitehead draws our attention in the text to the symbolic expansion of Lila Mae's "small expectations." After Mr. Reed's spiel, Lila Mae tells him that *she* will find the black box. Because Lila Mae believes the security of her job has become a foregone conclusion, she adopts a forward-thinking agenda. But before she can influence power and act as the custodian of her own narrative—independent of the semblance of progress ingrained into her via cultural means—Whitehead tasks her with negotiating two critical paths: her unyielding detective work to locate Fulton's missing papers and her intellectual/intuitive growth as an Intuitionist. First, Lila Mae must navigate the antics of the industry and its cronies. Then, she will have to shed her own composed exterior and appropriate Fulton's "luminous truth" (230).

Women and the Politics of Roles

In *The Intuitionist*, Whitehead ties issues of gender to situations in which women occupy roles either subject to male dominance or replete with reserved behavior. Lila Mae's conversations with Mr. Reed bring issues of gender to the fore. Her present skepticism "involves taking assistance from this man Reed—and it is the acceptance, and not the aid itself, which galls her and makes her pride curdle" (56). Reed's condescension juts up against the pride Lila Mae takes in striking her own path—a pride she fights to maintain when declaring she will locate the missing pages of Fulton's notebooks. In addition, one experience to which Lila Mae flashes back, about her abrasive father, Marvin, tells readers of their strained relationship, particularly as it concerns her education. She recalls a childhood incident in which she gets out of bed for a drink of water. Thinking her parents are asleep, she encounters her father drinking whiskey and reading about elevators. He calls her over and asks, "They teaching you how to read, girl?" (119). Lila Mae nods, but when she begins reading, she cannot identify most of the words. Her father reads every word and warns her to listen to her teacher: "'What'd you come down here for?' he asked her, talking loud now, not like when he was reading and he whispered. 'A glass of water.' 'Then get it and get your ass in bed.'" While her father takes an interest in her literacy, this incident, the contrast between gentle father and scathing patriarch, have the effect of making Lila Mae reticent in matters of education. For instance, when she applies to IVT, she does not tell her mother or father. As a result, she experiences guilt over leaving her parents and moving to the North.

The reticence she maintains as a dutiful daughter and adolescent unravels as she matures. While a teenager, Lila Mae goes on a movie date with her childhood friend Grady Jr., who is set to attend a college in the fall. Grady's demure behavior stifles her last opportunity for affection with him; he gently kisses her and then pulls away after spying her father in the window of her home. Lila Mae "wasn't mad at all, she wanted him to kiss her more. But Lila Mae didn't say that" (132). This marks the final instance of her reserved behavior. After moving to what is ostensibly New York City, she has a one-night stand with Freeport Jackson, a traveling beauty-products salesman, whom she approaches with a methodical, almost mechanical assertiveness. Her earlier reticence morphs into a disregard for trivial words and a command of the situation: "He said stuff but she ignored it because it did not pertain to the case" (180). Lila Mae only "recorded the details of the investigation, his fingers and kisses, his slow tumble on top of her . . ." A 1999 interview with *Salon* magazine sheds light on what seems like an odd sequence, given the development of Lila Mae's character throughout the novel. In the interview, Whitehead acknowledged that, when he initially started writing *The Intuitionist,* he relied on a stock male character. Ultimately, the decision to feature a woman protagonist led him to Lila Mae, whom he saw as more compelling. As Whitehead puts it, "She is incorruptible, but she has her own set of rules." In other words, Lila Mae does not fit into some saintly or docile stereotype; her character can be understood as both a street-smart and pragmatic person who equips persistence[8] as a tool in her war chest not only to face the city but also to endure a less-than-accommodating elevator-inspector career.

Another woman in the novel, Marie Claire Rogers, faces her own gendered challenges, with which Lila Mae becomes acquainted. As James Fulton's former resident housekeeper (he has been deceased for six years before the story takes place), Mrs. Rogers literally had to bear the burden of Fulton's endeavors, weathering intimidation and multiple break-ins. Lila Mae even has her own speculation about Mrs. Rogers: "It is Mrs. Rogers's house now, by contractual agreement. There was no mention of it in the file, but there must be rumors that Fulton and Mrs. Rogers were lovers. Why else go to so much trouble for a servant. Did she start redecorating when he was alive, by creeping degrees?" (89). Despite Lila Mae's speculation, we learn that Mrs. Rogers moves in because Fulton could not tolerate any other housekeepers. We also see that, when someone from the industry tries to make an informant out of her, she refuses: "Like I was going to be a spy in my own house, because that's what this place became as soon as I moved in here. My house. I told them to get the hell out of my kitchen . . ." (91). When Lila Mae asks why she accepted Fulton's offer to move in, Mrs. Rogers responds, "What am I going to do . . . stay in that city with all that foolishness that goes on these days? There ain't much to do out here, but you don't have to think about some kid knocking you over the head for your money" (90). Mrs. Rogers articulates the same sense of deprivation Pompey had identified, created by job discrimination and the nefarious practices of housing speculators and politicians, which limits opportunity in urban areas. This lack of opportunity has a compounding effect in black communities. Mrs. Rogers uses the agency she possesses as a domestic worker to negotiate her living conditions and escape those exacerbated by uneven development and sluggish socioeconomic access for black Americans.

Recently, critics like Dubey have given attention to *The Intuitionist*'s interrogation of urban modernity. For example, Dubey argues that "Whitehead's novel undertakes a critical excavation" and that he "revises the emancipatory narratives of . . . urban migration that propelled African-American literature for over a century" (*Signs and Cities* 238). Lila

Mae, Dubey argues, follows a path of social mobility by becoming literate and later questioning modern society's tenets of equality and self-discovery. On a fundamental level, Intuitionist philosophy—the brainchild of Fulton, who publishes the book that initiates it—awakens Lila Mae. Fulton's philosophy "makes perfect sense to Lila Mae once she understands the connection between racism and modern reason" (239).

In a different vein, John Johnston argues that Whitehead's project portrays Lila Mae as inserting herself into a coming sociopolitical order. According to Johnston, *The Intuitionist* mostly "consists of Lila Mae's efforts to avoid or move between the treacherous intrigues and manipulations of her boss, who is vying for re-election, and his Mafia supporters on one side, and the faux haven of Intuitionist House on the other" (863). Unlike Dubey, Johnston stresses the idea that, amid the threats, Lila Mae not only seeks out Fulton's theoretical work but also Fulton's role. He argues that, at the novel's end, Lila Mae "assumes the role of the 'keeper,' assimilating Fulton's voice" (864).

A Lila Mae that negotiates the good-old-boy gender politics of the department and the patriarchal tendencies of bureaucracies could make her way toward new perspectives that are amenable to her social and politically fragmented moment. Such a turn would offer her enormous potential in wresting her career and future away from unscrupulous figures like Mr. Reed and Oliver Lever. With a sense of the limitations of her current conceptions of progress and self-deluding, puritan work ethic, Lila Mae could embrace the postmodern projections of Fulton and add to them her awareness of the industrial frenzy over the future, because this would be a viable position. With a sense of the coming sociopolitical zeitgeist (speculative and self-destructive), she could negotiate the various intrigues and co-optations from a position of strength that bewilders and confounds unchecked power.

A Postmodern Unravelling of Cultural Notions

Whitehead posits a commentary on ambition in *The Intuitionist* to address the complicated internal motivations behind black progress. The novel describes rank-and-file elevator inspectors as "men of little ambition who sweat out their days looking at the calendar for their retirement date"

(70). This description is in contrast to the work character of Lila Mae and Pompey, which is largely self-conscious. Lila Mae has striven to become an exceptional elevator inspector, and Pompey, who holds a deep-seated disdain for the department, has endured untold degradation to rise within it. One reason Pompey abhors watching Lila Mae follow in his footsteps is that he despises what he sees as a pseudo-progress. Lila Mae has also earned a perfect inspection record while Pompey has climbed the rungs of the civil service ladder just high enough to do the boss's dirty work. Chuck is another character described as having a "scurrying ambition." Like Lila Mae and Pompey, he occupies a marginalized position in the world of elevator inspectors. Chuck desperately wants to finish his manuscript and justify his expertise and its value to the guild. All told, the diminishing viability of Lila Mae's career forces her to rethink her assumptions about what it means to make progress as a black elevator inspector and to reach for an operating principle that is postmodern.

Early on in the novel, in a conversation with an internal affairs agent about Lila Mae's whereabouts following the elevator crash, Chuck remarks, "You have to understand something about Lila Mae. She's different than you and me. . . . With how she sees things. It's not easy for her to work here" (111). Whitehead's critique of ambition is embedded in Chuck's words and speaks to much more than race. The text makes it clear that Lila Mae is black and does not have the luxury of simply *doing* her job. However, though she is the target of racial resentment and the ideal scapegoat for the incident, Lila Mae is driven by an ambition that supersedes her status as elevator inspector. What Whitehead wants to convey is that ambition alone is not a reliable attribute in a world of competing interests and political corruption; nor will maneuvering around the microaggressions or racial potholes suffice. Ambition has to be a strategic enterprise, and this is where Lila Mae's efforts become stymied. She has to arrive at a sensibility that does not view diligence or proving oneself as a sufficient quality in an industry rife with duplicity.

Whitehead's message is that those willing to make new assumptions about progress and to locate new routes to achieve this progress can thrive in uncertain contexts. To this end, he concerns himself with the sphere of recently integrated black labor, with those who pursue opportunity. In doing so, he zeroes in on ordinary people seeking upward mobility through work. Because Whitehead presents this reality as a very common human endeavor, he never endorses the option of lowering one's ambition in a competitive society. Nor does he accept the misconception that work opportunities would necessarily lead to equitable life chances. Instead, he calls for a postmodern redirecting of worker energy toward infusing the structures of power with racial difference and the perspectives of marginalized groups. Charles Banner-Haley's *The Fruits of Integration: Black Middle-Class Ideology and Culture, 1960–1990* looks at the way black cultural experiences, decades after integration, remain weighted to the "ongoing struggle of African Americans to define themselves and their attendant vision of what America is and is becoming, a struggle that has often fallen to the black middle class to mediate" (xxi). Whitehead's convictions seem to align with Banner-Haley's and, at the same time, move a step further as the novel consistently suggests that any new vision of social possibility for black Americans, regardless of class status, depends upon the achievement of individual agency within society.

As Lila Mae's quasi-mentor, Fulton signals an epistemological struggle between industrial capitalism and his postmodern framework about elevators of the future. Fulton also serves another purpose. Just as *The Intuitionist* depicts government and business monopolies, it also showcases the contributions to modernization by those rendered invisible. While the notion of the residual in postmodern discourse often relegates blacks to an otherness outside postmodernism, Fulton's philosophy (Intuitionism) acts as both marginal and foundational to the current practices of elevator inspectors. In addition, Fulton's research and philosophical development represent intellectual warfare against the assumptions of dominant culture. From the beginning, Whitehead has Fulton write against the inherently biased "all safe" elevation theories of Otis (the founder of Empiricism). Characteristically, Fulton's theories are abstract and, by Lila Mae's estimation, "It was Fulton's odd perceptions that made him a technical wiz, his way of finding the unobvious solution that is also the perfect solution" (100). What Lila Mae finds in Fulton's work *Theoretical Elevators* is that he bases his theories on his social reality. As a child, he dreamed of places and of racial conditions more fluid than those he had experienced.

However, Lila Mae does not fully grasp the battle lines Fulton has drawn and therefore misreads the postmodern implications of Fulton's project—his strategy of using the societal forces of uncertainty and alienation to his advantage. For her, Fulton "knows the other world he describes does not exist. There will be no redemption because the men who run this place do not want redemption" (240). But Fulton neither pursues another literal world nor some transcendence he knows he can never find. In a metaphor for elevation, he offers a poignant, if puzzling, understanding of how one "moves without moving":[9] "At ninety [the ninetieth floor], everything is air and the difference between you and the medium of your passage is disintegrating with every increment of the ascension" (222). In short, Fulton longed for ascension, not perfection, in the way he approached precarious circumstances. Embedded in Intuitionism, his complex notion of striving absolves its devotees of the burden of fighting against the racial odds.

As it concerns Fulton's past, Whitehead shrouds it in anonymity. Fulton seems to have come from nowhere: "Fulton just appeared at the Pierpont School of Engineering one day, eighteen years old, slow of speech, tentative, and proceeded to astound" (100). It is Mrs. Rogers who tells the story of a visit from Fulton's sister that precipitated a stark change in him. Fulton's sister arrives in tattered clothing and delivers news of their mother's death. His sister does not disclose his racial identity, but Fulton later reveals it to Mrs. Rogers. Though maintaining business as usual at home, Fulton's work demeanor[10] drastically changes, often in violent outbursts toward his colleagues.

Fulton's transformation seems to comport with his racial subterfuge. To contextualize this, readers must consider the circumstances of his birth, which the novel seems to imply is the result of rape: "His sister says she knew he was coming that night when their mother came home torn. She says she knew by their mother's silence and crying after that night that something new was coming into their house, and it turned out to be him [Fulton]" (135). Aside from this presumed atrocity, Fulton has his own anxieties about racial difference as a child: when an old black man in a town store "steps aside to let him buy his candy" (136), Fulton becomes deeply aware of his ability to pass.

After we learn from Mrs. Rogers of Fulton's shift from embattled academic to trickster, we get a posthumous glimpse of a man who has suppressed the painful experiences of his childhood. His sister's visit signals the postmodern revision of his worldview, which will live on through Lila Mae. Mrs. Rogers recalls Fulton's deep laughter as he read "the first review to describe [his] approach as 'Intuitionist': postrational, innate. Human. No wonder he laughed. His prank had succeeded" (238). During the years that he passed, he developed a critique of the sight-based tenets of white supremacy and racism, turned that premise on its head, and then disseminated his theories as something applicable to industry. As Mrs. Rogers reports, "He [Fulton] told me—these are his words—'They were all slaves to what they could see.' But there was a truth behind that they couldn't see for the life of them" (239). Fulton's "postrational" (read: postmodern) subtext proves inaccessible to those preoccupied with appearance and with manipulating those appearances to their advantage. Intuitionism subverts the one-sidedness of that gaze; it locates truth in sociocultural subtleties that those who only look with insularity and bias cannot see.

The road to a postmodern perspective for Lila Mae runs through her encounters with Mrs. Rogers. We see Lila Mae's modern impulses unravel during her first encounter with Mrs. Rogers. Mrs. Rogers invites Lila Mae into her home because she does not act "like them other men been coming around here, in their city suits all full of themselves" (89). But then Mrs. Rogers challenges what she believes to be the department's assumptions about black solidarity: "And I'll just say what I've been keeping because we belong to the same club." Ever the inspector, when Lila Mae can no longer control the conversation, she reveals that she has come in search of Fulton's missing writings. Mrs. Rogers asks, "How'd you get mixed up with these people anyway?" (90). "You all dressed like them, but you must still have some sense." Mrs. Rogers's rejoinder brings to center stage the problem of Lila Mae's facade and performance. Because Lila Mae's misguided path of progress hinges on toeing the line from one conformist move to another, she gets embroiled into the morass of the elevator world. Mrs. Rogers makes Lila Mae conscious of her greatest need—to strike her own path and develop a sense of self, untainted by cultural directives.

The battle for perspective that marks their conversation speaks to Lila Mae's tenuous self-assurance in her job. When giving her credentials, Lila Mae reveals that she attended the IVT as a student of Fulton's teachings. Mrs. Rogers responds, "I used to see you walking all fast everywhere, like you had someplace to go and didn't have no time to get there. You were always walking fast by yourself" (92). Mrs. Rogers then asks, "Was it worth it? All the stuff they put on you?" Embarrassed, Lila Mae can only offer a canned response, "I have my badge. I earned my badge." The badge that she fondles in her pocket quickly becomes a marker of conformity that does not hold sway with Mrs. Rogers. Whitehead describes Lila Mae's face as a "crumpled ball of paper" with the badge itself signifying institutional control. The paper has everything to do with the ways in which political figures like Mr. Reed are able to write out Lila Mae's agenda and then discard her after she completes it. Put simply, by the time Lila Mae makes it to Mrs. Rogers, her success has been co-opted by those who disingenuously sanctioned it in the first place.

Lila Mae's second conversation with Mrs. Rogers shows a revised character. She now wants to do more than just clear her name or find the black box; she now questions things. When Mrs. Rogers opens the door, Lila Mae first asks: "He was joking, right? About Intuitionism. It was all a big joke" (232). This second encounter features a more candid Mrs. Rogers. She remarks, "Not the same girl who was knocking on my door last week, are you? With your chest all puffed out like a peacock. You've seen something between now and then, huh?" (236). Having excavated Fulton's works, Lila Mae develops a new literacy by "learn[ing] how to read, like a slave does, one forbidden word at a time" (230). Becoming self-aware, Lila Mae begins to see the elevator industry from the vantage point of a pawn moved about in a conspicuous power struggle. Interestingly, as Mrs. Rogers talks about Fulton's sacred and profane project, she picks up pieces of her porcelain horse collection, broken during a recent break-in intended to unearth Fulton's papers. Because thugs damage the collection beyond repair, she cannot restack them on the mantle. When we encounter Mrs. Rogers' collection, in contrast to the stone menagerie at Arbo, it represents a disruptive shift in Lila Mae's complacency. Lila Mae now refuses simplistic notions of success and engages a postmodern worldview instead.

Whitehead uses Lila Mae's vigilance to revise a modern meta-narrative, which saw integration as an apex of racial progress and as a panacea for America's racial ills. To fully understand the unraveling of cultural notions of progress in *The Intuitionist*, readers must consider Lila Mae's range of worldviews. Whitehead's protagonist morphs from a by-the-book technician and "modern city girl" into a complex character who questions her fidelity to the elevator industry and to Intuitionism. She also matures as a student—from one dependent on the ideas of her predecessors into one confident enough to formulate her own truths. Lila Mae no longer views progress as dedication to either a career or cultural logic. By realizing a postmodern outlook, she turns the tables on her earlier assumptions about transcending the imposed limitations of race and gender, and emerges as the puppet master of the elevator industry. Over the course of a harrowing journey, she arrives at a place of profound insight: "That she was a citizen of the city to come and that the frail devices she had devoted her life to were weak and would all fall one day like Number Eleven" (255). In short, she adopts the postmodern framework elaborated in Fulton's works. Lila Mae has asserted her right as an individual to create the world around her opposite the will of industry magnates.

Though Lila Mae starts out with an imagination limited by cultural notions and bureaucratic imperatives, Whitehead charges her with contextualizing what Fulton's theories might imply for a postmodern cultural politics. At first, Lila Mae rejects the notion that the black box will change the way the world looks at elevators. Questioning what the perfect elevator would look like, she concludes "We don't know because we can't see inside it, it's something we cannot imagine, like the shape of angels' teeth. It's a black box" (61). For her, Fulton describes in his works an *elevator* world, "and a world needs inhabitants to make it real. The black box is the elevator-citizen for the elevator world" (100). It is from the imagined perspective of the citizen of this futuristic world to come that Lila Mae begins rethinking the first volume of Fulton's *Theoretical Elevators*, which she first encountered at IVT.

Lila Mae notices one concept that seems to be the skeleton key to unlock the tenets captured in Fulton's writings: the second elevation. She interprets the notion of second elevation as a commentary on African American mobility. Lila Mae intuits that workplace integration, in and of itself, will not enable African Americans to become elevator-citizens (as savvy, self-aware, and mobile individuals) Moreover, the second elevation metaphorically links black progress with achieving a level of thinking that no longer uncritically follows cultural narratives, but comes out of one's own "articulate self-awareness" (229). The future the novel portends will require more viable ideological options.

Lila Mae's next phase involves squaring the elevator incident with the discovery that Fulton passed for white. She ponders, "Is his black box immune to the comet of the catastrophic accident?" (229). Here Lila Mae begins to interpret accidents (even contrived ones like the elevator crash) as opportunities for revision and reframing, "instructing the dull and plodding citizens of modernity that there is a power beyond rationality" (231). Further, she senses that one has to move beyond complete rationality to equip a postmodern perspective. In rethinking her ideas about progress, Lila Mae resolves to look beyond the "skin of things" (239). She distills Fulton's Intuitionist theories down to the reality of the thoroughly compromised agency of black workers and determines that profound meaning inheres in Fulton's critique of sight-based logic. Those who take the elevator industry at face value cannot ascertain the structures of power within it, and, in fact, their ambitions to advance are ground to a halt by these very structures. As a result, they find themselves in a futile search for opportunity in a sector that is not only bent on maintaining a status quo unblemished by racial difference but also vying for a technological future that subordinates racialized others to little more tokens and cogs.

Lila Mae learns to trust her own insight and eschews an overreliance on either the obvious or the abstract. Comprehending the ways in which white power brokers co-opt black agency and thwart true self-determination, Lila Mae finally discerns that she, though wholly disconnected from the seats of power, perpetuated their agenda. Reflecting on a lesson she learns from Pompey, Lila Mae thinks: "Pompey gave them a blueprint for colored folk. . . . How eager they would be for a piece of the dream that they would do anything for massa. She hated her place in their world, where she fell in their order of things, and blamed Pompey, her shucking shadow in the office. She could not see him anymore than anyone else in the office saw him." (239). Now, she begins to see Pompey as more than just a jaded worker and to read Fulton more deeply in the process. Grasping her own inner conflict, Lila Mae "knew he [Fulton] was joking because he hated himself. She understood this hatred of himself; she hated something in herself and she took it out on Pompey. Now she could see Fulton for what he was. There was no way he believed in transcendence" (240). Her own growth mirrors Fulton's as she shifts her focus far away from transcending racial barriers and bootstrap uplift.

Another character aids Lila Mae in this shift. Urich, who penned an article announcing that searchers were close to finding Fulton's black box, gives Lila Mae the run-down about the political machinery of the elevator world, revealing the latent truth that whoever "owns the elevator owns the new cities" (208). Urich asks, "Did you think this was all about philosophy? Who's the better man—Intuitionism or Empiricism? No one really gives a crap about that. Arbo and United are the guys who make the things. That's what really matters. The whole world wants to get vertical, and they're the guys that get them there. If you pay the fare" (208).

Part two of the novel opens with the text of Fulton's lost notebooks, which presumably Lila Mae is reading. However, in nonlinear fashion, not long after we are introduced to Fulton's previously unseen and fragmented third volume of *Theoretical Elevators*, a subsequent encounter between Mrs. Rogers and Lila Mae unfolds, with Mrs. Rogers unearthing the notes from an old dumbwaiter in her kitchen. Significantly, one line from Fulton's notes seems to convey a timely message to Lila Mae: "the difference between you and the medium of your passage is disintegrating with every increment of the ascension" (222). While the relevance of this line to Lila Mae's circumstances is important at this point in the novel, the tone of the note holds meaning here because it speaks to the tenor of Fulton's writings, which implies that there is strategic value in circuitous thoughts and actions that obscure one's motives to those looking to capitalize on them. It is also significant that the technical contour of Fulton's writing does not obscure the gravity of his postmodern assessment for Lila Mae. The message is that all theories, tenets, procedures, and techniques are disintegrating around her and that, to find the surest footing in the chaos, Lila Mae has to marshal the detritus left over from Fulton's intellectual prank on the elevator industry.

Wielding the so-called black box as a weapon, Lila Mae dupes Urich, Coombs, Chancre, and several industry bigwigs by sending copies of Fulton's deliberately incomplete text. Isolating herself in an undisclosed location, Lila Mae plays upon the elevator world's obsession with the future. As they aggressively pursue the perfect elevator, "[i]f it is not time she will send out more of Fulton's words to let them know it is coming" (255). Lila Mae has situated herself to helm the confusion and steer the sociopolitical machine as puppet master of the elevator industry. What Lila Mae exercises is a postmodern form of agency that fuels the kind of resistance that destabilizes the system itself. The novel insists that submitting to the industry's whims or incessantly dodging its tentacles of influence is not an option that leads to agency. The main thrust of this comes through Whitehead's epistemological disruption via Fulton's research, which inscribes black intellectual thought and assumptions into the dominant cultural logic. Another instance of this disruption is Lila Mae's dissemination of the text, which further fragments it. She extends Fulton's semantic play into a one-woman nexus of influence. Given the premium placed on future projections about elevation concepts, Lila Mae's covert sway over the industry will open up more opportunities for other veiled interventions in the bureaucracy. But what is noteworthy is the way in which her political purview broadens as she goes on the offensive, cultivating postmodern alternatives to group narratives and institutional control.

Lila Mae rejects neutrality for an anonymity that restores her agency. The uncertainty that dogs her throughout the novel both compels adaptation and challenges the hegemony of industry. Lila Mae's transformation takes shape when she revises her assumptions about progress, which, in her case, had defined success as earning a formal education, leaving the South, and obtaining a coveted career. Having illuminated the sociopolitical tensions that arise among those who occupy token positions, Whitehead shows that those chosen few have little recourse than to reappropriate the otherness foisted upon them. By the end of the novel, the message rings clear: credulous individual ambition winds up tethered to the calculated schemes of the powerful and renders African American self-efficacy impotent.

The Intuitionist sets in motion the appropriation of system tactics by those marginalized within the system. In *Political Machines: Governing a Technological Society*, Andrew Barry argues, "All too often, postmodernism involves a different form of reduction—a reduction to complete fragmentation or fluidity—in which any sense of texture and difference is lost" (21). To avoid this trend, Whitehead elevates African American experiences to a significant level of sociopolitical importance. Specifically, the novel portrays the endeavors of black workers and the dominant political apparatus on an even keel in the ebb and flow of autonomy. In addition, he avoids glossing over the uphill battle the black characters face, particularly with their own assumptions about modern life.

Prior to Lila Mae's awakening, she thought of the future citizens of Fulton's elevator world as white elites, "the cosmopolitan darlings out on the town, tipped martini glasses and stroked silver cigarette cases engraved with their initials and called the bartender by his name" (176). Whitehead juxtaposes the future citizen/city concept Fulton heralds in his work with Urich's understanding of the present-day interworking of corporations, political campaigns, and elevator enterprises. In the novel, characters like Pompey, Coombs, and even Fulton (until his later years) are associated with striving to uphold some semblance of modern individualism, each dispirited in their own way, while Whitehead deems intuition a prime feature for those citizens with a postmodern worldview. For Pompey, the system of modern elevators "is a white man's world. They make the rules" (195). Coombs, the corporate spy, says, "I've paid my dues" and "is more surprised at being interrupted at his paperwork than at [Lila Mae's] appearance in his office" (248). Disillusioned, Fulton himself "secretes his venom onto the pages of a book. He knows the other world he describes does not exist. There will be no redemption because the men who run this place do not want redemption. They want to be as near to hell as they can" (240). Lila Mae's encounter with these distinct but not altogether different perspectives affords her "a space in which to imagine things differently." Almost prophetically, with a line scribbled in the margins of his notebook, "*Lila Mae Watson is the one*" (253), Fulton intuits that, if such a city could exist, at least in the minds of oppressors, Lila Mae would spearhead its construction and operation.

Ultimately, Lila Mae co-opts the othering process to which the industry subjects her from the beginning. She theorizes that "Intuitionism is communication. That simple. Communication with what is not-you" (241). For example, Lila Mae recalls attending church with her parents as a child and then no longer attending when she moves north. Yet she does not reduce religion to something useless but re-imagines it for her purposes: "Anyone can start a religion. They just need the need of others." In the end, we see Lila Mae strike a balance between fragmentation and fluidity, flouting Empiricism and Intuitionism alike.

Whitehead's novel probes the modern notions of rationality, humanism, and black progress that stall and subvert self-awareness. The text moves in opposition to modern discourse with a postmodern evaluation of black ideas about success and survival within industrial capitalism. In addition, Whitehead implements a revisionist stance to long-held, cultural assumptions about sacrifice and respectability. He does so by introducing nonconformist and oppositional theories like Intuitionism. Lastly, *The Intuitionist* concerns itself with social difference in a system that thwarts a variety of viewpoints and co-opts opposing ideas. Even as the novel tests the symbolic mettle of integration, it offers a critical take on the plight facing career-advancing black workers, their ambitions, and the politics that beset them.

2

RESTLESS QUESTIONING
Anguish and the Ethos of Black Struggle
in Alice Walker's *Meridian*

Twenty-three years before the publication of *The Intuitionist*, Alice Walker's *Meridian* explored group constraints and mainstream exploitation. *Meridian* prefigures the beleaguered African American female protagonist who opposes the practices of institutions intent on controlling and containing the impulses of their members. The postmodern cultural politics on display in *The Intuitionist* unfolds in *Meridian*, as well. While Lila Mae unravels defunct ideas about black progress to seize influence over a menacing elevator industry, Meridian Hill, Walker's eponymous protagonist, adopts a politics of restless questioning to demystify the top-down influence of Saxon College and the Atlanta movement. The way in which Whitehead situates Lila Mae in the latter parts of *The Intuitionist* suggests that she occupies the ideal sphere to antagonize an insatiable industry from within. In contrast, Walker focuses on constructing a separate and distinct activism for Meridian, which serves the masses and simultaneously undermines traditional movement leadership.

  Meridian provides a unique angle on the psychic anguish borne by black women and men who find themselves weighted with the ethos of black struggle and aware of their vulnerabilities to economic and cultural alienation in mainstream society. Meridian's goal is to sidestep these overwrought narratives by living out her beliefs and assumptions via social protest and considerable personal sacrifice. Profound self-awareness leads her away from a neutral politics to one that marshals her very health in the cause of resistance to political and intellectual domination. Opposite Meridian, Truman Held wants very much to abandon the freedom movement and embrace a middle-class identity of bourgeois decadence. Ironically, his penchant for avoiding the work of battling his own demons prevents him from really disengaging from the larger freedom struggle. Walker uses her considerable authorial skill to portray the psychological burdens of those toiling in the demonstrations and acts of civil disobedience common during the civil rights movement. Ultimately, Meridian and Truman become the perfect representatives of a generation of disillusioned intellectuals and activists compelled to pursue lives of purpose outside the traditional arenas of learning and resistance.

The postmodern here rises out of the questioning and reflection of individuals participating in rights movements. Problematizing issues like wholeness and stability, Walker hones in on the emotional and psychological forces that have always attended historical change. In the novel, Meridian arrives at a textured understanding of struggle and revolution. This comes about after deep reflection on two forms of civil rights' resistance: reformist politics in the Atlanta movement and militant notions espoused by the New York Revolutionaries. What unfolds for Meridian is a reframing of political resistance. Her experiences at Saxon involving the victimization of women, the critiquing of late capitalism, and the onslaught of an inexplicable illness lay the foundation for Meridian's ruminations. Her counterparts, Anne-Marion Coles and Truman, are engaged in their own battles to construct meaning out of their inner struggles with the goals and effectiveness of movement activism. Anne-Marion ultimately becomes a capitalist, shunning militancy and embracing the right to economic privilege in which she had anchored her zeal for resistance. On the other hand, while Truman's efforts to leave the movement behind are successful, he maintains a connection to its ideals. His dormant idealism eventually allows him to see Meridian's postmodern path as a viable and necessary option, if he is to work through the trauma and loss he endures. Walker's novel is able to address the overlooked psychological anguish borne by civil rights workers by offering a postmodern consciousness premised on the restless questioning of hierarchical and inflexible social movements. As movements sideline individual perspectives, the will to continually reflect on one's distress and efficacy as an activist becomes paramount.

As a postmodernist novel, *Meridian* has formal elements that range from brief chapters, to epigraphs, to repetition, along with other features. Yet these can be understood in relation to tangential asides. For the most part, Walker centers on three different volunteer experiences in the civil rights movement: militant/revolutionary, moderate/reformist, and radical. Very much a nonlinear narrative, the novel uses in medias res and flashback effects to situate readers in each of these dynamic forms in a cause/effect perspective. Even as jump cuts and temporal shifts abound to capture the jostling of bodies in protest and other pivotal moments, Walker's use of asides is most effective in enriching the text's meaning. Seemingly unrelated asides direct readers' attention to the background processes shaping the contexts and lives of the protagonists. When this element is appreciated, it opens up space for the consideration of political machinations and private and public policies that undercut the lives of black individuals. Walker has created a nation-in-crisis in *Meridian,* and the ramifications—which she inserts through intriguing asides—seem to be that apprehending the veiled mechanisms and structures repressing people is a precursor not only to mounting resistance to those existing structures but also to erecting alternative ones.

Walker encourages a tangential focus on cultural and ideological processes in the background. Describing this structuring of time and space as one that links "political-economic and cultural processes" (201) in *The Condition of Postmodernity: An Inquiry into the Origins of Cultural Change,* David Harvey offers an idea that becomes useful in reading these elements closely. For the most part, the efforts of activists in *Meridian* are influenced by assumptions and policies that are in motion behind the scenes (in different eras and locations). For example, in Meridian's town, unseen television executives decide that "Black people were never shown in the news—unless of course they had shot their mothers or raped their bosses' grandparent . . ." (69), and a patriarchal black church shapes movement politics and agendas. Insight into this veiled activity appears via brief asides and sequences, which highlight the nature of entrenched mindsets and biases and pinpoint the outsized influence they have on everyday people who hold little authority and are deliberately cut off from the corridors of power. By allowing Meridian to unveil power and put pressure on its structures through localized resistance, Walker sends the message that revealing and resisting unscrupulous configurations of power is the only way to subvert them.

In *Meridian*, the use of transitions highlights postmodern cultural headwinds: context shifts, insoluble problems, and a reckoning with the limits of political influence that circulate through the narrative. When one thinks about transitions in *Meridian*, one of the first that emerges is the definitions page that adorns the opening of the novel, before the story begins. In one sense, this page is invested in the myriad context shifts that characterize the postmodern era unfolding in the novel. According to Alan Nadel, the definitions page implies that "Walker tests the ways one gives meaning to objects, to self and to others. *Meridian* is a lesson in the power of language, the power to retain as well as to distort, to affect as well as to deny" (267). While Nadel rightly highlights Walker's attention to meaning and language, she most profoundly implies the sense that contexts can be altered as abruptly as the shifting sociopolitical ground underneath Meridian's feet.

The transition from the definitions page to the novel's first chapter is jarring in the way it disorients the reader who meets Meridian for the first time, ten years after her political awakening. Ironically, the different contexts mentioned on the definitions page (astronomy, geography) in relation to the word *meridian*, indirectly speak to moments of change in Meridian's life. Astronomy, which speaks of all things cosmic, can be read as a reference to her spiritual experiences, which are couched in cosmic terms. For example, early in the novel when Meridian stands in the Indian burial mounds of the Sacred Serpent, "there was at first a sense of vast isolation," and "She was a dot, a speck in creation, alone and hidden" (52). Reckoning with this experience years later (after the mounds become a public park that is eventually desegregated), Meridian has to grapple with visitors "attempting to study the meaning of what had already and forever been lost" (54). This cultural headwind involves the razing of sacred spaces for public consumption and recreation and features empty gestures of racial parity, which Meridian must endure.

Inserting transitions into the narrative allows Walker to insert what she terms insoluble problems into Meridian's world. The novel reflects on these problems in "The Recurring Dream," a chapter that serves as a transition from a chilling encounter between Meridian and Truman in the previous chapter. Prior to "The Recurring Dream," Truman asks Meridian to commit to a relationship with him on the basis of what he perceives as their sexual compatibility. Unknowingly, his proposition comes on the heels of an abortion and a demeaning encounter with her doctor. Abruptly, Walker places readers within Meridian's dreams, thus bringing two worlds in confrontation and illustrating Brian McHale's contention that one "dominant of postmodernist fiction is *ontological*" (10). McHale's sense is that postmodernist writers like Walker are concerned with posing questions about the worlds projected in their novels—and the existential modes of those worlds. Walker writes the following sentence three times to convey Meridian's problem of being: "She dreamed she was a character in a novel and that her existence presented an insoluble problem, one that would be solved only by her death at the end" (121). The passage not only details the dream but also sets up an instance of intertextuality, which helps clarify one of Meridian's conundrums: the difficulty of willing oneself to be and exist in a world of trauma, injustice, and death.

In her description of the changes impacting Meridian, Walker highlights Meridian's inner battle with the question of death and with her role as an activist, who would be called upon to risk death for her convictions and for black communities. Above most other challenges, this becomes one of the strongest cultural headwinds in Meridian's path because it engenders uncertainty. Walker writes, "She [Meridian] felt as if a small landslide had begun behind her brows, as if things there had started to slip. It was a physical feeling and she paid it no mind. She just began to take chances with her life. . . . She walked for miles up and down Atlanta streets until she was exhausted, without once paying any attention to the existence of cars" (121–22). Meridian's daze reflects Walker's own process with constructing Meridian's roles: her life as a student, mother, activist, black woman, lover, and spiritual person. In the novel, Walker fleshes out Meridian's struggle with the insoluble problem of death by allowing her to inhabit many roles and then to invest fully in her activism.

In *Meridian*, Walker reckons with the limits of political influence in the "Pilgrimage" chapter. One of the last chapters in the book, "Pilgrimage" features Meridian and Truman canvassing a small town for voter registration and taking a detour to a local prison, which held a thirteen-year-old girl who had killed her baby. The narrator discloses, "Yes. She had bitten her baby's cheek, bitten out a plug, before she strangled it with a piece of curtain ruffle. So round and clean it had been, too" (234). As gruesome as the details are, they are framed as the product of serious mental illness: "Where I am (she continues) no one is. And why am I alive, without my heart? And how is this? And who, in the hell, are you?" In their zeal, Meridian and Truman are there to offer the girl the means of political participation, which could possibly alter the conditions of her confinement, but they are greeted with suspicion, mocking laughter, and blunt rejection. The girl says, "If you can't give me back my heart [her deceased baby] (she says suddenly, with venom), go the fuck away" (235).

In a scene that strikes an unnerving note, Walker offers a critique of a postmodern headwind that sparks resistance to the idea that political involvement is a panacea. In this chapter, Walker juxtaposes the feelings of shame and gloom that wash over Meridian and Truman overnight—after encountering human failure at a level that renders politics moot—with the sight of a political victory intended to protect children. When Meridian awakens, she watches "workmen from the city begin to clear the debris from the ditch, preparatory to filling it in (yes, the voters had won this small, vital service). . . ." Yet, this *small* victory does not soothe their invisible wounds; nor does it comfort the particular feelings of sadness that visit Meridian, who made the decision to give her son up for adoption to afford him a good life. Opting for a stronger salve than politics can provide in that moment, Meridian writes intensely, "i want to put an end to guilt / i want to put an end to shame / whatever you have done my sister / (my brother)." For Walker, the realization that there are some human concerns that are so profound that they make voting, laws, and politics a distant matter is a reality that must be understood in the midst of both great change and times of political impotence.

Claudia Tate's *Psychoanalysis and Black Novels: Desire and the Protocols of Race* explores the presence of desire in African American fiction. In her 1998 study, she uses psychoanalysis to investigate the multiple ways black writers might convey "unsocialized desire," which has to do with implicit meaning that "complicates the explicit social message of the text" (9). Tate argues that these discourses around unsocialized desire elicit discomfort in readers because they do not constitute a familiar (or collective) racial discourse. In turn, literary criticism has the effect of repressing this phenomenon by freighting black authors with the weight of U.S. racial history, even when they attempt to affirm personal experiences, as does Walker. Not seeking to psychoanalyze authors, Tate investigates "novels that reflect how their respective authors uniquely combined emotional and cognitive meaning in the production of the works" (15). She also questions "how black texts construct textual meaning out of specific material and cultural circumstances as well as personal authorial longings—conscious and unconscious" (15). Her investigation, which does not dismiss racial politics, can advance a reading of novels premised upon psychological anguish. Significantly, an emphasis on anguish lodged deep in the psyche of characters shows up in African American literature as writers illustrate diverging perspectives on historical eras.

Writers have deployed psychological anguish to imagine the gutwrenching nature of resistance and the toll it takes on individuals. A close observation of consistent struggle reveals two things—that individual concerns in movements often get dismissed in favor of a group agenda, and that there is much distress visited upon those who voluntarily execute the mission handed down by figureheads. Such protagonists are often besieged not only by their respective communities and society but also by their personal convictions.

Alice Walker's Range and Representation

Along with authors like Toni Morrison, Toni Cade Bambara, Paule Marshall, and Gloria Naylor, Walker brings an informed perspective to the portrayal of the emotional and spiritual strivings of black women. Out of the incorporation of agrarian folk elements and an emphasis on the thwarted energies of women by these novelists, contemporary notions in black feminism and black women's studies[1] have emerged. Undoubtedly, Walker's oeuvre has weathered much attention, as several literary theorists, including Marjorie Pryse, Debra Walker King, Houston Baker, and Susan Willis, have written about her impact on African American literary studies and theory.[2] Several social science–based readings of Walker's fiction rest alongside literary criticism, as her work stretches disciplinary boundaries. For example, anthropologist Faye Harrison describes Walker as "one of anthropology's less visible interlocutors" (123) because of her inclusion of discursive systems, communal configurations, and cultural contexts. Similarly, Melvin Dixon in *Ride Out the Wilderness: Geography and Identity in Afro-American Literature* provides a geographical reading of Walker's fiction in its vacillation between the North and the South and concern with land and identity.

Most explicitly, Walker's novels exemplify her notion of a womanist[3] view, and her concern for the spiritual and cultural needs of women and men. In this context, she links the road to consciousness and commitment to history. Contemplating several challenges African Americans have faced throughout American history, Walker's *The Color Purple* examines the post–Civil War/Reconstruction period, *Meridian* critiques the civil rights movement, and *Temple of My Familiar* connects ancient history and African cosmology with late-twentieth-century life. I focus on *Meridian*, which Deborah McDowell describes as Walker's "most artistically mature work" (168).[4] I find *Meridian* relevant to my reading of the personal adjustments to culture and society that individuals must make in a postmodern context. In addition, the novel is very much about facing off against oppressive structures. Lastly, Walker's earlier novels tend not to focus on the renegotiation of black political projects that is central to *Meridian*.

My reading diverges from these critical observations of Walker's writing in that it examines political and institutional repression. I consider the mainstream institutions Walker portrays, group politics, and how they impact African Americans. In *Meridian*, Walker interrogates the alienating nature of the civil rights movement with sharp perception. Tone-deaf leadership creates a space where activists find their views eclipsed by a hierarchical organization. In complicating this state of affairs, Walker considers the movement from the activist's perspective and highlights the individual's restless will to question staid protocols. Ultimately, the individual autonomy that sparks change also opens up new possibilities for realizing the convictions of those committed to political struggle.

In *Reconstructing Womanhood, Reconstructing Feminism: Writings on Black Women* (1987), Hazel Carby's disavowal of the term *tradition* established a strong foundation from which to explore psychology in black women's literature. Focused on acknowledging the historical reality behind black women's fiction, Carby takes as her point of departure the uneven relations around race, class, and gender and provides "a materialist account of the cultural production of black women intellectuals within the social relations that inscribed them" (17). A reading of anguish hinges on the representation of social and political prohibitions in black communities and white institutions. Barbara Christian "characterize[s] Walker's work as organically spare rather than elaborate, ascetic rather than lush, a process of stripping off layers, honing down to the core" (*Everyday Use: Alice Walker* 124). This thought-provoking quality marks Walker's process as a deep exploration of historical events that have had lasting effects both within black communities and on the consciousness of America. Likewise, her fiction captures the weight of black women and men's historical memory, does not allow an easy cathartic release, and necessarily engenders uncertainty and ambivalence. Novels about inner turmoil demonstrate how the emotional and spiritual undercurrents of race inform social reality. As a characteristic, such texts feature interiority in a way that provides insight into the minds of beleaguered individuals. What comes across in Walker's works is a profound preoccupation with self-confrontation. African American writers who deploy this theme enter into an ongoing cultural conflict brought on by inattention to the particular strivings of black individuals.

While a reading about psychological and emotional confusion appears to privilege interiority over exterior concerns like material deprivation, many black writers do not engage the former without equitable attention to the latter. Walker especially possesses a discerning eye for the historical realities and racial politics depicted in her work, through which she has written herself into the ranks of the foremost twentieth-century writers. Novels about anguish must grapple with issues such as displacement, education, and late capitalism/globalization. As writers bring Tate's "authorial longings" and "unsocialized desire" to the fore, they verbalize the nagging notions of activism. And by angling the lens to show a different perspective, writers can make the fictionalized personal relentlessly political. Still, what emerges in a novel like *Meridian* leans less toward a linear critique and more toward an indirect perspective. Walker seems to prefer ambiguity to the erasure of black anguish. When we read Walker's views on the constraints of intraracial tradition in *Meridian*, we hear her elaborate on a kind of oppression that is often unremarked upon.

The emphasis on the black psyche that has characterized African American literature since the 1970s has gained political import. Gene Andrew Jarrett squares the sociopolitical value of African American literature with the sense that "racial representation in African American literary history has consistently endeavored to overthrow racial injustice" (*Representing the Race* 6). One literary tool has been narrative representation, intended to make readers question their attitudes and assumptions about race in America. Sociologist Robert Washington, in *The Ideologies of African American Literature: From the Harlem Renaissance to the Black Nationalist Revolt,* considers the impact of African American literature on American race relations and black communities. Yet he concerns himself with the notion that mainstream ideological forces, which shape prominent literary works, may have eclipsed black social consciousness. Skeptical of mainstream notions that exclude the perspectives of marginalized groups, in *Meridian,* Walker rejects the conferring of legitimacy upon people and ideas by hidebound power structures.

Just as the literary sphere wades into ideological battles playing out in society, in the wake of racist backlash against movements during the 1950s and 1960s, the political sphere was called upon to sway perceptions about race. Garth Pauley's *The Modern Presidency and Civil Rights: Rhetoric on Race from Roosevelt to Nixon* evaluates presidential rhetoric on racial crises in American history. Throughout the mid-twentieth century, integration forced the intervention of Dwight Eisenhower and John F. Kennedy. Their respective national addresses described racial issues as sullying "the national reputation in the eyes of the world" and as a "moral issue" (215). Black Americans have undoubtedly harbored a healthy skepticism about the motivations and efforts of any leadership for good reason. While Pauley highlights broader misconceptions about black social movements, James Fendrich's *Ideal Citizens: The Legacy of the Civil Rights Movement* looks at misconceptions about civil rights activists. Though several grassroots efforts centered on student politics, war, race, and gender sprang up amid the civil rights movement, "popular psychological theories of mindless, irrational contagion" called into question the commitment of activists (xxi).

Social commitment in black communities, because it tends to be grounded in history, has become an interesting concept for writers. Keith Byerman argues that "contemporary narratives are trauma stories in that they tell of both tremendous loss and survival; they describe the psychological and social effects of suffering. More important, perhaps, they tell of the erasure of such history and, as a consequence, its continued power to shape black life" (3). Because Byerman concerns himself with black suffering, he turns to the notion of recovery in trauma theory, which requires an acknowledgment of the stories of lives crushed by repression. As it concerns fictive representations, however, Byerman inserts a caveat about the difficulties of ascribing therapeutic possibilities to literature. *Meridian* demands that it be taken seriously as literature because it complicates our understanding of the pivotal struggle for civil rights in America, not because of its clinical merit. In particular, Walker portrays activists' tense relationships to autocratic systems and highlights the ways individual autonomy can rebuff rigid methods. Moreover, *Meridian* provides a portrait of Fendrich's "ideal citizen" who relentlessly challenges the status quo whether through campus, state, or national politics. If *Meridian* tackles questions that arose out of rights movements, then it must pose answers that complicate ideas about reform or, its militant counterpart, revolution. Karen Stein, in her essay "*Meridian:* Alice Walker's Critique of Revolution," discusses the evolution of Walker's thoughts on revolution. For Stein, Walker's appraisal of the civil rights movement in 1967 changed when she wrote *Meridian* a few years later to favor spiritual transformation and psychological stability over militant resistance.

In acknowledging the psychological burdens borne by women during this era, Walker explores the complexities of their marginal roles. Evelyn White has suggested that one of *Meridian's* "most incendiary complaints was that of black women who had given their lifeblood to the movement only to be forsaken by black men" (285). Twenty years after the movement, several core assumptions made by women were mentioned in Anne Standley's essay "The Role of Black Women in the Civil Rights Movement." Standley suggested that, in hindsight, black women activists tended to identify the movement with its "liberating effect" on their sense of self, with it becoming an "inseparable part" of their identity, and with blacks "overcoming circumstances that degraded them" (185–87). Walker's and Standley's works inform the ethos around a movement championed by black women, bolstered by their endurance, and sustained by their commitment to self-sacrifice.

Black Struggle and Lived Reality

The novel explores the weight of ambient black struggle in the life of a precocious student turned activist. Meridian attends Saxon College, a southern institution for the black middle class, where she is exposed to bourgeois values and a confluence of social perspectives, though a patriarchal foundation is apparent. The college is a kind of elite, academic oasis with green lawns and buildings bearing the names of philanthropists that is also surrounded by economically depressed communities. Distinguishing itself via class and pedigree, "Most of the students—timid, imitative, bright enough but never daring, were being ushered nearer to Ladyhood every day. It was for this that their parents had sent them to Saxon College. They had learned to make French food, English tea, and German music . . ." (27–28). Saxon College acts as a mainstream space that is invested in imposing a very narrow form of womanhood on its students and, perhaps even more so, quashing any inkling of political ire. For instance, during the funeral of a homeless young black girl from a nearby ghetto—known as the Wile Chile—Meridian pictures the campus president chiding the students for not going "through the proper channels" to access the campus chapel.

When the students are refused access to the chapel, they riot, ultimately hacking away at the Sojourner, the largest magnolia tree in the South, until it is destroyed. Ironically, although this act seems to contradict the projected "Ladyhood" ethos as Saxon, in reality it falls in line with the wishes of the administration, who wanted to remove the tree "for a spanking new music building that a Northern philanthropist—unmindful that his buildings had already eaten up most of Saxon's greenness—was eager to give" (34). In this way, Saxon exploits the political energies of its students, including Meridian, who was unsuccessful in redirecting the students' outrage and getting them to dismantle the president's house.

As a mainstream space, Saxon's ultimate goal is to institutionalize and socialize its students into normative ways (traditionally Anglo norms) of operating in society. Set in Atlanta, the college exists as a prestigious institution established on the notion of refinement through higher learning and exposure to the liberal arts. Transgressive behavior around sexuality as well as equity between the student body and the administration are shunned. Saxon is vehemently opposed to sharing power with students it identifies as both socially vulnerable as African Americans and as desperate to join the ranks of the black elite.

While Saxon does provide spaces like the honors house, in which Meridian lives, for its high-achieving students, even this space largely leads students to feel disempowered and disconnected from countercultures. The only sensibilities Meridian has access to that run counter to collegiate customs are transmitted via television. A significant moment occurs as Meridian watches the funeral of John F. Kennedy; she "slump[s] forward with grief, she did not bother to raise her hands from her lap, where they lay palms up, empty" (22). The same chapter also remarks that, in response to the assassination of Medgar Evers, "Meridian had planted a wild sweet shrub bush among the plants in the formal garden in front of the honors house." These miniscule acts of quasi-pushback pale in comparison to Meridian's later activism, so much so that her actions attract the pity of Anne-Marion Coles, a fellow honor student. Nonetheless, they are foundational to her budding sense of resistance. This is also the point at which the vortex of Saxon begins to numb and sublimate Meridian's inclinations and awakening, so that it becomes a defanged "perverse curiosity." In one scene, Meridian finds herself talking to a white divinity student: "This curiosity was the way she was, sometimes, with whites. Mostly they did not seem quite real to her. They seemed very stupid the way they attempted to beat down everybody in their path and then know nothing about it. She saw them sometimes as hordes of elephants, crushing everything underfoot, stolid and heavy and yet—unlike the elephant—forgetting" (115).

To understand what makes Meridian vulnerable to the influence of Saxon's bourgeois agenda, which seems to circumscribe, and therefore, exploit its feminine community, one has to consider the assumptions she makes about herself. Having dodged a future of domesticity in her mother's house, earned a scholarship, and "appropriated all the good qualities of black women to herself" to get to Saxon, Meridian "thought of herself as an adventurer. It thrilled her to think she belonged to the people who produced Harriet Tubman, the only American woman who'd led troops in battle" (112). Though telling, Meridian's self-perceptions alone do not throw her into a crisis of contending against Saxon and a powerful group narrative as much as her relationship with Anne-Marion does.

The inescapable ethos of black struggle under which Meridian and her counterparts learn and strive represents the overarching constraining group narrative in the novel. Pressure to go along with the militant form of activism Anne-Marion adopts (which refuses communication and reconciliation) is part of this ethos and is very real for Meridian. While Meridian's activism comes out of a sense of group solidarity tempered by tenderness and a deep sense of loss, Anne-Marion exposes Meridian to a political philosophy that embraces violent resistance. After severing ties with Meridian and the reformist Atlanta movement, Anne-Marion takes up with a group called the New York Revolutionaries. In the novel, Meridian recalls meeting with the revolutionaries one summer and sitting silent as Anne-Marion and others questioned her loyalty to extremist ideas (using violence, shedding blood) because she could not affirm that she would kill for the movement.

What Anne-Marion and her revolutionaries cannot comprehend is that Meridian is torn between at least two group conceptions. On the one hand, Meridian is face-to-face with students and intellectuals turned revolutionaries who take her through a ritualized process designed to get her to swear allegiance to kill and die for revolution. On the other hand, her familial past looms large, replete with notions of dignity in black striving, agrarian practices, and spiritual resonance. Meridian ponders, "But what none of them seemed to understand was that she felt herself to be, not holding on to something from the past, but held by something in the past" (14). It is not a simple proposition for Meridian to divest of long-held cultural moorings. In this sense, she is both hemmed in internally by the stalwart idealism of black struggle and, externally, by the sting and brazenness of the notion of social change through violence.

Meridian's politics depart from Anne-Marion's in that she foregoes material desire and does the heavy lifting of inner questioning. When reflecting on her encounter with Anne-Marion's compatriots, she ultimately admits her inability to kill anyone and deems herself a failure in terms of their brand of revolution. Still, the weight of this group narrative stays with her and complicates her ideas about activism. Ten years later, Meridian still retains the notes and letters that she received from Anne-Marion, which amount to "a litany of accusations" (9), chiding Meridian for being weak and lacking priorities. While others agonize over the toll the movement has taken on them, Meridian imagines that she will continually rise up singing the freedom songs that have held black communities together for generations. Though Meridian is uncertain about what form her activism will take, the image captures her desire to be a vessel through which the "songs of the people" flow and to carry the burden of animating the political vitality of African American communities.

Even before Meridian's encounter with the revolutionaries, she was already questioning the more moderate reformist movements, which constrained the impulses of its foot soldiers via staid strategies. During one summer, Meridian succumbs to battle fatigue after committing to one demonstration after another. For the most part, Meridian seems to question the unspoken expectation of self-sacrifice tacitly demanded by the "Reverend in charge." Walker writes, "But even as she marched, singing, to the courthouse square, which was across from the jail, Meridian could not figure out how it was supposed to work. The earlier demonstrators, she felt sure, would not be set free because a few singing people stood peacefully across from the jail. And the jail was too small to accommodate any more bodies" (81). After enduring much abuse at the hands of law enforcement, Meridian is in a state of constant anxiety. Even when she takes on less danger-prone duties, tears flow ceaselessly.

The ability of the movement to garner the sympathies of most black southern townspeople in the vicinity is what leaves Meridian powerless to critique openly some of the desegregation strategies at one end and to reveal to her mother that she was heavily involved in what her mother saw as unnecessary agitation. Meridian also struggles with the tension of serving black people (demonstrating, typing, teaching) and being deployed as a docile collective by race men who see activists like her and, by extension, disenfranchised black Americans "as a lump of homogenized matter that could be placed this way or that way, at will, to affect change" (114). In short, Meridian has no quibble with self-sacrifice on behalf of ordinary black people. Her problem rests with the high-level limiting of independent spontaneous passions and Individual acts of resistance

Meridian's counterpart in the novel, Truman Held, is saturated in mainstream bourgeois intellectualism at R. Baron College, an all-male school near Saxon. While Truman resides under a conspicuous class politics at his college, Walker situates him in disparate environments: the South and the North, international sites like Paris, and within the Atlanta and Mississippi movements. Even with this geographical mobility, Truman is ultimately boxed in by the kinds of elitist exploitation common at his college—signified in its satirical name. Labeled the "Conquering Prince" in one of the novel's brief chapters, Truman busies himself philandering with three white exchange students. He justifies his sexual indiscretions to Meridian by saying he does it for reasons of agency and because of implicit taboos against interracial relationships.

Truman's relationship with the exchange students suggests that R. Baron functions, in one sense, to co-opt his political energies. While the institution makes his connections with these students possible, the encounter serves a specious purpose. On the one hand, his interaction speaks to a kind of social liberation, freeing him to view white women as sexually available. On the other hand, the intellectual premise that allows him to qualify his desire for white girls to Meridian as "essentially, a matter of sex," indicates that his consciousness is caving to the social arrangements often advertised and facilitated by institutions like R. Baron. The very fact that the white students are northern points toward the kind of historical, regional connections that have vested interests in southern colleges educating African Americans and imparting to them a distinct cultural capital. Significantly, Truman fetishizes the thrill of indulging in whiteness, and in so doing, he convinces himself that devouring white bodies and Eurocentric communication (that is, his lionizing of the French he learns studying abroad) is a meaningful and foremost endeavor. What is at stake here is what Meridian identifies as Truman's potential to impact the movement and her life: "He was, in any case, unlike any other black man she had known. He was a man who fought against obstacles, a man who could become anything, a man whose very words were unintelligible without considerable thought" (100).

As a result of a kind of institutional carrot and stick, R. Baron compromises Truman's intellectual curiosity. For instance, after spending months with the exchange students and not seeing Meridian, Truman mentions reading *The Souls of Black Folk* to her and beams with the desire to share the insights he's come across. However, the text indicates that his preference would have been to rhapsodize about the book with the erstwhile exchange students. And while he has been moved by the text, the implication is that Du Bois's seminal work gets reduced to an exemplar of black rhetorical and cultural genius as opposed to being utilized in matters of social urgency to which Meridian is connected.

Truman finally confronts his hedonism when he works at a country club and subjects himself to the condescending remarks of wealthy whites—possibly some of the same moneyed individuals who gave liberally to R. Baron. Truman complains that he has "to just stand there and grin and bear it. I despise them,' he said vehemently . . ." (117). Because he cannot enjoy the pleasures the members lord over him, Truman consumes himself with attaining prowess on the campus of Saxon and elsewhere. Finding himself in a demoralizing position, Truman feels powerless, socioeconomically, to achieve equal footing with the country-club barons. He decides instead to voraciously indulge in bourgeois capitalism—thereby rendering himself even more psychically vulnerable to dismissive elites who are fine with him diverting his nascent political energies from freedom struggle to frivolousness.

In *Meridian,* Walker uses Truman to comment on the individual activist's almost adversarial relationship to the movement. As an embattled artist and activist, Truman[5] contrasts with characters like Meridian. In understanding Truman, readers may consider a couple of questions: What are his politics? How does he practice activism? And how does the movement influence his sense of individuality? Though vigilant in the freedom struggle early on, his commitment becomes ambiguous: "[a]s a rule, [Truman] said, he didn't march any more, 'because what I believe cannot be placed on a placard'" (108). The mainstay in Truman's personality is his insatiable appetite for a bourgeois lifestyle, a tendency he assimilates from his background with a well-to-do father and an esteemed education. Unlike Meridian, whose activism leads to withdrawal from fraternization and bourgeois pleasures, Truman seems to struggle with the contrived nature of the movement—the jail-packing strategies and operations that come out of closed-system-type practices.

Truman also has a desultory relationship with Meridian that is stained by his patriarchal assumptions about women. As Meridian saw it, he "did not want a general beside him. He did not want a woman who tried, however encumbered by guilts and fears and remorse, to claim her own life" (112). Eventually, Truman's and Meridian's lives diverge and intersect at multiple points. Shouldering the cause of freedom as an unaffiliated activist, Meridian engages in a perpetual squaring off against the political agendas of figureheads who diminish black ambition. Maintaining ties to the movement, Truman witnesses the fragmentation of black freedom movements, the rise of the black middle class, and the fluctuations in politics and race relations during the 1960s, all of which are tarred with sociopolitical alienation and apathy. Unfortunately, Truman finds himself in the middle of one of these tectonic shifts, namely internal racial animus within the movement, which leaves him jaded.

The group constraints Truman faces in *Meridian* are linked to the overwhelming need for group affirmation among activists—the need to affirm black solidarity in word and deed. Walker initiates a clash within the Mississippi movement over Truman's relationship with a white Jewish woman named Lynne Rabinowitz. The two marry and move to Mississippi to join the effort there. Though Lynne is phenotypically white, her marriage to a black man and residence in the black belt of the South cordons her off from white society. After a racially motivated shooting in which fellow activist Tommy Odds gets hit exiting a church, Tommy and Truman argue over what precipitated the shooting. After Tommy blames Lynne's whiteness for the racist backlash, Truman ponders her culpability and then deeply considers, in a way he had not before, how race has factored into the mistreatment of black individuals. For Truman, blacks bear the burden of their skin color and all its negative associations, which are lodged in the consciousness of white America. Truman contextualizes the shooting incident in the realm of the taboo of black and white relations and the purported protection of white womanhood by white men. Ultimately, he links the shooting to the racial terrorism that went unchecked throughout much of American history.

In Mississippi, Truman and Lynne experience discrimination and witness the closing of ranks around black members as the movement spreads. Truman notices the fear Lynne engenders in the young men at their first meeting, even though, despite her whiteness, they develop an affinity for her. Still, "while this building of trust and mutual liking was coming into being, the Movement itself was changing. Lynne was no longer welcome at any of the meetings. She was excluded from the marches. She was no longer allowed to write articles for the paper" (146). Just as the leadership marginalizes his wife, they ostracize him for his attachment to her and insist that he not discuss sensitive information with her. These examples of exclusion constitute the kind of group-inspired ostracism that leaves Truman little wiggle room for brokering any power in the movement. Walker offers readers a window into a dynamic show of ideological force based on prejudicial assumptions. She further insists that the decisions of a few serve to carve out a worrisome undemocratic space for the many. One crucial point is that in Truman's mind this stance by the leadership effectively crowds out other grassroots options. Even as an experienced civil rights worker, Truman finds it impossible to operate in any leadership capacity. Likewise, marshaling the agendas of the movement for his own interests, as his colleagues are prone to do, seems implausible.

Unable to conceive of an activism that does not rely on group affirmation, Truman not only estranges himself from Lynne but also moves to New York. He retreats into the arts, painting his first mural for the Atlanta movement, and then exclusively painting and sculpting figures of black women. Whereas he once decried the voluptuousness of black women's bodies to Lynne, "in the end, he had stopped saying those things, at least out loud. It was as if the voluptuous black bodies, with breasts like melons and hair like a crown of thorns, reached out—creatures of his own creation—and silenced his tongue. They began to claim him" (184). Even so, it does not follow that his art represents a kind of aestheticized recuperation of his earlier commitment to cooperative struggle. Instead, Truman attempts to find himself, or rather, center himself, through his art. In a later encounter with Meridian, during which time he lectures her on thinking too much about the revolution, Truman asks: "Do you realize no one is thinking about these things anymore? Revolution was the theme of the sixties: Medgar, Malcolm, George, Angela Davis, the Panthers, people blowing up buildings and each other. But all that is gone now. I am, myself, making a statue of Crispus Attucks for the Bicentennial. We're here to stay: the black and the poor, the Indian, and now all those illegal immigrants from the West Indies who adore America just the way it is" (206).

Just as the political resonance of Truman's statue is overt, capturing a shift in America, which hinges on difference and militates against the denial of cultural pluralism, his conversation with Meridian speaks volumes. Meridian's follow-up question, "Then you think revolution, like everything else in America, was reduced to a fad?" remarks on the ability of American capitalism to fetishize even the most poignant symbols and icons of resistance, which is a staple feature of late capitalism. Though some spark of consciousness remains, Truman has no desire to recover the freedom struggle and has taken a capitalist off-ramp. To move beyond the state of resignation in which he finds himself, he will need to champion his ambivalence. In her own way, Meridian does this by contemplating pertinent questions about resistance with obsessive regularity.

Civil Rights Battle Scars

By observing the impact of the civil rights movement on budding revolutionaries, Walker delves into the commitment of black activists to reformist aims. She captures the depth of individual restlessness and the toll the movement exacts. Through the novel's exploration of conflict between politics, ideological turns, education, and society, Meridian's own development becomes symbiotic with the growth of the movement. As she advocates for democratic ideals (such as voting rights, nonviolent resistance, and demonstrations), she begins to look at the freedom struggle from a different angle, questioning its effectiveness. Because the novel takes as its backdrop the nonviolent protests and voting-rights efforts of the 1960s, Meridian is ideally situated to take reformist ideals to task. Left to champion the values of the movement after her counterparts (Anne-Marion and Truman) leave it behind, Meridian faces an existential crisis. Not only does she combat the threat of co-optation by distant leadership in the movement, but also she comes to terms with her own ambivalence about prescribed political action.

As Alan Nadel's essay "Reading the Body: Alice Walker's *Meridian* and the Archeology of Self" explains, "*Meridian* can be read as an attempt to mend the ruptures and reconstruct an alternative black tradition from its contemporary American artifacts. The novel conducts a historical search in that it tries to recontextualize the past" (56). In *Meridian*, Walker signifies on the many unnamed activists, volunteers, and grassroots efforts for enfranchisement by privileging the unarticulated psychological angst and the snubbing of individual input. Walker's discourse champions the disregarded individuality of those participating in broad-based movements. While we tout the mass countercultural sway of social movements, many people who initiated and sustained the struggle for civil rights did so for the purpose of realizing their autonomy. Walker's *Meridian* does not take this particular facet of struggle for granted. Rather, it criticizes the idea that unquestioning solidarity existed as a staple in our most celebrated social movements. Still, Walker makes the point that, when it comes to on-the-ground resistance, intellectual nuance among supporters is value added.

In the novel, the civil rights movement constitutes a system with a hierarchy that alienates Meridian and other volunteers. In fact, this system encourages individual sacrifice for the benefit of the group. Even as the movement makes meaningful strides and is largely celebrated by the communities it occupies, it can neither account for the battle fatigue endured by individual volunteers nor the psychological trauma endured by people who give not only their bodies to the struggle but also their emotions. Like the strivings of workers devoted to racial integration in *The Intuitionist*, these efforts tend to go unsung both inside and outside the halls of domineering organizations. In a flashback, Meridian recalls inviting a young woman named Anne (distinct from Anne-Marion) to join in a demonstration. Anne gets separated from her during a lunch-counter melee. After they are arrested, Meridian can hear Anne's screams from a distant cell, "and though she never saw her again, she began to imagine she did, and the screams became an accompaniment of the guilt already weighing her down" (96). Because there is no space to voice the concerns of volunteers, their pain and critical observations gets swallowed up in the urgency of protests.

Before joining the Atlanta movement, Meridian witnesses as protest movements become infectious in her community and surrounding areas. While the novel suggests that Meridian typically lives in a fog of unconcern, the violent backlash against this groundswell becomes eye-opening for her. After sauntering through her neighborhood one day and passing a black family's house where she noticed white people milling about, Meridian returned home to hear the television announce that a voter-registration drive would begin at that house and spread through the neighborhood. The following morning Meridian learned that the house, along with other homes on that same street, had been firebombed, and three small children were killed. Walker's insertion of this event calls to mind the tragic 1963 bombing of the Sixteenth Street Baptist Church in Birmingham, Alabama, which resulted in the death of four young black girls. This experience causes a collision with American racial reality for Meridian and stirs an emotional response: "it was that one day in the middle of April in 1960 Meridian Hill became aware of the past and present of the larger world" (70). With her innocence shattered, Meridian ponders whether those risking their lives to canvass neighborhoods hold some understanding that she lacks.

Meridian's chilling introduction to the tensions of the civil rights movement has a profound effect upon her sense of awareness, so much so that, afterwards, she sits in front of her bedroom window to reflect on her life. There Meridian undergoes one of several transformations: "At first it was like falling back into a time that never was, a time of complete rest, like a faint. Her senses were stopped, while her body rested; only in her head did she feel something, and it was a sensation of lightness—a lightness like the inside of a drum. The air inside her head was pure of thought, at first. For hours she sat by the window looking out, but not seeing the pecan trees bending in the wind, or the blue clouded sky, or the grass" (71). Though seeking pureness of thought proves to be a futile endeavor, Meridian is able to wade through ignorance to emerge more conscious of her own circumstances. At the time, Meridian is a young mother and wife mired in domestic responsibilities. However, she perceives something beyond the burdensome nature of a loveless marriage and recognizes a future for herself that has yet to unfold. In this frame of mind, Meridian ventures beyond her usual confines into activism. For Walker, the space of black protest into which Meridian enters affords her more mindfulness because she moves from curiosity to volunteering in a neighborhood voter-registration drive—the same event that was shrouded in violence days earlier.

Meridian becomes determined to empower others with the vote and with political participation. The black people in her town commend her for "doing a good thing: typing, teaching illiterates to read and write, demonstrating against segregated facilities and keeping the Movement house open when the other workers returned to school" (82). Like her father, Meridian has a political core that kindles her indignation. Unlike Lila Mae, who looked to strong women that followed a one-dimensional notion of progress, Meridian is able to anchor her impulses in the cultural sensibility her father exhibited when she was a child. Meridian's advantage over Lila Mae is that her father was invested in cultural difference as opposed to patriarchal control. Mr. Hill identified with Native Americans and their marginalization and had fought for land reparations for the wrongs perpetrated against them. Meridian's mother, on the other hand, did not share his sentiments and is hostile toward civil disobedience. Beyond denigrating protestors, Mrs. Hill tells Meridian, "you've wasted a year of your life, fooling around with those people. The papers say they're crazy. God separated the sheeps from the goats and the black folks from the white. And me from anybody that acts as foolish as they do" (83). Mrs. Hill also clamps down on the fact that fallibility runs through every entity and resigns herself to an apolitical life.

In the novel, the civil rights movement takes advantage of crisis points. The decision to engage locales in several former Confederate states is anything but a deliberative, democratic process among rank-and-file volunteers. This leads to groups of demonstrators being deployed to hot spots of injustice, which tend to be teeming with opposition. For the greater cause of freedom, leaders harnessed the energies of masses of disenfranchised black college students. The will of some students gave way under the crushing weight of mental injuries worse than bodily harm. Meridian remarks about the demoralization that accompanied this strategy, which crept up on her and other supporters: "She [Meridian] saw small black children, with short, flashing black legs, being chased by grown white men brandishing ax handles. She saw old women dragged out of stores and beaten on the sidewalk, their humility of a lifetime doing them no good. She saw young black men of great spiritual beauty changed overnight into men who valued nothing" (95). Walker does not paint a superficial picture of young foot soldiers as heroic and invulnerable to the personal inner turmoil that came with combating racism and staunch resistance to black civil rights. For example, while other volunteers fear violent confrontations with police and angry mobs, Meridian welcomes the clashes. What is significant is that Meridian witnesses secondhand as much pain as she endures firsthand. Perhaps Walker's most important construction is the notion that there is a sociopolitical exchange at work. Volunteers do not simply expend themselves without creating friction throughout the movement; likewise, the movement exerts itself on them, in both meaningful and devastating ways.

Despite the flaws associated with the direct-action protocols, Meridian's involvement is pivotal. After graduating from Saxon, Meridian has no intention of leading a life of apathy but identifies wholly with the disenfranchised. Unfortunately, her personal challenges are compounded by her participation: "Meridian found, when she was not preoccupied with the Movement, that her thoughts turned with regularity and intensity to her mother, on whose account she endured wave after wave of an almost primeval guilt" (96). The challenge is that she lacks a coherent politics that is not wrapped up in her feelings of vulnerability and guilt for both embracing the movement and being marginalized by it. In writing an interrogation of mid-twentieth-century civil rights struggles, Walker seems to carve out a space for her protagonist, which adheres to the definitions offered for the term "Meridian" in the first few pages of the novel. In the (a) clause of definition number 6 ("a place or situation with its own distinctive character"), Walker seems to hint at the possibility that Meridian can draw from the wealth of critical knowledge available in the arenas of activism and higher education. Then she can begin informing her impulses and following her own politics.

Women and the Sway of the Movement

In *Meridian*, Walker paints a clear picture of the civil rights movement's impact on women, including those whose circumstances the proverbial agenda ignored. In particular, Walker challenges dehumanizing practices against women by allowing those practices to incite Meridian's political fervor. Quiet and unassuming, Meridian gets whisked into adult life and marriage after becoming pregnant by a high-school lover. At seventeen years old, she marries her lover at the behest of her mother, drops out of high school, and assumes the role of wife and mother, though unprepared for either. At first oblivious to the racial and gender politics that beset her, Meridian matures into someone capable of challenging traditional assumptions. Just as writers like Toni Morrison and Gloria Naylor often imbue their female characters with nonconformist sensibilities, Walker infuses Meridian's character with the acumen to discern the unsavory politics at play in various contexts. Throughout the novel, Meridian scrutinizes multiple ideological fronts: the ladyhood-obsessed arena of Saxon, the male-dominated Atlanta movement, and rural southern communities. These spaces serve as a gauntlet—forcing her to come to terms with the broader struggle for civil rights while at the same time navigating the mental deprivation that stems from it.

Exposing herself to several stories and incidents involving female tragedy at Saxon, Meridian colors her understanding of patriarchal power. First, Wile Chile gets pregnant (presumably from rape) and then is killed by a speeding driver. Meridian also hears about the timeworn tales of Louvinie and Fast Mary. Louvinie, an enslaved West African (on the former Saxon plantation), has her tongue cut out for telling a ghost story that literally frightened the master's son (who had a heart problem) to death. Fast Mary, who was once a student at Saxon, concealed her pregnancy out of shame, murdered her baby, and then committed suicide three months later. These tragic events converge for Meridian at the site of the Sojourner, which becomes a target of student rage. Lastly, at the beginning of the novel, the "Marilene O'Shay" circus exhibit displays the corpse of a murdered woman. The back story reveals that the woman's cuckolded husband strangled her and shot her lover, dumping both their bodies into a lake with impunity.

While the novel's southern patriarchal ethos rehearses severe punishment for those who violate conventions of decorum, Meridian's resistance throughout serves to disrupt such practices. Walker reacts against this system by creating an environment in which Meridian neither takes on the weaker sex role nor the mule-of-the-world mantle historically prescribed for black women. Walker's general critique is aimed not only at bearing witness to sexist atrocities but also forcing patriarchal authority to own them. Meridian's will to resist the diminishment of the politics of women who struggle alongside her (in their respective spaces) can be read as extending Walker's critique. For instance, Meridian synthesizes the philosophies of two influential people in her life—namely Miss Winter, a black professor at Saxon, and Anne-Marion—to cultivate her own brand of struggle.

Miss Winter grew up in the same community as Meridian, graduated from Saxon, and acts as a contrarian figure in the novel. While the text does not speak specifically to her involvement in any auxiliary of the civil rights movement, she has made a career out of combating repression. We learn about the radical politics Miss Winter held when she taught Meridian in high school, which is the same politics she ascribes to at Saxon. At the former, when Meridian objected to reciting a speech on the virtues of the U.S. Constitution, she quelled her reservations. At the latter, she mentors Meridian. One of three black faculty members on campus, Miss Winter has a misfit reputation—and contrary to Saxon tradition, teaches jazz, spirituals, and blues in her classes. She stands in opposition to the administration's efforts to either have her conform or to oust her: "her fights with the president and the college dean could be heard halfway across the campus" (125). Further, in the midst of Miss Winter's bureaucratic contestation, she becomes a surrogate mother for Meridian, who is struck by a mysterious illness. While in bed, Meridian dreams about her strained relationship with her actual mother, an overburdened yet driven woman, whose expectations Meridian feels she cannot live up to. In this moment, Miss Winter acts as a healing presence for Meridian because she is one of the few people able to reach Meridian's inner self in ways that neither religion nor politics ever has. In a sense, Miss Winter offers Meridian forgiveness on behalf of a legacy of black women who were born in an age shaped by necessity and limited in opportunity.

Because Meridian has a penchant for purpose and not distinction, she has no desire to follow in Miss Winter's career footsteps. Instead, she rebuffs the bureaucratic structures that insist on black middle-class conformity. Like Miss Winter, Meridian starts to feel that she no longer needs to attach herself to a hierarchical movement to impact others. She moves away from a collectivist politics to leverage what she has distilled from Saxon and the Atlanta movement. In an era of cultural fragmentation spurred by social movements, Meridian has learned to challenge apparatuses of power alongside those who are disenfranchised and seeking to eke out a meaningful existence.

Anne-Marion is a rebellious and, at times, complicated figure in the novel, but not solely because of her embrace of militancy. At Saxon, Anne-Marion cuts off all her hair, dismisses bourgeois refinement, rebuffs male advances, and risks harm to "discover the economic causes of inner-city crime" (28). Irreverent as she is, Anne-Marion believes that by participating in the movement she is paving the way for a fuller life for black people. This awareness leaves her conflicted in her views about what the goals of the movement ought to be. In a veiled way, the conversation between Anne-Marion and Meridian about capitalism is really a debate about the lasting meaning of the movement. Walker states, "Both girls had lived and studied enough to know they despised capitalism; they perceived it had done well in America because it had rested directly on their fathers' and mothers' backs" (122). The separation comes when we learn that Meridian's objections rest on a strict notion of equality while Anne-Marion wanted "blacks to have the same opportunity to make as much money as the richest white people." And she herself flirts with the idea of a "capitalist fling" that could weaken her adoration for socialism. Ultimately, Anne-Marion wants to see black people have the opportunity to profit from America's free-market system as others have and to experience ownership on a wide scale. Her activism seems to be premised on material progress for blacks and not public-policy concessions. It is little wonder, then, that Anne-Marion becomes a well-known poet, enjoys the luxuries that her writing affords, and even comes to own a lake. The text's silence on the New York Revolutionaries group suggests that they soon dissolve, and that Anne-Marion abandons her militancy for the opportunity to become wealthy.

Meridian adopts Anne-Marion's earlier loathing of capitalism without ambiguity and inverts her militant sensibility. Meridian's aim is not to live a life of bourgeois comfort or leverage her education into a lucrative career. Instead, she opts for a nuanced position that is decidedly people-centered. When Meridian reflects upon her priorities, she repudiates the simplistic notion that she should leave a violent enough impact that would thrust the black poor into opportunity. In looking for something deeper than capitalism, Meridian chooses to live penniless and socially powerless. Her overarching goal is to act as a cultural fount of resistance for black people. Anne-Marion embraced a kind of racialized economic self-interest: "When black people can own the seashore, she said, I want miles and miles of it. And I never want to see a face I didn't invite walking across my sand" (122). In contrast, in an era marked by the triumph of social movements, Meridian wants to advance the rights of the people. But she does not seek to control the masses through traditional leadership. Nor does she want to be the type of revolutionary who self-consciously renders the masses dependent on her political whims. Rather, Meridian wants to see the soul of the people "transformed by the experiences of each generation" (221).

Meridian's Restless Questioning

A more complex understanding of what signals a postmodern moment in African American literature lies in looking at the questioning and reflection of individuals in black social movements. Meridian embodies these postmodern inclinations throughout the novel. Having witnessed social, political, and racial upheavals that awaken her consciousness, Meridian cannot easily move past these experiences in her inner life. Walker's concern for how individuals might harness the inner anguish that is often a by-product of movement politics leads her to imagine an activism built on the revolutionary practice of restless questioning and critical reflection.[6] This becomes an overly self-conscious (and imprecise) attempt at maintaining a critique of the efficacy of movement politics and of individual struggle against the status quo. That said, Meridian demonstrates the postmodern when she goes against the agendas pushed by leadership, when she imposes on herself the responsibility of changing society, and risks harm to her own psyche to combat indifference. When I mention *the postmodern* in the context of the wherewithal to act on one's compulsions, the term is not confined to a particular era. Instead, it implies the marshaling of one's agency strategically and from a nonconformist perspective. In particular, Meridian's postmodern practice involves the voluntary shouldering of psychological burdens and physical pain for the radical cause of social equity.

Throughout the novel, Meridian shows the capacity to adapt and change. She operates according to Linda Hutcheon's sense of the postmodern: "The postmodern impulse is not to seek any total vision. It merely questions. If it *finds* such a vision, it questions how, in fact, it *made* it" (48). After leaving the confines of young motherhood, Meridian becomes invested in this paradigm. In spaces like Saxon and organizations like the Atlanta movement, which are filled with ambiguity, she survives by questioning the deeper meaning of struggle. While her queries alienate her from loved ones and fragment her politics, they also enable the kind of reflection that buffers distressing experiences and sustains her resistance efforts outside the context of a formal movement.

In her interrogation of the civil rights movement, Walker has Meridian reflect on the protracted struggle itself, the endless battles, and the losses that have attended it. At one point in the novel, Meridian takes a walk and ponders the thoughts of martyrs like Christ, King, and Malcolm. In the chapter "Free at Last," Walker recasts the funeral of Martin Luther King Jr. as an affair with the expected pomp and circumstance, but absent any grief. Meridian witnesses an odd distancing from death by the spectators who engage in loud conversation, laughter, and create "a feeling of relief in the air, of liberation, that was repulsive" (203). In a subsequent conversation with Truman, Walker seems to parse Meridian's thoughts: "She could not help struggling with these questions. Just as Truman could not help thinking such struggle useless. In the end people did what they had to do to survive. They acquiesced, they rebelled, they sold out, they shot it out, or they simply drifted with the current of the time, whatever it was. And they didn't endanger life and limb agonizing over what they would lose, which was what separated them from Meridian" (207).

This passage highlights Meridian's refusal to settle for anything less than giving her whole self to serving the downtrodden, because any other path would mean self-defeat and acquiescence. In opposition to the notion of "going along to get along," Meridian ruminates on the novel's most pressing questions. Walker frames this agonizing need to question as postmodern because it not only clarifies her political core but also rouses her activism. Ironically, ambivalence is also part of this peculiar process that sustains Meridian, though it cuts against the grain of her activist training and certainly runs counter to the protocol-based, movement politics. Further, Meridian's postmodern inclination to compulsively ponder large questions becomes her crucible, which she enters without compulsion.

A number of studies on *Meridian* give attention to reflection and self-identity. Lynn Pifer in her essay "Coming to Voice in Alice Walker's *Meridian*: Speaking Out for the Revolution," for instance, suggests that, "when she [Meridian] finds that she cannot conform to authorized notions of appropriate speech (public repentance, patriotic school speeches, and the like), her only rebellious recourse is silence" (77). As Pifer explains, Meridian works out the brunt of her personal struggle through nonconformity vis-à-vis the status of southern black women.[7] According to Donna Winchell, individuality gets repressed in the civil rights movement's group agenda. Moreover, "Before Meridian can successfully define her role within the revolution, she must first successfully define herself . . ." (59). In explaining the protagonist's conundrum, Stein remarks that "*Meridian's*

eponymous hero enacts this quest in her journey from adolescent unawareness to mature self-knowledge, from death to rebirth, from confrontations
with revolutionary ardor to a spiritual vision" (130). If Meridian is on a
quest, then it is a restless pursuit that is decentered from modern agendas
or goals and framed by postmodern individual consciousness.

At the beginning of the novel, we meet Meridian, more than a decade
after the civil rights movement, leading a demonstration in the small town
of Chicokema against the city's segregationist policies. Black schoolchildren can only see the Marilene O'Shay circus exhibit on Thursdays. In
protest, Meridian faces down a tank and a phalanx of police alone: "The
town of Chicokema did indeed own a tank. It had been bought during the
sixties when the townspeople who were white felt under attack from 'outside agitators'—those members of the black community who thought equal
rights for all should extend to blacks" (2). Several components make this
demonstration peculiar: First, the "deep silence" of black onlookers instead
of a robust outcry is a stark feature of the march. Second, Meridian dons
the garb of a train conductor, as opposed to that of a charismatic leader.
Lastly, we see small schoolchildren follow behind Meridian, but they never
burst into song as a bystanding Truman anticipates. After the children and
some adults view the demonstration, the crowd disperses without much
ado. Then Meridian almost methodically collapses, and the townspeople
cart her home.

In a departure from the Atlanta movement, Meridian neither seeks
to recruit volunteers for a drawn-out struggle nor dismisses them. Here
she neither adopts movement practices nor rejects them. Meridian's act
of resistance is postmodern in that it is very much in the moment and
not tethered to a stable narrative or proposed end point. When Truman
remarks that she cannot expect the townspeople to take on a tank, Meridian responds with the town's adage "[t]hat if somebody had to go it might
as well be the person who's ready" (11). Unlike Truman, Meridian cannot
walk away from the movement as if it never happened. She contemplates
the victories and defeats of the past incessantly. Committed to battling racial domination, Meridian meets the imperatives of fighting for civil rights
with the immediacy they necessitate.

In the novel, a bizarre sickness grips Meridian days before her gradu-
ation from Saxon. Her illness begins with blindness, loss of appetite, and

then culminates in catatonic fainting spells. When Anne-Marion (her roommate at the time) feeds her what little she will eat, Meridian "discover[s] herself becoming more and more full, with no appetite whatsoever. And, to her complete surprise and astonished joy, she began to experience ecstasy" (124). At this point, Anne-Marion misreads Meridian's condition as escapist or as capitulation. Anne-Marion soon leaves Meridian behind with the parting comment—"Meridian, I can not afford to love you. Like the idea of suffering itself, you are obsolete" (131). But Meridian's illness is not a retreat of sorts. And there is a measure of transformation that occurs in her isolation and physical decline. The novel portrays her illness as sociocultural, with implications for the realm of liberation in which she operates. For instance, Meridian embraces the inquisitive mindfulness that suffering brings, which later becomes a feature of her activism. When Truman visits Meridian in a small Alabama town a decade removed from their college days, he remarks on the kind of parallel course in her psyche: "Meridian, no matter what she was saying to you, and no matter what you were saying to her, seemed to be thinking of something else, another conversation perhaps, an earlier one, that continued on a parallel track. Or of a future one that was running an identical course. This was always true" (149). Meridian also exuded a restlessness, wherein "the future might be short, but memory was very long" (150). In essence, what Truman describes is Meridian's rejection of futurity—her choosing to live in the urgency of the moment, incessantly questioning, in an endless loop of reflection. Similar to James Fulton in *The Intuitionist*, Meridian is tasked with fashioning the new cultural formations and practices that will be put to use in the future. In that respect, Meridian occupies the role of the visionary whose black box contains emergent forms of activism that cannot be fully comprehended in her political moment.

To grasp the tensions that saturate postmodern critical reflection among movement activists, observing an encounter between Lynne Rabinowitz (after her marriage to Truman has ended) and Meridian is useful. The occasion for the visit is Lynne's well-founded belief that Truman wants to rekindle a relationship with Meridian. During her visit, she offers a brazen perspective on the contradictions between black male and female activists. As Lynne puts it, "Black men and women *are* scared to death of each other, you know. Not your *average* black men and women, of course, who accept each other as only natural, but people like you and Truman who have to keep analyzing each other's problems" (156). In a blatant, if presumptuous, manner Lynne touches on something interesting. The regularity with which black activists find themselves wrestling with each other's inner burdens is a fraught enterprise—one brought on by a lack of introspection on the part of the larger movement and somehow devolved to the rank and file.

One impetus for Meridian's and Truman's reflection and their refusal to ignore their battered psyches is their identification with the ordinary people they fight with and for. An example shows up as Lynne and Meridian watch a TV program featuring a black man who, after gaining the right to vote, starts to process the reality that he does not know how he will earn money to buy food. The bemused look on his face forces Meridian and Lynne to question the modicum of freedom available to the enfranchised poor in a nation run by and for those with capital and the knowledge to use it for their benefit. The black man's face mirrors their own contemplation: "It sought to understand, to encompass everything, and the struggle to live honorably and understand everything at the same time, to allow for every inconsistency in nature, every weird possibility and personality . . ." (190). Walker's novel suggests that the movement never accounts for this dynamic. In the same way that differences get flattened out in institutions like Saxon, the bureaucracy of civil rights activism sought to paper over class and socioeconomic difference within its ranks.

Meridian concerns itself with the complexities of sacrifice. An interesting thing happens in the chapter "Visits," which initiates Meridian's postmodern understanding of her social position as an activist in a long line of martyrs and freedom fighters. She recalls an earlier time in which she embraced her illness as cultural currency: "she could summon whatever energy a task that had to be performed required, and like them [enslaved Africans], this ability seemed to her something her ancestors had passed on from the days of slavery when there had been no such thing as a sick slave, only a 'malingering' one" (154). Meridian takes a long walk and begins to question the idea of martyrdom. Interestingly enough, this walk precipitates a revision of the ancestral connection, which she welcomes: "[O]ne thought had preoccupied her mind: 'The only new thing now,' she had said to herself, mumbling it aloud, so that people turned to stare at her, 'would be the refusal of Christ to accept crucifixion. King,' she had said, turning down a muddy lane, 'should have refused. Malcolm, too should have refused. All those characters in all those novels that require death to end the book should refuse. All saints should walk away. Do their bit, then—just walk away" (162).

While Meridian knows this "new" thing has not yet materialized, she is seeking something besides compulsory sacrifice and imagines martyrs walking away alive after having done their part. When Lynne tells Meridian that she cannot change people in the South, Meridian replies, "But I can change, [and] I hope I will" (163). Here Meridian is willing herself beyond her ontological limitations. She has come to believe about her humanity "that this existence extended beyond herself to those around her because, in fact, the years in America had created them One Life" (220). In cultivating a unique ontological perspective, Meridian recalls her squeamishness about killing and resolves to move away from the untenable urgings of rage in search of a new understanding of martyrdom. Rather than invite death, Meridian chooses a posture that stares death in the face.

Walker uses Meridian's reflection on spirituality and political action to offer a postmodern reading of both. Meridian easily identifies with her father's spirituality, which incorporated Christian hymns and Native American rituals, but she can neither understand her mother's unquestioned love for the Baptist church nor confess her belief in God. Early on, Meridian experiences a tangible spiritual encounter at the Serpent's Coil, a large mound on her father's farm shaped similar to Indian burial mounds. Meridian's spiritual intoxication at the burial grounds stands opposite her indecision in the black church. The former is a fleeting moment while the latter holds unnerving immediacy for her. As an adult, Meridian begins irregularly attending a large Baptist church. The church has a stained glass image of B.B. King, and the congregation sings dirge-like lyrics to freedom songs. Because she has always connected with freedom melodies, Meridian notices that the songs have become much less revolutionary since the culmination of the movement.

While the first preacher to grace the pulpit rehearses the exact cadences of Martin Luther King Jr.'s homilies and delivers a politically charged message, the congregation responds half-heartedly. Another preacher introduced himself as the father of a civil rights martyr pictured on a large photograph in the church. Hearing the buzzing congregation, Meridian gathered that the sacrifice made by this man's son had resonated with them. Taking stock of her own sacrifices, she "understood finally, that the respect she owed her life was to continue, against whatever obstacles, to live it, and not to give up any particle of it without a fight to the death, preferably *not* her own" (219–20). Questioning the sermon's impact, Meridian senses the congregation's desire to share in the preacher's loss and their longing to weave something more palpable (invoked by the death the preacher often referenced) into the language and culture of the church. While the gravitas of death strikes a chord in an institution becoming increasingly absent in grassroots struggle after the civil rights era, the red-eyed preacher only makes such appearances on the anniversary of his son's death to remind the people of his loss. Walker uses this scene to comment on the changing cultural sensibilities and the absence of political ire among black churches in the late twentieth century.

Ultimately, the novel paves the way for Meridian's postmodern subjectivity by having her question her way through her parents' belief systems into conceptions that suit her temperament. The Serpent's Coil spiritual experience—though key in her father's embrace of the natural and the supernatural—proves inaccessible to Meridian. Nonetheless, in her psychological, burden-bearing approach to resistance, Meridian equips parts of her paternal grandmother's (Feather Mae's) spirituality and reappropriates her mother's Baptist proscriptions. Meridian's restless questioning and reflection are spiritual in nature, a form of asceticism.

In an early chapter containing an epigraph of assassinations from Medgar Evers to Viola Liuzzo, Walker weaves in a passage that comments on the 1960s:

It was a decade marked by death. Violent and inevitable. Funerals became engraved on the brain, intensifying the ephemeral nature of life. For many in the South it was a decade reminiscent of earlier times, when oak trees sighed over their burdens in the wind; Spanish moss draggled bloody to the ground; amen corners creaked with grief; and the thrill of being able, once again, to endure unendurable loss produced so profound an ecstasy in mourners that they strutted, without noticing their feet, along the thin backs of benches: their piercing shouts of anguish and joy never interrupted by an inglorious fall. They shared rituals for the dead to be remembered. But now television became the repository of memory, and each onlooker grieved alone. (21)

This passage captures a profound cultural shift in America from community solidarity to individual burden-bearing. The absence of solidarity mentioned in the final sentence not only signals a bygone era that readers might bemoan, but it also implies a reflective and questioning tone as it directs our attention to the onlooker who now grieves alone for the fallen, outside the confines of community or group grief. Throughout the novel, Walker offers individual autonomy as an option for resistance and refuge as successive eras witness society coming unmoored from a sense of community.

Walker's postmodern exploration of the civil rights movement has implications for the conceptions of power we see emerge throughout *Meridian*. Walker's civil rights conditions are indexed by the struggles not of affluent movement figureheads but of minor participants determined to sacrifice for freedom in the most personal ways. Suffocating leadership becomes the nemesis of the individual in *Meridian*. It seeks to silence women, quell deep intellectual and emotional energy, and mandate a contrived solidarity. Within this dynamic, sacrificing oneself for a movement becomes the order of the day. Yet the novel challenges this trend. Discussing 1960s radical politics, Marianne DeKoven's *Utopia Limited* highlights a "conception of power and resistance as shifting, multidirectional, local, partial . . . dynamic flows rather than massive dualisms of domination and revolution" (256). DeKoven's observation speaks to the activist's ability to conceive of a social movement not as a monolith but as a program with competing ideas both inside and outside its ranks. Finally, Alan Nadel suggests that *Meridian* does not lend itself to one reading, but cycles through several alternatives, options, and points of view. In this way, Walker offers readers a postmodern perspective on the significance of meaning-making for communities and individuals alike.

In *Meridian*, Walker offers a portrait of the psychology behind revolutionary practice. She explores its capacity to spread from one person to the next and become infectious. The corollary to that is the trauma that gets shared and passed on as well. Without an activism tweaked to process this trauma—or to wield it in Meridian's case—movement participants are left vulnerable. Henry Kariel's *The Desperate Politics of Postmodernism* observes the politics behind movements. He describes this politics as one that gives attention to the need to maintain "one's balance in a world in which crisis and emergency are not discrete moments but a universal condition . . ." (92). In Kariel's text, inclinations like reflection and questioning accompany resistance and are unavoidable in a political or cultural sense. In the final chapter, "Release," Meridian finds the strength to return to her cause through these impulses. Truman's hope that she "would return to the world cleansed of sickness" (241) falls flat. Instead, Meridian "had discarded her cap, and the soft wool of her newly grown hair framed her thin, resolute face." Her conversation with Truman in this scene is telling as it concerns whether Meridian's postmodern questioning is a suitable paradigm that can be reappropriated and deployed for his circumstances. At one point, Truman says to Meridian: "Your ambivalence will always be deplored by people who consider themselves revolutionists, and your unorthodox behavior will cause traditionalists to gnash their teeth. . . ." In response, Meridian explains that she values her separation from group interests and leaves him to his own questioning. To manage his afflictions (the death of his daughter, the sting of being blacklisted by the movement) Truman must engage them—he must take the weight of a cause on his shoulders and bear it for others. Taking the capitalist route of selling his artwork has not sufficed.

In this scene, he climbs into Meridian's sleeping bag (a symbolic crucible), initiating what is a difficult postmodern turn for him. Truman "had a vision of Anne-Marion herself arriving, lost, someday, at the door, which would remain open, and wondered if Meridian knew that the sentence of bearing the conflict in her own soul which she had imposed on herself— and lived through—must now be borne in terror by all the rest of them" (242). Truman comes full circle, from activism to hedonism to recuperating his role in the liberation of the downtrodden. Ultimately, he will need to willingly shoulder the calamities of his own life, not to find complete psychological relief, but to become, as Meridian does, "strong enough to go."

Walker's novel leads her to acknowledge the pitfalls of civil rights activism, which result from top-down politics that alienate volunteers and workers. She pinpoints the sense of abstraction marking black experiences in not only activism but also education and capitalist society. Through it all, *Meridian* explores the individual's sense of resistance and opposes an essentialist, one-size-fits-all approach to the struggle for change. Even as Walker illuminates the psychological toll and inner trauma that accompanies taking a stand against oppression, she makes the case that the political fire is not entirely extinguished in those who are left jaded. In the midst of deep social and cultural fragmentation, a postmodern perspective is the perfect catalyst for retooling the psyche and channeling the energies that remain.

Critics should explore the contribution of *Meridian* to postmodern black cultural politics. Among other things, taking a look at the barriers to individual action erected during the civil rights era can provide insight into the alienating conditions of contemporary black life. If the absence of such an extensive reform movement represents a cessation of broad political stratagems around race, then why does so much informal struggle continue to play out among middle- and working-class blacks? In short, the unquenchable urge to resist oppression rests not with the auspices of political or cultural organizations but with ordinary people. Ultimately, I encourage the exploration of the benefits and detriments of group consciousness and institutional access. Critics might especially consider the struggle for autonomy, which traverses both cultural and institutional landscapes. Finally, postmodernism might be reconfigured by including Walker's discourse as insight into historical and recent crisis points in African American experience.

3

RESISTING CONSENSUS
Class-Driven Politics in John Oliver Killens's *The Cotillion*

The Cotillion evaluates class-driven resistance to social conformity and critiques bourgeois class consciousness. The culture work John Oliver Killens does, which involves demystifying and comprehending the politics of cultural entities, sets the stage way for the maneuvering through group constraints and mainstream insularity. *The Cotillion*'s plot features the Lovejoy family (Matthew, Daphne, and Yoruba) and Ben Ali Lumumba, an erstwhile neighbor, in their individual quests to map out resilient social identifications. Set in the late 1960s during the height of black nationalism, the flourishing of blackness creates a backdrop not only rife with the cultural capital of black pride but also sullied by an insidious class consciousness. Yoruba Lovejoy comes of age in this environment and attempts to question both the shallowness of some presentations of working-class nationalism and the calcified high-society notions of what constitutes "refined" ideals. Lumumba, a self-proclaimed citizen of the world, hopes to raise consciousness and introduce social heterogeneity into the class equation. Killens positions both of them to challenge parochial ideas about decorum and tradition. In doing so, he diverges from narratives of racial uplift highlighted in *The Intuitionist* and from the ethos of black struggle shown to impose group constraints in *Meridian*. Shifting from the misdeeds of white mainstream institutions in the previous novels, he foregrounds a black organization, which appropriates a mainstream ethic and perpetuates class chauvinism. Ultimately, Killens wants to make visible the misapplied effort that goes into the decision for blacks to distinguish themselves over and against each other.

Killens creates a postmodern context that not only resists consensus but also resists the tendency of groups to collapse into particularistic black experiences by class. His vision of a postmodern moment revolves around resisting cultural consensus enough to make cultural identity something flexible. The postmodern hastens the withering of arbitrary boundaries within or between cultural institutions that share a common heritage. In exploring the complexities of African American class mobility, Killens illuminates the extent to which some groups aspire to repressive politics in their respective communities. For example, in *The Cotillion,* the Femmes Fatales, an exclusive social club Daphne hopes to join, welcomes only middle-class individuals while inviting in the children of working-class blacks like Yoruba for the sake of reforming them. But this kind of exchange is precisely what eventually infuses a politics of difference into the organization. Individuals fend off exclusion by spreading their norms as opposed to capitulating into like-minded ways of thinking. Indeed, a postmodern perspective problematizes the rigid distinctions around class made by entities like the Femmes Fatales. In the novel's predominantly black setting, readers see diverse black experiences bloom in close proximity to one another, and the flexibility around identity and status enabled by this flowering not only invites dissent but also throws the need for consensus into crisis.

In *The Cotillion,* formal satirical features work to capture the witting and unwitting tendencies of black social organizations—each aspiring to create lasting comradery and belongingness. Poetic epigraphs, epistolary form, and intertextuality flourish in this satirical work as it lampoons the black bourgeoisie and offers a corrective on the appropriation of self-defeating cultural practices. Killens uses an open-ended structure to facilitate dialogue around these issues and to invite complex arguments regarding diverse and diffuse black experiences. This feature stands out because it serves as the perfect literary apparatus upon which to hash out concerns over the implications of class mobility and black social connectedness. What Killens's open-ended narrative does, then, is avoid an easy resolution. Instead, it offers a sounding board for African American experiences en masse, one equipped to absorb and disseminate the views of critics, sycophants, and interlopers alike.

Killens's open-ended humor speaks to the shuttling of postmodern ideologies across contexts and situations to generate satirical critiques, namely of popular culture, public indifference, and invocations of protected liberties and democracy. Alongside the novel's many popular culture references, the sequence involving the *Johnny Carson Show* and its featured guest, Jomo Mamadou Zero the Third, offers an interesting commentary on the interfacing of black radicalism and popular culture. Joined by Yoruba, Lumumba looks forward to watching his former shipmate appear on one of the most popular television shows of the era. Lumumba remarks on the artificiality of Zero's black radicalist act: "I want to tell you, it took beaucoup creativity and imagination to put his fine Black thing together. He ain't hardly been in jail them years he was supposed to've been in Ossining . . ." (159). The satirical element here is really the contrast between a show that epitomizes white American mainstream humor and the portrayal of a black revolutionary caricature.

After Carson welcomes Zero to the couch and the audience applauds, Zero says, "I wished [*sic*] all of you pale-faced pigs a bad damn evening, you swinish cannibalistic motherfuckas! And after them few kind words of salutation, I'm going to say some mean things to you" (162). After Zero's caustic words, the audience explodes in hysterical applause. While laughing at Zero's brutal salutation, Lumumba realizes that, even in the midst of Zero's demeaning tone, the white audience has actually signified on them both. Through Lumumba, Killens makes the poignant observation that, "No matter what we say to Whitey, we always end up as his entertainment." Moreover, Killens offers a more nuanced assessment, which Lumumba articulates a couple pages earlier. In response to Yoruba's remorse about doubting his political resolve after he cuts his hair and joins her in the cotillion preparations, Lumumba says that "It's [his missing afro] a symbol of our Black and beautiful selves, and that's a great thing, but it's not the revolution. There ain't no revolution yet" (160). If there is to be a revolution, Killens implies, it will emerge through the unsung cultural and political labor of ordinary people on the ground, working in communities to imagine different arrangements outside the capitalist, popular culture—which are distant from the orbit of black radical iconography and the white curiosity.

Killens creates the sort of unambiguous allegory McHale describes in *Postmodernist Fiction* where, "instead of exploiting indeterminate allegory to destabilize ontological structure," the author opts for "relatively transparent, univocal allegorical narratives" (142). In his ridiculing thoughts on indifference in the novel, Killens works within two frames of reference: the cotillion as a metaphor for the willingness of middle-class blacks to imitate misguided white traditions and the debutante process as an unwitting pursuit of tainted cultural capital and transference of it. An allegory on sociocultural credulity and indifference shows up in Killens's description of the political and global events unfolding in the background, which render the cotillion a mindless distraction. Killens writes, "The rains came, the leaves fell turning golden brown, some trees seemed to have struck fire with fall-time happenings. Burn, baby! Then came the quiet of the snow. Law-and-order[1] was the thing in winter. Wars were fought all over the earth. Men died for freedom and democracy and Blackness and liberation and communism and socialism and capitalism. Planes crashed, automobiles collided, casualties soared, especially on holidays. Some men just lay in bed and died, mundanely, and without imagination. Through it all the girls prepared for the Grand Cotillion. It was indeed a tribute to their singlefulness-of-purpose" (113).

Along the same lines, Killens remarks later in the book, "Blacks laid down their lives for freedom as riots raced throughout the country, especially in the urban centers. Yet with great religious fervor, debutantes in Crowning Heights went ever forward to their goal of the Grand Cotillion. A tribute to the Femmes Fatales!" (171). Killens's critique here is aimed at community projects, which do not lead black people or other minorities toward liberation. Referring earlier to the majority of the debutantes as "the children of Frazier's Black Bourgeoisie and Hare's Black Anglo-Saxons" (67), Killens indicts the middle-class blacks whom E. Franklin Frazier and Nathan Hare criticize in the well-known works named above. As Killens sees it, not only does the black middle class shun and abandon the black urban and working poor but, worse, they condescendingly reach out to select poor youth only to impose on them self-defeating traditions and practices.

Killens satirizes off-kilter references to constitutional protections in *The Cotillion* to make a point about the imbalance of power that governs encounters between middle- and working-class blacks. These references have an open-ended quality to them as they touch on broad concerns for which there are no easy solutions and reverberate beyond the text. For instance, at the end of the novel, when the debs plot to make the Grand Cotillion black and beautiful is revealed, Ann Brasswork shouts "Search their purses! Tear their dresses off! Investigate their funky drawers! Don't let them plead the First Amendment!" (224). Then, furious about the situation, she screams "Fifth Amendment!" At this point in the novel, tensions between the Femmes Fatales and their Harlem recruits are at their highest level of absurdity.

Using this hilarious moment, Killens underscores the Femmes Fatales' ulterior motives in bringing Harlem girls into the fold. They violate not only the "free speech rights" the girls have to express themselves and to challenge agendas with which they disagree but also they deny them the opportunity to articulate the consciousness behind their actions (the "due process" that Brasswork's invoking of the Fifth Amendment implies). Instead, they are deemed "little Black Harlem hoodlums" who are incorrigible and, thus, cannot be civilized by elite black women. Ultimately, Killens elevates the critique even further on the final page of the novel. Killens writes that "you can take democracy and freedom and integration and due process and all them damn amendments too damn far. Particularly when it comes to colored people" (239). For Killens, even when blacks develop their own social organizations and pivot toward in-group concerns, they are still plagued by the dubious threat of either misapplying mainstream customs or appropriating traditions that were designed to undermine the ability of blacks to thrive in America. Killens is concerned that a false sense of class nobility could take root in black communities—one that curtails self-esteem and cultural pride and subjects individuals to an insidious notion of status and mobility.

James Smethurst's essay "The Black Arts Movement" accounts for the cultural, social, and political legacy of the black arts era, which Killens's novel champions. Smethurst suggests that the era changed the creation and reception of artistic endeavors and that it produced conflicting tenets which, for better or worse, took culture seriously. Commenting on the debates among artists and activists, Smethurst remarks, "One thing that bound Black Arts and Black Power together was that their ideas and even organization work moved through shared institutional spaces" (304). For instance, "activists who were also artists would travel to various cities to participate in some political event or activity and would also find the time to do some cultural work (e.g., a poetry reading, the staging of a play, and so on)." Doing culture work (making cultural production accessible or taking a critical position on cultural experience) within urban spaces reclaims those sites for oneself and others. Particularly, they are made available to those languishing in the monotony of social climbing. With this observation, Smethurst hones in on the energy behind a key move in 1970s African American literature, wherein black writers began *working* culture in advantageous ways for black communities. Literary culture workers have functioned to support, criticize, and educate emerging intellectuals and the general populace by creating an aesthetic infrastructure that demystified intraracial difference.

The African American culture-work narrative delineates the cultural fluidity one needs to equip in a postmodern context. As *The Cotillion* demonstrates, this type of narrative situates numerous cultural practices, questions allegiances to those practices, and decries partisanship. Inasmuch as *The Cotillion* riffs satirically on a longstanding southern tradition (cotillions), Killens also ironizes various rituals practiced among different classed groups. In sum, he creates an environment in which inflexible traditions[2] jar with more flexible and open practices.

James Emanuel's 1971 essay "Blackness Can: A Quest for Aesthetics" discusses the burden that authors have, due to a lack of diversity within publishing houses, in helping black America discover and preserve the range of its stories. Emanuel outlines the cause for which authors themselves have become culture workers and have reproduced this role in their fiction. Writers like Ishmael Reed, Gayl Jones, and Sam Greenlee present the culture-work narrative in multiple ways. Whether using themes that push against Western monocultural impulses, circulate an Afrocentric ethos, or cultivate political consciousness among the working class, these authors speak to the necessity of socializing others to different cultural realities. This includes working to bridge class and political divides that remain after the collision of civil rights and nationalist populism. African American literary culture, having benefited from reform movements on the ground and gained a foothold in academia through student fervor, cannot afford to flatten out different viewpoints among everyday black Americans. That said, the culture-work narrative relishes the circulation of multiple traditions, but its goal is neither a consensus of ideas nor an agree-to-disagree compromise. Instead, it rejects such false dichotomizing of human experience for vibrant cultural expression.

Ideas about culture make their way into African American literature because they abound in debates about education. Sociologist Amy Binder in "Friend and Foe: Boundary Work and Collective Identity" looks at divisions created among black activists that "go cultural" in the 1990s in order "to press for changes in their own and the majority population's acknowledgment of their contributions to world and national history" (222). Binder examines the different ways in which Afrocentrism and multiculturalism, as discrete racial projects, comprehend the academic terrain and work to change traditional approaches to education. Yet separation seeps in as each program views the other as suspect. To this point, Binder references Manning Marable's and Leith Mullings's essay "The Divided Mind of Black America: Race, Ideology and Politics in the Post–Civil Rights Era." The authors typologize racial-identity projects that have their roots in 1960s and 1970s social issues. In discussing the separatist and inclusive perspectives espoused by black nationalism and post–civil rights liberalism, respectively, they observe that black intellectuals chose to work within the sphere of their separate ideologies and institutions.

The valuing of discrete experience over common culture is a current that runs through black cultural studies. Writing about the post–civil rights era, Marable's *Beyond Black and White* remarks that we "cannot really speak about a 'common racial experience' which parallels the universal opposition blacks felt when confronted by legal racial segregation. Moreover, contemporary black experience can no longer be defined by a single set of socioeconomic, political and/or cultural characteristics" (128). Marable's comments go to the heart of rifts around class and culture within black communities. They speak to a reality that was taken up at the height of black nationalism and has been scrutinized in African American Studies departments since the 1970s. Amy Ongiri's *Spectacular Blackness: The Cultural Politics of the Black Power Movement* points out that the "Black Arts movement began its negotiations around class, inclusion, and cultural production precisely when changes created by the Civil Rights movement and the end of legalized segregation fostered opportunities for economic advancement and inclusion" (103). Literary projects during the era included correctives for culturally disinvested blacks who favored identifying with black American reality over ideas about African heritage. Those kinds of negotiations played a major role in pushing against the generalization of black identity.

Among features of black experiences in the 1960s, socioeconomic change signaled class conflict. Class tends to be a thorny issue because it encompasses one's assumptions about and tendency toward certain sets of behaviors. Determining that an investigation of class relations would yield an understanding of black socialization, *The Cotillion* portrays what Linda Hutcheon describes as "differences that go beyond class; differences that challenge from within the possibility of mastery, objectivity, impersonality . . . (69). In defining difference, Killens's novel provides evidence for Hutcheon's idea that the complexities of class are invariably engulfed in crisis and rife with meaning. This becomes a particularly vexed situation in postmodern culture when class issues are aggravated by socioeconomic shifts and a sense of decenteredness.

Killens's Polemical Writing

Shaped by the cultural consciousness of black civil rights and nationalism, Killens's political activism was part and parcel of his polemical writing. In *The Indignant Generation*, Lawrence Jackson discusses Killens's sociopolitical grooming and looks at his artistic ties. Because Killens wanted to compose a politically engaged black subjectivity, he found multiple aesthetic conventions through which to analyze the black experience. He created a composite out of satire and a fluid narrative voice, which was built on community-based black lexicons, commentary on the cultivation of a black psyche, and reflection on televisual African American identity politics.[3] Alan Wald's *Trinity of Passion: The Literary Left* looks at how Killens organized numerous conferences during the 1960s for the purpose of compelling young writers to "join a crusade to decolonize the minds of black people" (62). Joyce Ann Joyce recalls a 1966 writer's conference during which he articulated artistic issues fundamental to today's understandings of the African American literary canon. Moreover, the *Journal of Blacks in*

Higher Education dedicated its 2004 issue to Killens for influencing upcoming generations to use writing to promote black sociopolitical agendas. Killens initiated his artistic foray when his first novel, *Youngblood*, grabbed the attention of readers and critics alike for its emphasis on unionism among black and white workers in the South. From there, his novel *And Then We Heard Thunder* examined racism abroad and situated black racial reality within a global context. While each of these works confronted race relations, neither featured the kind of racialized, in-group cultural tension that is germane to *The Cotillion*, which focuses critically on class: exclusionary practices among the black elite, Afrocentric influence among black intellectuals, and vernacular tradition within the black working class. The novel is also replete with a cultural nationalist sensibility. Killens takes a perspective on the era of black nationalism that not only reads the divisions between activists, artists, and elites into the ideology but also looks at the overprotectiveness around tradition in each arena. Capturing this reality, *The Cotillion* does not privilege or reinstall one tradition over another but arrives at an urban context in which multiple viewpoints clash and flourish.

As black nationalism emanated from leaders and intellectuals, incarnations like the black arts movement and black power developed and called for cultural self-determination. Much has been written about the ripple effect of this seminal moment in black culture. Ongiri makes the case that "the very contradictions inherent in Black radical notions . . . critically formed the ways in which we continue to understand Black identity, Black community, and Black cultural production" (27). In this sense, contradictory social notions undergird Killens's narrative because he believed that the recognition of a common heritage and of socially specific experience could reinvigorate the cultural consciousness of working-class blacks in particular.

Remarking on a topical vision for his novel, Killens explains, "Well, first of all, the history of *The Cotillion* was something that had been going around in my head for some time, how to satirize what I deem to be the folly of black middle-class imitators of the white people who oppress them" (Lehman 86). Killens argues that affirming one's own sense of racial identity (developing a black psyche) challenges cultural inferiority. In effect, those who would embrace cultural nationalism must reject essentialist notions of black respectability, avoiding as they do the pitfalls of mistaking white imitation for enlightenment. As Killens saw it, certain middle-class blacks demonstrated an unawareness of their own agency: "I think they think that they are for the uplifting of the race with these cotillions. That's because their values are completely white. What is white is right. What is black is negative. Some of them, I think, when they read [*The Cotillion*] were deeply hurt. But I think it made some of them think" (86). Published in 1971 and set in Harlem and Brooklyn, *The Cotillion* purposely critiques the narrow assumptions about black life that abound even in the midst of a wealth of black experiences. Awareness of the various identities that surround, engulf, and make up blackness represents not only a prime concern for Killens but also the most important step toward acknowledging nonessentialist ways of being.

Some of the most useful studies of Killens's interrogation of intraracial class tension, I think, focus on satire and nationalism. Darryl Dickson-Carr, emphasizing the text's satirical design, for example, argues that "Killens's explicit project of trying to find a common ground on which the different *intraracial* classes can meet is remarkably rare, if not unique" (143). Dickson-Carr suggests that Killens satirizes "tensions that should be familiar to those readers who have witnessed the absurdities of class conflict" (144). Observing the nationalist self-display in *The Cotillion*, Rolland Murray remarks that it "[r]egister[s] the exalted status of language in nationalist ideology at the same time that it undoes the instrumental deployment of that speech . . ." (156). Ultimately, Killens's satire functions to insert a politics of difference into the class equation and to pave the way for varied social relations across family, cultural ties, and social organizations.

Much current reassessment of the legacy of nationalism centers on its installation of a masculine, patriarchal foundation. In some ways, Cornel West takes up this issue in the "The New Cultural Politics of Difference," where he critiques the legacy of black nationalism as negating difference for a repressive acknowledgment of shared heritage. Nonetheless, West seems to define the contemporary culture worker as one who carries on the legacy of nationalism's dissenting struggle. Killens is such a writer who interrogates the "profoundly hybrid character" of blackness, race, and nationality (7). Embedded in *The Cotillion* are instances of the postmodern articulations that undergird West's prospective vision for a redefining of cultural ideology in the American social fabric. In terms of redefinition, the value of the culture-work narrative rests in its suspicion of prescribed allegiances and suppositions.

Class-Driven Politics: Resistance and Respectability

Early in the novel, class-driven resistance appears in the form of cultural nationalist and bohemian ideologies. This resistance acts as a group constraint for Yoruba because it stylizes black identity to a degree that it creates pressure for her to own a contrived identity. In Harlem, Yoruba encounters throngs of countercultural groups and hears the melodies of jukeboxes blasting the jazz classics of artists wailing freedom sounds. Two entities in particular speak to the strategies deployed by various groups to resist social conformity: Café Uptown Society and Way-Out Restaurant. Café Uptown Society is a place where Yoruba is mesmerized by the rhythms and cadences of spoken-word poetry, tinged with nationalist rhetoric and bawdy humor. While this space gives voice to racial uplift, pan-African solidarity, and notions of authentic blackness, the hyperbolic performativity renders its overarching messages too theatrical for Yoruba to adopt as guiding principles on her way to a sense of identification. For example, the satirically named Kool Krazy Kats featured at Café Uptown Society not only speak an inscrutable language but presumably engage in violent action: The "KKK got themselves together and rapped and blew each other's minds, and some say they blew other things and sundry" (55). In terms of resistance to a white supremacist mainstream, Café Uptown Society acts as an outlet for working-class blacks with cultural nationalist sensibilities—for those who gravitate towards a competing narrative that reclaims the beauty and complexity of blackness and utilizes those elements as a means to engender solidarity. This is done not only in light of racial hostility but also amid the pull of the mainstream pursuits.

Way-Out Restaurant is full of sights and sounds, a mix of cabaret and coffeehouse emerging out of the sexual revolution: "Psychedelic happenings adorned the walls. Cats came there some special nights to do their things and plunk guitars and howl sad songs of happy times and great-gittin-up-mornings" (81). Interestingly, the restaurant is a common meeting space for "proper bourgeois rebels" who philosophize about revolution and cultivate a sensibility rooted in both nationalism and black middle-class culture. Way-Out Restaurant's resistance strategy is built around trafficking in a bohemian ideology that is decidedly idiosyncratic and nonconformist. Yoruba witnesses handshakes described as a "combination of hand-grip, Indian-wrestle, chest-pounding, hand-grip, again, finger snapping." That the greetings vary by neighborhoods, cities, and states, makes their appropriation nearly impossible. From lengthy greetings to uninhibited hair growth, the idea seems to be to resist the prevailing assumptions about social climbing by creating not only distance from it but also by nurturing an intellectual critique of the capitalist system, which makes bourgeois life something desirable. Unfortunately, the distance from social climbing has negative implications for Yoruba, who has both intellectual and material ambitions. Yoruba is provided a critique of bourgeois culture in this space but is not offered a snapshot of what it might look like for a black individual to pursue socioeconomic mobility and maintain folk consciousness—to remain identified with and engaged with lower- and working-class blacks. *The Cotillion* avoids linking the two sites mentioned and renders the experiences of cultural nationalism and bohemian ideology distinct. Further, Killens does not portray cultural nationalist and bohemian experiences as always already philosophically congruent, though the adversary on the receiving end of their ire (conformist society) is the same. This becomes a textual strategy for the later entwining of these paradigms.

Amid robust, class-driven resistance to conformity, Yoruba continues to seek a stable self-identity. Observing the plurality of culture surrounding her as she travels to and from her summer job downtown, particularly aboard the "A" Train, Yoruba feels nearly assaulted by "Black and white humanity of all sizes and denominations. An air swindled concoction of sound and sweat and soap and perfume and beaucoup talk, Afro-Americanese, West Indianese, Italianese, Jewishese . . ." (2). On the other hand, she is fond of the black-power mothers, black picketeers, and self-appointed nationalist figures in Harlem. Feeling relieved after reaching her block, "All of the memories that came back to her now from that faraway [childhood] age were good times to her" (13). In this instance, a moment of nostalgia stings Yoruba, but a longing for the past does not ensnare her. Yoruba lives very much in the moment: "she could not turn back the clock. She never really wanted to" (17). At eighteen, Yoruba has come of age in a class-diverse environment where she sees herself as flanked by an array of identities but having few suitable options from which to choose.

Another reason Yoruba struggles to assert what she sees as her "real" self is the friction between her own budding self-concept and her mother's perception of her as an upper-class, posh-black-woman-in-training. "Deconstructing the 'real me'" for Angela McRobbie in *Postmodernism and Popular Culture* "has involved showing [this process] to be a social and political requirement, a form of enforcement, a means of regulating legitimate ways of being . . ." (70). The process to which McRobbie refers requires that Yoruba assert her individuality: "How do you tell your mother you don't want to be a lady? That you would rather be a good Black woman. . . . Sometimes she felt like shouting: 'Will the real Yoruba Evelyn step forward please. And assert yourself?'" (46). Unfortunately, throughout much of the novel, Yoruba sees herself as powerless to shape her own destiny.

Daphne Lovejoy's assumptions about being cultured are very much wedded to the social-climbing ideas of Brooklyn high society and not Harlem, where she resides. She has literally attempted to mold Yoruba from childhood to one day debut in society, having the culture of the first black families of Brooklyn bestowed upon her. Because of this, Daphne commits, to an extreme, to keeping Yoruba away those she deems culturally deprived and lower class in the neighborhood. Scolding her husband, Matt Lovejoy, for not buying into her narrative, she says, "I try to teach my daughter to stay away from these wort'less pickaninnies on the block. But the more I try to culturize her, the more you pull the other way" (14). Daphne's worst nightmare would involve Yoruba adopting the mores of the poor and working class. Even though the Lovejoys reside in the same neighborhood as the so-called "low class," Daphne elevates her family, at least in her mind, by diminishing those around her in ways that betray self-hate and colorism. If the goal is to prevent Yoruba from becoming "as common as all the other no-good darkies in this ratty neighborhood," then Daphne's plan of action is about ingraining this idea into her family.

In her own way, Yoruba counters the identities either directly or indirectly imposed on her embracing disparate constructions of blackness. Yoruba talks boldly of her decision to attend Howard University, a historically black university. Regarding an institution that nourishes dynamic black experiences and touts a legacy of recruiting prominent black intellectuals, Yoruba envisions Howard as a place that will enable her to live an authentically black life. Moreover, Yoruba is content to educate herself into the black middle class. When her mother suggests historically white colleges like Sarah Lawrence and Radcliffe, Yoruba counters by offering City College as an option, which would put her with black working-class students. At the same time, in her personal life she embraces Lumumba, whom her mother had long deemed too lower class for her, as a love interest. Ultimately, though, Yoruba gives in to the emotion Daphne displays to coax her onto the path toward upper-class privilege. Yoruba not only agrees to submit to the bourgeois tutelage of the Femmes Fatales, whose goal is to civilize one culturally deprived Harlem girl and usher her into high society, but also she appeases her mother by promising to debut in the year's Grand Cotillion. Because Yoruba does not embrace the concept of black respectability as attained through the emulation of whiteness, she must rely on her working-class consciousness as a safeguard against Daphne's highfalutin and contrived expectations.

The group constraints Lumumba (formerly Ernest Walter Billings, Yoruba's childhood playmate) faces take the shape of the triviality behind black cultural politics. As Lumumba puts it, "The Black folks of the world are lost. . . . It's okay to wear boubous and dashikis and change your name and all that jive. And Afros. Dig it. I got a closet full of African identity, like authentic from the source and jive. But most of the Black hip people up to now have been only *acting* Black" (91). This group narrative implies that such trends are a defensive effort, a matter of resisting the reality that blacks were barred from enjoying and reaping the benefits and excesses of capitalism. If it means commodifying a movement, then, the stakes on the ground, according to some, dictate this strategy. Nonetheless, these efforts have the effect of impeding the cultural mission Killens gives Lumumba, which is to galvanize the black masses and to facilitate the cultural cross-pollination of discrete black communities. Because Lumumba is invested in creating social tipping points, the state of black American consciousness is crucial to him. As he puts it, "Everything depends on the Black brothers and sisters in the Movement right here in the USA. . . . We're the hippest, purest, beautifullest [sic], most dedicated, most disunited, most together, most opportunistic, most naïve, most corrupt, most humanistic on this planet." While the group narrative of trivializing and commodifying blackness does not douse Lumumba's personal political fire, it places limits on his social reach and reins in the global influence of black America—which served, particularly in the 1960s, as a bellwether for the larger black liberation struggle.

Because the inclination toward "acting" black is what hinders Lumumba, he wants to compel Harlemites (and Brooklynites) to become "Black doers." By this, Lumumba implies that blacks should reject posturing and, instead, adopt a meaningful sociopolitical stance based on realizing their cultural agency. This involves communicating with and moving each other to action through black nationalist principles such as self-help and black empowerment. What stand in the way are disillusionment with movements, disunity, and an embrace of white social norms. In myriad spaces, *The Cotillion* paves the way for Lumumba to stir up people to act as doers through the boundary-crossing, class-bridging tactics he utilizes. To understand Lumumba's complex and contradictory ideological and cultural repertoire, I ask basic questions: What approach to class and tradition does he espouse? How does he differ from other characters? How, then, do other characters respond to his instincts? Commenting on the function of postmodernist art, Gerald Graff, in "The Myth of the Postmodernist Breakthrough," suggests that the dissolution of ego-boundaries dismantles identity and acts as a prelude to consciousness expansion (227). As Graff explains, the Western ego represents a rational mode of consciousness opposed to conceptions of difference. Lumumba perceives difference the opposite way. He has an instinctive ethos when it comes to class and culture, which enables him to improvise when faced with ego-boundaries; therefore, the surplus of class distinctions in Harlem does not sway him.

Still, Lumumba has to find a way to corral a wayward flock that has opted for a middle ground between nationalist tenets and bourgeois vanity. While this middle ground is opportunistic, it is also littered with housing, employment, and legal skirmishes with whites like the case brought against Matthew Lovejoy when Yoruba was a child. Matt's slumlord, Mr. Shyler, attempted to have him evicted for nonpayment of rent. Ultimately, the judge ruled in Matt's favor because the landlord had neglected repairing seventeen violations. For two years, however, Mr. Shyler had also collected "fifteen dollars per month rent above the legal amount" (88). While

Matt received some justice (he would have had to sue to recover the over-charges), it is easy to imagine that numerous others blacks, at one time or another, ended up on the receiving end of ample injustice. The weight of this reality is what fuels the group narrative keeping Lumumba at bay.

One of the clearest examples of how the commodification of black-ness snowballs comes through an observation made by Yoruba: "there were other hustlers . . . who had skimmed through a few books and memorized a few catch phrases, bought a few dashikis, put their do-rags in hiding for a season, washed the process out of their hair, changed their names, got themselves a niche or corner and gone into the business of Black Na-tionalism" (61). Among other things, the business of nationalism involves hawking black accessories like dashikis, adopting African monikers, and donning Afros, and so on, but the novel suggests that, as a proposition, this enterprise has a corrosive effect. Lumumba employs a metaphor about prostitution to suggest that Harlem blacks have sold themselves out in an illicit deal with white society. Not only does a white police officer transact business with a black sex worker, he also "saunter[s] down the avenue and get[s] his Sunday payoff from the junkman and the policy director" (62). Another metaphor that Lumumba offers concerns a man who sleeps in his yellow El Dorado instead of purchasing a home and joining "the white man and the Black petit bourgeoisie." Lumumba surmises that "our El Dorado man can put distance between him and Charlie in his all-purpose mobile housing unit, but you can't make no getaway with one of them brownstone houses on your back." The message is that blacks are better off mobilizing their political power than anchoring themselves to trivial "monuments to all them bourgeois insecurities."

Primed to act as a purveyor of culture, Lumumba possesses the skill set of adapting to traditions[4] while infusing them with his own assump-tions and values. A poet and artist, he proves to have a cosmopolitan dis-position. Lumumba speaks of Africa, Asia, Europe, and South America, describing himself as a world traveler on a journey to galvanize the black diaspora. When clubs close ranks along the lines of difference, as do the class-stratified Femmes Fatales, Lumumba's first goal is to disrupt their politics. He eventually achieves this by socializing in different spaces (ban-quets, parties, and cotillions), and then using those spaces as a palimpsest upon which to write his own idiosyncrasies. Ultimately, Lumumba shatters class barriers and brings culture to bear on the Grand Cotillion.

The Cotillion tasks Yoruba and Lumumba with navigating the mainstream exploitation embodied in the Femme Fatales. While this is not a white institution, it exists in a white-identified framework, in the sense that it maintains ties to exclusive entities, appropriates white traditions like the cotillion, and sees part of its mission as reforming and refining blacks outside its cultural loop. To maneuver through this heavily classed terrain, one has to assimilate multiple subjectivities while appearing innocuous enough to inhabit such a space. What Killens portrays is the kind of social flexibility warranted by the societal dynamic African Americans found themselves in during the early 1970s, which not only came about as a result of the entrance of numerous blacks into the middle class but also the surge of black pride among the working class. Lastly, in navigating the world of the Femmes Fatales, Yoruba and Lumumba seem to betting on the idea that the element of social difference can be so potent that class bias cannot quell it.

From the outset, the Femmes Fatales' debutante process objectifies Yoruba and exposes her to the pretentiousness of black upper-class life, but the soiree hosted by Zenith Jefferson poses a different challenge. Initially, Yoruba is viewed with suspicion because her burgeoning friendship with Pam Jefferson, a prominent daughter of Brooklyn's Crowning Heights, earns her the derision of the other debutantes. Beyond that, the Jeffersons adorn their home without pretense, display "original paintings on the wall of Black happenings by Black artists. Okay? There was even one of Malcolm" (109). In addition, the Jeffersons also enjoy speaking "Afro-Americanese." The spectacle of it challenges Yoruba not only because of her ambivalence toward middle-class culture and the cotillion crowd but also because the Jefferson soiree compels that she adapt to a peculiar environment, one which seems to teeter between high-society posturing and a love of black iconography. Still, this situation does not convince her to buy into bourgeois culture en masse. And while the debutante process is aimed at driving Yoruba into "singlefulness of purpose" (113), her identity cannot be pegged into any one slot. Further, one of her cultural buffers is her partiality to nationalist sentiments, which, prior to beginning the deb process, appealed to her: "all her inhibitions, even those Lady Daphne instilled, gone with the selfhood-ship of words . . ." (91). Lastly, to help her overcome the pressure of her mother's bourgeois ideals, Lumumba makes the case that the Femmes Fatales, with their fixation on pedigree, acted as unaware agents of black cultural oppression.

Yoruba's next foray into the mainstream of white-inflected mores occurs after she is invited to dinner by Brenda Brasswork, a debutante who both adores and abhors hers. Brenda and her mother tended to be overbearing all evening and obsessive about such mundane matters as dieting and legal jargon. The text adds some perspective: "Blacks laid down their lives for freedom at race riots throughout the country, especially in the urban centers. Yet with great religious fervor, debutantes in Crowning Heights went ever forward to their goal of the great and Grand Cotillion. A tribute to the Femmes Fatales!" (171). In addition, the very plastic that adorns the furniture in the Brassworks' home conveys the message that Yoruba will have to navigate the artificialities that surround her and not allow herself to be duped by them. A tendency of Brenda's is her tasteless linking of Yoruba's features to Africa. Ironically, this is the one barb that leads Yoruba to a moment of triumph in this setting where the predominant customs diverge from hers. While rhapsodically fondling Yoruba's hair, the "dear sweet-tempered Yoruba slapped the raving girl [Brenda] clear across the plastic dining room, and split the scene post haste with all deliberate speed" (170). In this moment, Yoruba violently rebuffs an arrangement that wants to turn her into a puppet of sorts, on display for the pleasure and voyeuristic gaze of black elites.

Committed to undermining the mainstream instincts at play, Lumumba clips his locks, dons a tux, and joins Yoruba in her upper-class excursions with affluent debutantes. Lumumba rebuffs the notion that black bourgeois values will rub off on him: "If I'm that insecure, my Black Consciousness must be pretty thin and superficial" (180). Preempting co-optation, Lumumba observes and informs his assumptions about the black upper class. Ironically, one reason he participates in these bourgeois activities is to "dig the source" and gain material for a novel he wants to write. At one party, Lumumba sees white girls wearing Afros and pretending to be members of the "near-white Black bourgeois." At another party, a group of

African students and Ivy League black men debate Negritude and sartorial choices. Lumumba, "an obvious hybrid of the two contingents" (176), plays both sides when one African student deems him Nigerian and a black American questions why he does not wear an Afro.

It is not until working the Long Island cotillion (a prequel to the Grand Cotillion) that Lumumba begins working to undermine the influence of the bourgeoisie, black and white. There in a serving capacity along with Yoruba and Daphne, Lumumba notices that, after the pomp and circumstance of the cotillion dance, the evening takes an unsophisticated turn: "Lumumba never failed to call Miss Daphne's attention to the same. . . . 'Look!' Over to the right of the bandstand, a couple of exuberant youngsters of the gentler sex were stripping down to the very nitty gritty of the bare essentials" (195). Not invulnerable to the callous privilege of white elites himself, Lumumba is asked by one girl if he is anyone of a few prominent black figures. He also gets called a bad militant by someone else and has to listen to the insincere sympathies others claim to have for black organizations like the Urban League. While Lumumba engages in his own antics, the tide of unruliness turns to Daphne: "a misty veil was slowly lifting from her eyes, even as she struggled valiantly to remain behind the veil of her darling innocence" (198). But perhaps his greatest act of subversion is in stirring the pot a bit among the white elite by periodically playing the role of the humble servant on the wait staff and then becoming the trickster who "Mess[es] up their little old white minds."

Lastly, Lumumba plans to offer a counter-narrative at the Grand Cotillion via an ad-libbed demonstration. Unbeknownst to the Femmes Fatales, Yoruba and some of the other debutantes plan to wear their hair natural without product. Lumumba decides to put on African garb and make a final appeal to the black masses. Panicking over their plot, Yoruba thinks about ditching the cotillion before she debuts. Lumumba sympathizes with her but also equivocates: "But look at it this way. We won't be messing it up. We'll be beautifying it. We'll be making it Black and beautiful and significant instead of white and pretty and meaningless" (232). As the final blow to the postulates of the Femmes Fatales' tradition, this act of defiance will signal a new cultural paradigm intended to expose the mainstream pretense of sophistication.

Black Nationalist Discourse

In *The Cotillion*, Killens portrays the black nationalism of the late 1960s as it engulfs Harlem. Galvanizing poetry and militant rhetoric flourish, igniting a sense of shared black consciousness in the area. However, even as the radical language of black empowerment and self-love spurs and sustains social movements, the performativity around it seems less substantive. For example, the public rantings of Billy "Bad Mouth" Williams, a self-styled nationalist leader introduced early on, draw laughter from crowds. The text says, "Yoruba thought, It's preachers today. Yesterday it was 'Negro' leaders. The day before that it was the 'white Communist liberals.' Tomorrow he would be doing a putdown on something else. The labor movement. The NAACP. The President. It was always something, or somebody" (12). Though Bad Mouth fails at articulating specific strategies for economically disenfranchised blacks, the satirical tone and folk tenor of his speech (call and response, the dozens) is magnetic. And his bombast nourishes a respect for the nationalist critiques of racism, hedonism, and consumerism.

In the novel, the era of nationalism represents a moment of calling things into question, particularly class divisions, though Killens has many targets. Nowhere in the novel is Killens's portrayal of class division more precise than in the groups with whom Matt and Daphne associate. Matt, a rural man from Georgia, comes to Harlem in 1928 and, believing himself business savvy, pursues entrepreneurial success, which never pans out. He marries Daphne Braithwaite, a self-identified aristocratic beauty from Barbados, who cherishes her Scottish heritage and, soon after migrating to New York, decides against domestic work. The stock-market crash of 1929 and the Great Depression see to it that Matt's businesses neither take root nor grow into a fortune. As a result, Matt clinches his blackness as a source of great pride and joins the nationalist and working-class movements of Harlem. He runs the gamut of global black solidarity, "march[ing] behind every Black man who ever raised his voice in Harlem, including Garvey, Powell, Ben Davis, Paul Robeson, and very very naturally Brother Malcolm" (31). Afterwards, Matt identifies entirely with the working class and settles into his job as a Penn Station redcap.

Interestingly, Matt refers to some of the most prominent voices that informed black nationalism prior to and during the 1960s. So it is no coincidence that Matt's armchair observations, which begin in his favorite chair at Jenkins Palace Barbershop, stem from nationalist perspectives. While the barbershop is a place of signifying, its insulated environment makes it the perfect site for humor and critique. One conversation about the state of black America transpires between an old man described as shabbily dressed and impoverished and a young man sporting processed hair and a pastel do-rag, which suggest middle-class status. The old man contends that blacks have never known as much progress as they have made in the context of nationalism. A fan of nonviolence, the young man takes exception to that view and, quoting Shakespeare, insists, "The only way the solution can be solved is through the weapon of love. We have to teach the white man to love us by the example of our undying love for him. Shakespeare said it. 'Love is not love that alters when it alteration finds'" (26). Matt's sense of the young man's overwrought seriousness before he even speaks provides a modest critique that is in tune with the nationalist zeitgeist sprawling across Harlem: "Matt thought, 'He's lost his colored sense of humor. That's the danger of the white man's bourgeois education'" (25).

The nationalist tone of Matt's jab at bourgeois education becomes even more pronounced later when Daphne criticizes him for offering an explanation of the not-too-distant folk origins of the cotillion. Matt describes the cotillion as a trend rooted in cattle-farming practices, which evolved into a white social custom designed to pair young women up with eligible men of status. Embedded in his words is a plain-spun evaluation of Anglocentric symbols and customs, which he believes have no intrinsic benefit for black people but function to stoke class division. This framework allows Matt to critique middle-class education by deeming his black vernacular and working-class intelligence superior to the knowledge doled out at prestigious white institutions. According to Matt, "I graduated at the top of the class from the University of Hard Knocks and Disappointments. I got my degree in Mother Wit. I took my classes where I found them on the streets of Harlem U. I trickulated at the University of Pennsylvania Station. That oughta qualify me as a expert on white folks and colored peoples. I know the white man cause I done handled all his baggage. I'm a expert on the Negro on accounta I been one all my born days. I know what the white man putting down, cause I been picking it up for almost thirty years, and long before!" (126).

Killens's critique of Anglocentric education in *The Cotillion* is similar to Whitehead's assessment of the Institute for Vertical Transport and Walker's appraisal of Saxon College. The bigotry to which protagonists are subject in academic spaces has the effect of narrowing their perceptions and inducing them to identify as racial pawns in a game being played by social and political interest groups. Matt's invocation of black intelligence grounded in material reality speaks to the crux of black nationalist ideology, which has to do with an embrace of distinctly black definitions and considerations as a road map to cultural self-determination. The phrase "the Great Debate," which is mentioned at several different points in the novel, arguably points back to the overarching debate over the viability of black-identity-based ideologies and over the detriment done to black people by white mainstream notions.

The white bourgeois values that Matt undermines are a major target because they not only capture the ethos of black nationalism that pervades the text and touches each main character, but also they serve as a point of departure for other critiques. One of the extended critiques in the novel revolves around the cotillion and has its strongest valence not in the suggestion of the practice as black folly but in the indictment of it as a symbolic impediment to cultural unity—the kind Matt once marched in support of and for which Lumumba advocates. For example, Matt offers an incisive socioeconomic critique of the cotillion when he says, "But colored folks just do these things cause they see white folks doing them. It ain't no investment like it is with white folks. All the money ends up in Whitey's hands again. To the dance teacher, to the beauty peoples, to Mr. Waldorf. It's just some more white folks' foolishness that don't git Black folks nowheres except in debt" (126–27). In making the connection between adopted bourgeois values and black economic standing, Killens raises the stakes on what it means to pursue prestige or status over more substantive forms of social uplift.

Another issue that surfaces within the orbit of Black Nationalist ideology is the matter of black solidarity, which Lumumba's cotillion critique taps into incisively. According to Lumumba, "The Black Movement is going all out to rally our people to a sense of peoplehood. . . . The Cotillion says: 'You don't need no power. You don't need no people-hood. You don't need to be no nation. You going to be integrated'" (140). Lumumba's message of solidarity is potent throughout the novel because it is premised on realizing empowerment for the bourgeois and the working class and every stratum in between. Lumumba, whose name is a nod to the legacy of Patrice Lumumba, the first democratically elected leader of the Democratic Republic of the Congo, is someone whose name signifies on black independence. When he speaks of a black nation, he has in mind the masses of black people who are both victims and perpetrators in their failure to develop a black agenda free of white influence.

Lastly, black nationalist sentiment rises in matters of black socialization. In the community realm, socialization is a critical matter, which leads some institutions to become suspect because they are viewed as either contaminating the black psyche or diluting black interests. Early on, the novel highlights protests against organizations like the Black and Beautiful Burlesque (BBB), a strip club featuring black dancers. One nationalist group demonstrates against "Black nudity" and another against permitting "white voyeurs" in the club. Similarly, near the end of the novel, the Femmes Fatales are concerned about race-rioters known to be vigilant in their efforts to scrub black communities clean of cultural degradation. Having chosen "Slavery in reverse—Crow Jim!" as their theme, the Femmes Fatales hire plainclothes policemen to safeguard against militants who, rumor suggests, could riot at the Grand Cotillion.

Religious tradition also figures into the issue of black socialization. For instance, The Cotillion portrays the Brooklyn Memorial Episcopal Cathedral as disconnected from black life. Because Daphne designates it the family church, it denies Yoruba a religious option amenable to her cultural identity. The cathedral, once an all-white church in the exclusive Crowning Heights district, undergoes a drastic change in becoming an all-black congregation. The parishioner Father Madison Mayfair succeeds Father Thatcher, who, in the wake of the full-scale retreat of white congregants, only then invited black parishioners to join. Thatcher's desperate gesture does not placate Yoruba or Matt, who remain suspect about the motives of the church.

When Yoruba and Matt accompany Daphne on Sundays, she sees them as occupying a state of "complacent ignorance" because they adamantly resist her efforts to expose them to middle-class manners. Still, Daphne relishes forcing her family to join her every Sunday, which she believes is for their benefit. Though she favors appropriating black middle-class traditions, Daphne's actions ascribe a disproportionate value to white religious traditions. We soon learn that the church's prior membership left for racial reasons, "as the onward Christian soldiers sought the Blessed Saviour in less dark, more illumined quarters. Preferring not to brighten the corner where they were, as they were called upon to do by the blessed Vicar" (35). Nonetheless, church represents a status symbol for Daphne. She sees a connection between associating with the middle class, absorbing their cultural capital, and attaining prestige for her family.

The cathedral, in contrast to cultural nationalism, offers only a one-dimensional experience and marginalizes black conceptions of spirituality.[5] Nevertheless, Daphne sees Father Mayfair as a self-sacrificing Christ figure because he follows suit with the former pastor in permitting black attendance. In one instance, Daphne scolds Matt, "The dear Vicar is giving up his entire career as a white man, just to give us an integrated experience. He's the only white person left in the entire congregation. You should get down on your Black knees and thank God for progressive men like Father Mayfair" (36). Ironically, Mayfair's silence suggests that, while he takes up the previous vicar's integrationist stance, he makes no turn toward incorporating black spiritual traditions; even more so, the absence of white congregants speaks volumes about the ostensible integration experience. Lastly, divorced from any movement that attaches to the lived reality of black working-class or middle-class life, Mayfair's democratic gesture falls flat. Killens does not present him as an agent of change but as an emissary of white paternalism. Matt himself deems the black congregants complicit: "All them black damn sheep with a white damn shepherd . . . Calling a white man Father in these days and times" (36). Indeed, Mayfair's pastorate implies a non sequitur: it does not follow that the church's feeble efforts at racial reconciliation will grant blacks any social parity with whites.

Lastly, the sway of black nationalism, through the backdrop of militant protests, black power conferences, and nationalist book stores (as well as references to James Brown, H. Rap Brown, and Stokely Carmichael) ignites a conversation about black cultural production and black pride. When it comes to cultural production, the issue takes center stage when Beverly Brap-bap of the Femmes Fatales assumes a nationalist voice when she confronts a well-known but unnamed black movie star about his frequent roles in "shucking and jiving" movies. The movie star himself acknowledges that he would like to produce his own films. In addition, *The Cotillion* makes reference to the debutantes and their escorts who "waltzed with a distinctly different idiom that was definitely un-European" that the liberal integrationist dance instructor would have to "teach." Killens sees black culture as steeped in its own traditions that can serve as greater catalysts for liberation than social-climbing within white institutions and absorbing white aesthetic practices. As a buffer to assimilationist practices, Killens locates the onus of black pride on the shoulders of Lumumba and Yoruba. Prior to their Afro-natural debut at the Grand Cotillion, Lumumba remarks, "these colored cotillions are aimed against our race pride— against our sense of Black identity . . ." (232). Ultimately, Killens celebrates class-bridging tactics that are aimed at achieving the goal of black unity, which was foundational to black nationalist movements.

Gender and Its Ramifications

In *The Cotillion*, working-class black women occupy a mythic and adored status rhetorically, as descendants of African queens. This contrasts with the mainstream proclivity to degrade black women and elevate white womanhood. In different ways, Yoruba and Daphne encounter paternalism, which the narrator underscores early on in a description of Yoruba as "[p]ure, beautiful, untampered-by-the-white-man Yoruba" (1). Yoruba inhabits this role in a milieu that declares, "*Keep the Hunkie's eyes off our Beautiful Black women!*" (7). This nationalist logic, which sees women as defenseless objects in need of protection, embraces a patriarchal notion of masculinity.

In two particular instances, Yoruba and Daphne combat white masculine privilege. Yoruba fends off her gay dance instructor who holds racist assumptions about the sexual vitality of black women. Daphne has to work through the hurt she internalizes as a result of her white father's sexual misconduct. First, the attempt to exploit women for sexual favors figures into Yoruba's experience with her dance instructor, Mr. Phil Potts. His stereotypical assumptions lead him to ascribe to Yoruba a kind of generative sexual vigor, and then to attempt to consume this imagined energy for his own purposes. In one satirical scene, with tears in his eyes, Potts begs Yoruba to save him from sexual ambivalence by having sex with him: "I can be a man! I know I can, and only you can help me find the way. . . . We are both unloved!" Beyond the sexual harassment and potential offender implications, his words suggest that by some bizarre illogic Yoruba's "Black beauty" will propel him into heteronormativity because she too belongs to a marginalized group. Killens's rendering of Potts's homosexuality is a thinly veiled indictment of Western cultural values as aberrant in the face of black ability and determination. Potts has not only witnessed the subordination of his sexuality in mainstream society but also the subordination of his masculinity as a male dance instructor hired by the Femmes Fatales. In addition, he fancies himself an expert on the color question and on latent attraction between blacks and whites. Though this situation is crafted satirically, it indicates that Yoruba and Potts are both othered and relegated to the position of culturally unwashed by the Femmes Fatales, who are invested in shaping and exploiting the usefulness of those they recruit to help advance their unwitting cause.

After Yoruba escapes Potts's clutches, the novel goes silent on him until the Grand Cotillion. Unfortunately, in the same vein that society denies Potts masculine privilege, he attempts to reduce Yoruba to a mere gateway to his own ascendance. The novel paints Potts as a ridiculous character, whose preoccupation with heteronormative masculinity and association of it with sexual prowess are his own undoing. Just as he embraces this problematic conception, he also puts stock in the racist notion of black womanhood as a kind of source of transformative capabilities. Fortunately, Yoruba grows accustomed to wading through wrongheaded notions and comes to redefine black womanhood for herself. She looks for ways of owning her identity that repel exploitation and move her into autonomy.

A kind of emotional victimization becomes apparent in Daphne's unquestioned admiration for her white father and disregard for her black mother. In the fondest memory, Daphne declares, "After Angus Braithwaite was created, my dears, they threw away the mold" (39), yet she believes "her mother didn't understand the limitations of a concubine's prerogatives. In a word, she was a sassy Black woman, gave ol' masser word for word" (38). If Daphne privileges her father's promiscuous legacy of having eleven black concubines and fathering two or three children by each instead of the implied agency behind her mother's decision to leave him, then that might help explain why she despises the indefatigable quality of working-class culture. Daphne has a culturally fragmented psyche. As she later confesses, "My mother and her folks was the humble people. Wherever my white father walked, Black men bowed and scraped, so I despised the Black in me" (202). This window into Daphne's soul links the damage done to her with the overvaluing of whiteness—a common practice within the ranks of the Femmes Fatales. Daphne and the Femmes Fatales illustrate the ways in which this dilemma functions as more than some isolated quirk. Both represent the feelings of racial inferiority within black social institutions that privilege whiteness.

Resisting Consensus

Through his critique of class division in *The Cotillion*, Killens weaves in threads of dissent that undermine group consensus and bolster a postmodern sensibility. This sensibility enables the dissolution of class conflict because it stretches perceptions of cultural experiences to the extent that culture becomes a more flexible construct. This class tension in the novel can be understood through the inextricable cultural connections between working- and middle-class black individuals. Even as these connections become frayed in organizations like the Femmes Fatales, new ones emerge. A postmodern outlook makes this recurring process intelligible. As Lyotard puts it in *The Postmodern Condition: A Report on Knowledge*, "A *self* does not amount to much, but no self is an island; each exists in a fabric of relations that is now more complex and mobile than ever before. Young or old, man or woman, rich or poor, a person is always located at 'nodal points' of specific communication circuits, however tiny these may be. Or better: one is always located at a post through which various kinds of messages pass" (15). Exploring class tensions across black communities, *The Cotillion* shows how individuals (namely the Lovejoy family and Lumumba) connect to an ever-evolving "fabric of relations" and receive numerous social messages. Moreover, Killens suggests that cultural experiences in the novel are linked to many subjectivities and ideas that move against consensus.

Lyotard's postmodern understanding of dissent suggests that organizations like the Femmes Fatales and the Kool Krazy Kats will evolve in relation to language and the mores surrounding them. Similarly, the Crowning Heights and Harlem debutantes come to explore other social realities among their racial and class counterparts. Even those outside the conspirators who don Afros at the Grand Cotillion "heard about the plot through the grapevine and joined it of [their] own volition" (224). However thorny, social and cultural exchange in the novel is inevitable, laying the foundation for opposing views that can coexist in place of a repressive group consensus.

Nested firmly in the middle and upper class, the Femmes Fatales pride themselves on being an exclusive organization. Thomas Vargish, in *Rewriting Democracy*, reveals that this type of organization functions as an absolute system, which is an entity isolated from external influence and instilling its order through self-aggrandizement. The Femmes Fatales tout that they have "always been more than just a social club. More than a social club. We have always been civic-minded and interested in helping in the uplift of our fellowman, those less fortunate than ourselves. . . . To brighten darkened corners wherever they may be" (73). Tellingly, this history of civic engagement exposes their distance from the poor and working class. For years, they have "served" the community in accordance with a flawed value system that is disconnected from social projects and other efforts in lower-class communities. Having focused on imposing a certain classed identity onto so-called disadvantaged debs, it is ironic that the Femmes Fatales' mission actually lays the groundwork for the debs' own project: animating a postmodern cultural politics that resists consensus.

The opposing views that exist within the ranks of the Femmes Fatales bubble up at the Jefferson soiree. Here it becomes clear that the unabashed Jefferson and the outspoken Beverly Brap-bap maintain a subculture of nonconformity within the organization. Offering herself as the voice of reason, the Femmes Fatales as shortsighted, and the debs as participants in a problematic social experiment, Brap-bap's rhetorical quips speak to the difficulties of creating a functional social organization without dissent. Reacting to the initial treatment of the Harlem debs at the beginning of the debutante process, Brap-bap remarks, "I mean, let's don't look down on each other. And don't get started reading pedigrees, cause I can read quite a few of the sisters of the Femmes Fatales" (76). Brap-bap had settled into a nip-and-tuck critique, and, of their signature event, Jefferson "thought the whole Cotillion bit was one big good joke, which she went along with, strictly for the laughs . . ." (108). While neither Brap-bap nor Jefferson pursues the obliteration of their organization's operating principles, the decision to verbalize their dissent is significant. This element speaks volumes because so much African American fiction portrays opposition to staid institutions but does not introduce ways of subverting the constructs that maintain them. Because there is a redemptive power in resisting consensus for social organizations nearly undone by uncritical practices, Killens's novel suggests that groups should engage in the postmodern practice of welcoming dissenting voices and questioning their own assumptions.

Regrettably, because the Femmes Fatales preoccupy themselves with the august lore of their traditions, the diverse class heritage within their own ranks goes unacknowledged. In one instance, Brap-bap interjects a measure of historicity into the false recollection of another member. Reflections on the good old days, when aristocratic black families "had a splendid staff of servants," act as revisionist history arrived at through mutual agreement. However, Brap-bap's corrective includes an explanation of "cousin clubs": "Migrant workers. They would have them shipped up here from Virginia, Georgia and Barbados and South Carolina, right out the cotton patch and the cane fields, and live with them to help them pay them mortgages. They were paying guests, but since the colored muck-the-mucks were not supposed to let rooms for rent, these people were palmed off to everybody else as first cousins, second cousins, distant cousins. High-yaller families with jet-black cousins" (130). In correcting the historical record, Brap-bap recuperates the erased individuals who, because of their mischaracterized experiences, do not exist within the selective annals of the Femmes Fatales. Corrections such as this create a context in which the organization can acknowledge the actual lineages among its membership and use them as a launch pad for expanding and invigorating the anemic dialogue around heritage. Such a posture would only serve to strengthen the Femmes Fatales by making them responsive to their own cultural needs.

Having a stake in the organization, Yoruba and Lumumba are uniquely positioned to disrupt any form of class-biased consensus and usher in a more flexible politics. In response to Yoruba's displeasure with the whole deb process and her sense that she has compromised too much for her mother, Lumumba puts the larger plight in focus: "I'm on your side, my queen. And we're both on the side of Black folks. And your mother is not the enemy. If she is, then we are in a real big hurt. Cause your mother is where a whole heap of the Black and beautiful people of the Black Nation are at. . . . She just got her head all messed up with bourgeois aspirations. I mean, your mother is the Black masses that we're supposed to be fighting for. If we can't dig what's bugging her, forget it" (183–84). Even in the midst of experiences that seem to fragment her socially, Yoruba entertains Lumumba's reading of the situation without losing her own. In fact, she brings her own impulses to bear on her experiences. Possessing a flexible sense of self, Yoruba opens herself up to the social possibilities that exist across the spectrum of black middle- and upper-class life. Through her connections to Matt, Daphne, Lumumba, and the Femmes Fatales, Yoruba arrives at an evolving postmodern identity that resists total consensus with any particular group or set of ideological tenets.

Killens analyzes Yoruba's newfound postmodern framework by highlighting the tensions that emerge during her debutante training. When preparing for the cotillion, Yoruba struggles to affirm a particular conception of beauty. During a moment of reflection, she finds herself before a mirror taking inventory of her features: "Gazing narrow-wide-eyed at the mirror. She turned her back and stared behind her. Then went into her dance, turning, spinning, pirouetting. I am Black and beautiful, O you daughters of Aunt Hagar" (144). In a Jungian sense, Yoruba poises herself for social determination, but a kind of determination that does not settle on a fixed identity. At the Grand Cotillion, Yoruba debuts "short-and-nappy-haired" (238)—neither donning a wig to appease her mother nor suppressing her own anxiety about what is a blatant disruption of custom. Narrowly escaping the angry grasps of the Femmes Fatales, Yoruba is the first to debut. She takes the stage to mixed reactions that mirror her own mixed feelings—"there was one loud gasp from the audience, then a murmur went over the ball room, then wild applause from some" (237). Still, her entrance represents a genuine postmodern moment of instability and a flouting of others' expectations. Yoruba tears up, and her mother instantly finds herself torn between fidelity to the Femmes Fatales and her family.

When Yoruba follows through with her plan to make the event black and beautiful, the novel says that she possesses a kind of "nervous dignity"

(237). As she waits backstage at the cotillion, she contemplates the question: "Was everything in this crazy world only fun and games when you got down to the nitty-gritty?" (227). Killens describes Yoruba's debut by saying, "Yoruba was the first natural woman to make her grand debut in the annals of cotillions, and when she debutted [sic], it was like the living end . . ." (237). What this passage describes is the disruption of staid traditions and the ambivalence that overhangs the shattering of deeply sedimented notions.

Yoruba activates the postmodern at the Grand Cotillion in a way that imbues her with the courage to resist the consensus around future mobility touted by the Femmes Fatales. She chooses to live in the moment—to avoid resolving issues beyond the moment, such as future college plans and her tense relationship with her mother. Yoruba, in effect, jettisons her burdens, in part by casting off the middle-class wishes her mother has imposed on her since childhood. But how does Yoruba own the freedom she has granted herself at the Grand Cotillion? The answer lies in understanding that Killens posits dissension and uncertainty in place of stability. While the novel suggests that Yoruba is in a strong position to blaze her own trail, her debut does not represent a moment of transcendence or freedom. Instead, it represents the possibility of the interplay of myriad black experiences that have been colliding all along. Certifying Yoruba's postmodern subjectivity, Killens ends the narrative by having her harness the symbolic power of the cotillion. She debuts as an individual, not as an honorary recipient of all things bourgeois. Having waded through class division, survived her sojourn into an overbearing middle-class culture, and even ferreted out her cause within the confines of the Femmes Fatales, Yoruba embraces her decentered self. She exits the cotillion toward an uncertain, but viable, future.

As a work that rejects totalizing narratives, *The Cotillion* succeeds in democratizing an array of ideologies. Not at all invested in triumphalism, the novel closes open-ended and resists a concrete resolution. Killens's aim is not to leave either the discussions raised in the novel or the characters stunted or locked into one frame of reference. The structure is all about arriving at a broadening and flexibility around classed perspectives. Killens is targeting those who are unyielding in their cultural ideology, which he satirically describes this way: "The Black extremist demagogues who can't be bribed, and so you know they can't be trusted. That's the thing you go to watch. Understand?" (239). Overall, the novel's open-endedness strategically makes it ripe for the reflections and discussions of readers invested in black life. Finally, because *The Cotillion* concludes open-ended, it allows insights from the novels discussed in previous chapters to reverberate in the absence of a simplistic wrap-up.

Passing through the circuits of disparate lived experiences (through the boroughs of New York City and abroad), Lumumba's investment in denying consensus its stagnating role is true to postmodern form. His notions, which do not limit an individual's capacity for the mastery of many epistemologies, are an affront to modern conceptions of fragmentation and self-consciousness as crisis points. Lumumba best embodies Susan Lundquist's description of a trickster figure—as "a being who continually exposes those behaviors and thinking processes that have been marginalized. [The] [t]rickster is continually deconstructing ideologies and calling attention to foolish human behavior" (89). Further, Lumumba inhabits what Linda Hutcheon terms the "inside-outsider" position, in which one rejects a totalizing tradition while simultaneously participating in it. For instance, Killens hints at Lumumba penning his own novel about the cotillion, a text capturing the kind of postmodern politics that flourish amid disparate ideologies like black nationalism, bohemianism, and the black bourgeois culture. Joining Yoruba's deb process as her escort situates Lumumba as someone who exemplifies a postmodern conception of exchange that holds implications for those concerned with shattering class divides.

In the novel, Lumumba's postmodern aesthetic is premised on cultural collision. As a poet and writer, Lumumba will no doubt use the madness and spectacle at the cotillion as material for his novel. But his aesthetic contrasts with what we see in Truman's paintings and sculpture in *Meridian*. While they are both artists, Truman wanted his aesthetic to be in the service or larger ideals—that is, black women or historical figures. His crutch lies in trying to pursue meaning in a situation riddled with depthlessness. Lumumba, however, is able to dive headlong into the morass of confusion and allow his art to speak through the discordant registers of race, nation, and class.

Signifying on the reader, Lumumba suggests that the novel he has been writing all along is actually *The Cotillion*. The other layer to Killens's play on a frame narrative is that Lumumba's aesthetic is based on his recollection: "I don't mean I've actually been putting it down on paper, but I've been soaking up the experiences" (185). This effort on Lumumba's part is what illuminates his capacity to act in subversive ways. The time he has spent soaking up peculiar experiences and the acknowledgment of his slippery relationship to the truth (in his personal foreword to the novel) make him an ideal, if unreliable, dissenting voice. Even before the Grand Cotillion takes place, Lumumba himself leaks the secret that the debs will "blacken" the event. Once the stage is set for a raucous encounter, his postmodern agenda involves setting off the pent-up anxiety and opposition in the room and fragmenting everyone's preconceived ideas about what would take place before their eyes.

In the final scene, as Lumumba chants "Up the Black Nation!" the Grand Cotillion becomes a postmodern space of dispersal, rather than an arena favoring one class politics over another. To realize this effort, Lumumba uses the Grand Cotillion's stage to explode assumptions about black respectability. Admonishing the crowd, he declares, "Be done with false illusions! Come with us to the real world" (238). His words are ironic, in that he himself has used artifice and an Afrocentric, nationalist veneer to liberate the minds of black people. The distinction between the "really real thing" and the kitsch not only falters, it collapses in *The Cotillion*. Killens, through Lumumba, exploits issues of authenticity to give voice to different classed experiences, which tend to overlap.

Unbeknownst to many at the Grand Cotillion, Lumumba has indirectly paved the way for Matt's poetic drunken stupor, inspired Brap-bap's voice-of-reason admonition that "It'll be a different kind of cotillion and it'll make history" (238), and incited Daphne's momentary indecision, "I need a clear head, she told herself, to find my way to the really real world." Neither person persists uninterrupted in this space or is permitted to explore or delve into their instincts for long. When Lumumba calls out to a black nation, he does so ironically, neither invoking the totalizing narratives of black nationalism nor denigrating the comradery of the Femmes Fatales. Though *The Cotillion* foregrounds black cultural entities with either resilient histories or communal foundations, it does not instigate a competition for the figurative soul of the race. Nor does it answer the question of which entity puts the most nimble finger on what happens to be in the interest of black people. Instead, Killens furnishes a model of a black nation where diverse experiences become intelligible to blacks othered unnecessarily by class, pedigree, counterculture, or tradition.

Throughout the novel, Lumumba pushes against the modern notions of reason and objectivity, which often stall the practice of resisting consensus. On the one hand, ideas around unanimity and fidelity have served blacks well in the course of building resistance movements over and against forced exclusion. On the other hand, a defensive and protectionist sort of logic also sprang up, which led blacks to appropriate some of the self-defeating practices of the majority. Critiquing the toxicity of such ways, Brap-bap says, "Just because we're colored we don't have to look on the dark side all the time." Further, in describing his aim to usher in a context where postmodern cultural sensibilities could be realized, Lumumba says in his foreword to the reader: "I will intrude, protrude, obtrude or exclude my point of view any time it suits my disposition. Dig that." Ultimately, Lumumba reveals that in a constellation of middle-class, working-class, and nationalist values even the most durable cultural silos have fissures through which varied assumptions will collide and mesh.

In *The Cotillion,* the consensus-fracturing values of Yoruba and Lumumba prove both paradoxical and practical in destabilizing the status quo. As the novel's ending alludes to, a postmodern perspective favors disruption. In contrast to Daphne's approach of siding with the upwardly mobile and disparaging lower-classed others, Yoruba and Lumumba subvert pretentious institutions by imposing difference on them. Lumumba's character, in particular, demonstrates the idea that attention to class politics can facilitate an inside-outsider critique of black organizations that suppress diversity of thought and experience.

Killens's culture-work narrative derives its value from not shying away from the divergent socioeconomic realities that abound in black life. For this reason, *The Cotillion* fictionalizes numerous black experiences within the cultural terrain of an inherently conflicted, yet useful, black nationalist movement. One viable solution to class division is often an insistence on encounters that force one group to see and comprehend the other. Killens meticulously renders this process to readers. He juts a postmodern sensibility up against stagnating, marginalizing, and repressive class traditions. Lastly, the novel infuses flexibility into the cultural and historical legacies recognized in different organizations. In doing so, *The Cotillion* addresses intraracial class tensions—taking as its backdrop a politics of difference within black communities around race, class, and gender. Inasmuch as the novel satirizes the postmodern interplay of different social customs, it also assesses the viability of such a project in black life. Using these thematic elements, Killens teases out a postmodern cultural politics through which African Americans can navigate complex social arrangements formed around class.

4

SELF-RENEWAL THROUGH INTROSPECTION

Endless Journeys, Endless Becoming in Toni Morrison's
Tar Baby

The novels discussed so far illustrate that the cultural and social predicaments black men and women face in society stem from a thorny nexus of group narratives and mainstream manipulation. Lila Mae and Pompey are hemmed in by competing corporate interests whose tendrils reach into neighborhoods and news media alike. They have little choice but to either resist the bureaucratic and industrial behemoths or do their bidding. Meridian and Truman flee diminishment at the hands of academic institutions and out-of-touch leadership. Neither can stand to have their lives circumscribed on the basis of mission statement or movement protocols that diminish their individuality. As toxic as these conditions are for these characters, they are equally so for Yoruba and Lumumba, who find themselves plagued by intraracial class tension between middle-class culture and working-class ideology. Similarly, in Morrison's *Tar Baby*, the protagonists' lives are shaped by the rat-race compulsions of modern society and the weakened family ties that point to the further compromising of social conditions. *Tar Baby* offers a milieu that is the social and cultural culmination of the previous decades of political struggle teased out in the work of Whitehead, Walker, and Killens. In particular, the novel features male and female characters grappling with, navigating, and embracing uncertainty in the post–civil rights era. Morrison's portrait of black life becomes a source for reconsidering shared cultural experience and probing individual aspiration.

Tar Baby portrays seemingly endless personal journeys and moments of becoming that characterize the culture of the post–civil rights generation. Characters embarking on these journeys do so to get around the dilemma of group constraints and mainstream alienation—yet these paths do not lead to some neutral space away from this sociocultural bind. Caught in the throes of a changing fashion career in Paris, Jadine Childs contemplates returning home to the unarticulated family commitments she always felt unable to live up to. In addition, these commitments could threaten her cosmopolitan way of life. Leading the life of a vagabond—principally to escape a past that left him broken—Son (William Green) moves about frenetically, critiquing institutions like the military, which he believes exploit, compromise, and impose norms incompatible with black life. *Tar Baby* moves away from the black experiences consistent with steadfast racial traditions and leans toward more fluid and advantageous cultural sensibilities in the post–civil rights era. Alongside this element, the novel's postmodern tension is perhaps best captured in its title, which refers to a nineteenth-century folktale. Near the end of the novel, Son rants the "Tar Baby"[1] story in a heated argument with Jadine. Son uses the story to convey why he is unwilling to accept Jadine's money (which comes from dividends on a bond given to her by Valerian Street, her aunt and uncle's white employer and her benefactor) to finance his college education (which Son never pursues). What is interesting about his version of the tale is that he abridges it; as opposed to recounting the ending of the story where Br'er Rabbit outsmarts Br'er Fox and escapes the stickiness of the farmer's tar baby doll, Son ends the tale by saying, "He made him a tar baby. He [the farmer and now Valerian] made it, you hear me? He made it" (270). Ironically, the part of the tale Son omits is most significant because it not only alludes to the cultural and societal snares they will encounter on their respective journeys but also the capacity they must harness to either sidestep these conditions or maneuver through them.

Morrison offers a portrait of this era that pinpoints the problems around socioeconomic mobility and racial identity that remain in the aftermath of America's civil rights struggle. The unresolved social dilemmas and the bare-bones solutions characters deploy to cope with them represent a moment just as pivotal as the 1950s and 1960s yet devoid of organized resistance and social redress. In African American fiction, even as individual journeys lead to the prospect of new social and cultural paradigms, the black individual's fragmented mentality is consistently on the chopping block. Therefore, Morrison's *Tar Baby* explores the existential challenges that come with personal journeys—the losses and gains in terms of one's sense of self.

Morrison's main characters achieve the kind of self-renewal necessary in an era teeming with decenteredness and dislocation. One path to renewing the self—or one's intellectual and social perceptions—in *Tar Baby* seems to be through postmodern introspection and the will to act on personal convictions that embrace flux and vulnerability. Postmodern introspection involves grasping different epistemologies, social perceptions, and cultural ideas about ways to move through the world (navigating disparate communities, situations, and societies). Self-renewal does not necessarily imply a positive state as much as it implies the mettle to embrace new perspectives and begin again on a trajectory of one's own choosing. As someone adopted into a wealthy home, and then raised by her aunt and uncle (Ondine and Sydney), Jadine struggles to find her familial footing. After living and studying abroad, she returns home to determine her next path, but Jadine wrestles with a budding racial awareness brought on by what she viewed as a spectacle of blackness. She struggles to access some notion of authentic blackness in herself until she accepts her own complicated and fragile idea about what it means to live as a privileged and educated black woman. Similarly, Son wants to square his opinion of himself with what society's systems wish for him. *Tar Baby* offers him a postmodern lifeline befitting an era filled with the whims and tensions that accompany black aspirations. He has spent nearly a decade living in opposition to mainstream norms while trying to contemplate a world he can occupy on his own terms—suspicious of money, identification, and education. Pursuing self-renewal through introspection, amid a cornucopia of assumptions and convictions, becomes the best option along the vexed journeys society compels one to take.

Tar Baby's postmodern formal elements give it a sense of distance and perplexity as Morrison attempts to pull different geographies (the Caribbean, Europe, the U.S. mainland) into the arena of a discussion about change and adaptability. Aside from the cultural politics attached to each of these sites, devices like foreshadowing, backstory, and shifting points of view bring particular lived realities into play. Perhaps fragmentation provides the most potent source of meaning in the novel in its structural and thematic impact. Fragmented experiences and bits and pieces of recollections are used to critique and dismantle notions of wholeness. In a world where characters seem to be at home in their respective livelihoods, Morrison chips away at everyone's sense of steadiness, either through discomfort, disaffection, or disillusionment. What she uncovers in the process is the considerable effort to feign contentment and the relentless latching onto the bare essentials undergirding one's station in life out of fear of either reprisal or displacement. Morrison uses fragmentation and fracture to dispel the fear of entertaining other life chances and prospects.

Morrison embeds sequences of interior, exterior, and expansive fragmented perspectives as formal elements. Her commitment to fragmentation and fracture allows her to center various ideological and intellectual positions and then gradually decenter them across chapters in *Tar Baby*. One result of this postmodern endeavor is that the novel levies a disorienting experience. In this way, the reader's experience serves to accentuate Morrison's overarching goal, which is to stress the point that the characters have internalized their own assumptions to the point that they cannot easily discard them without collateral damage to their own psyches.

Valerian's stroke is an example of interior fragmented perspective. The stroke happens after Valerian learns that his wife, Margaret, brutally abused their son, Michael, when he was a child. Upon hearing the news, "Valerian held on to the table edge as though it were the edge of the earth. His face was truly white and his voice cracked a little . . ." (209). The following day a subdued Valerian sits next to Margaret with his knees trembling as she recounts details about her actions. Soon Valerian interrupts her: "'I cannot hear anymore,' he said. 'I can't'" (232). Then, "Valerian did not move. I will never be that strong, he thought. I will never be strong enough to hear it. I have to die now or go to him [Michael]. When I move from this table I will do one or the other, nothing in between. I will never be able to hear it" (233). While the words Valerian hears would have a chilling effect upon anyone, Morrison uses this scene to highlight a resonant sense of fracture within the Street family.

Valerian's condition leaves him inwardly muted and closed off from the viewpoints of others, which essentially makes introspection a forgone conclusion. The statement "I will never be able to hear it" implies that his perceptions are fixed. The novel not only describes him as "oblivious to everything but 1950 when he heard for the first time his son's song" (231)—it also suggests that he cannot "shift his gaze." If Valerian were originally poised, in light of Jadine's return home and Son's squatting via intrusion, to reconsider his relationship to both his family and the small army of workers that surround him, then that capacity becomes stunted after he suffers a stroke. The stroke serves as an apt metaphor for the kind of fragmentation, which creeps in at a moment of unsettling enlightenment—that threatens to chip away at one's core sense of self. The tragic news about the abuse of his son is not what threatens Valerian's mental and physical stability as much as his stalwart resistance to learning new ways of grasping the world (read: postmodern possibilities) and viewing life after the difficult revelations. Valerian finds himself trapped in a bygone era and a defunct frame of mind.

In contrast, Son's exterior sense of fragmentation is bound up in his inability to prevent himself from obsessively revisiting past experiences and from studying the experiences of others in the present. For example, his mind periodically wanders back to his hometown, Eloe, and to his former crewmates, whom he refers to as the Swede and the Mexican. He also muses on the experiences of Gideon and Thérèse (Valerian's workers) and Jadine. And it is this unfortunate character flaw that limits his capacity to productively reflect on his life. We encounter this trait at the beginning of the novel when Son jumps from the *Stor Konigsgaarten* into the Atlantic and trudges toward the Street estate, L'Arbe de la Croix. This is a fragmenting sequence because Son treks "through darkness lined by trees muttering in their sleep," ruminates on the past, experiences meditative moments, and surreptitiously studies the inhabitants of the Street home.

At first Son approaches the house for water, but after looking through one of the windows and noticing a piano, he recalls Miss Tyler's piano. Miss Tyler was the only person in Son's neighborhood who had owned a piano he could use to learn to play. The memory itself clarifies Son's discomfort with deep reflection: "It made him tired, weak and tired, as though he had swum seven seas for seven years only to arrive at the place he had started from: thirsty, barefoot and alone. . . . He backed away, away from the light and the window into the protection of the trees that were still muttering in their sleep" (136). Son's backing away from the light is analogous to his retreat from palpable memories that force him to reckon with his past, namely, the time he spent playing the piano badly at a smoky joint (after being dishonorably discharged) while his soon-to-be-unfaithful wife Cheyenne waited at home. Son also thinks about his childhood friends Drake, Soldier, and Ernie Paul who all share a collective fear about their bodies (hands, balls, eyes, spine), which seems linked to their vocations, vices, and to the likelihood of their being drafted and sent off to the Vietnam War. Interestingly, Son is the only one who gets drafted. While Morrison mentions Son's fear of his hands, she also alludes to another, perhaps more deep-seated, fear of his true self, which is embodied in the moniker "Son." Morrison states, "It was the name that called forth the true him. The him that he never lied to, the one he tucked in at night and the one he did not want to die. The other selves were like the words he spoke—fabrications of the moment, misinformation required to protect Son from harm and to secure that one reality at least" (139). This passage brings to light Son's obsessive focus with walling his true self off from inner reckoning and from the possibility of mitigating the sense of fracture that blankets his life.

Jadine is the character whose fragmented perspective is expansive and sweeping. Throughout the narrative, Jadine's preoccupation with finding her way back to success and status after leaving Paris ebbs and flows and initiates a paradoxical trajectory in the latter part of the novel. When Jadine leaves Paris, she works as a social secretary for Margaret and flirts with the idea of opening a retail shop. All the while, her hunger for the grandeur of her previous life remains. Eventually, her frenzied affair with Son leads her to New York City, where she feels empowered. Jadine imagines taking the city by storm and becoming a success on her own terms, darting from the Hilton to a friend's apartment, vacillating over whether to call a former professor of hers who can help her find work, and fruitlessly toying with the idea of "opening a retail flower shop and boutique that they could call Jade and Son" (230).

Ondine and Sydney perhaps experience the brunt of Jadine's dizzying ambition. Her abrupt departure to New York plays a part in fracturing their relationship, particularly because Ondine and Sydney are left to ponder the retail-business idea Jadine sold to them, along with the possibility of living together as a family away from the Streets, which she later seems to thrust aside. When Jadine receives a harsh response to her postcard, by way of a letter from Ondine and Sydney, we learn that "she left the two sullen and confused old people at the kitchen table, their hearts steeled against her leaving, even though her New York trip, she said, was vital if she were to arrange things so all three could live together" (225). Jadine's fragmented and grandiose plans lead to a sense of instability across the island of Dominique and New York City. Ultimately, Morrison's utilization of the fracturing perspectives held by her characters gives the novel its postmodern contour.

Robert Butler's *Contemporary African American Fiction: The Open Journey* identifies a significant niche in African American literature, which portrays the individual journey as a process wherein the freedom to define oneself unfolds. Butler also highlights the symbiosis between the American and African American literary canons where it involves the sense of open-ended movement in fiction, which often illuminates the desire for social mobility. Writers "characteristically view movement and change as intrinsically valuable—a process of endless becoming rather than progress culminating in a state of completed being. Such open movement becomes a compelling metaphor of the American desire for the 'new life,' consisting of unlimited personal development" (11). What is ultimately being referenced is the journey motif, which has its roots in early twentieth-century literature and its extensions in later writing. This motif places a high premium on change and the need to continually renew one's *self* in contemporary times. In this way, it pivots off the social and cultural upheavals in American society. For instance, Butler's chapter on Morrison looks at the tendency of her characters to resist settling in a single place for long and, instead, to opt for the space upon which to expand conceptions of the kind of individual they want to become. Often situated in agrarian society, Morrison's characters must negotiate the politics of history, place, and tradition. Representing a dialectic that traverses the canon, the opposition between one's physical place and individual sense of space is perhaps what stabilizes and supports the journey motif.

In *Tar Baby*, Morrison utilizes the trope of the black runner to initiate journeys toward broader subjectivity for her protagonists. Phyllis Klotman in *Another Man Gone: The Black Runner in Afro-American Literature* has observed this trope in twentieth-century American literature. Specifically, Klotman's running-man trope has often been linked to some form of flight or freedom—a "protagonist who rejects the values of the culture or society in which he [or she] finds himself [or herself] by birth, compulsion, or volition, and literally takes flight" (3). Extending Klotman's characterization to include women protagonists, I find that her notion of "the runner as defector" bears useful implications for Morrison's *Tar Baby*. This running is "less a mark of alienation" than self-reliance and epitomizes a shift away from "the expectations for recognition of worth" (95, 129). For example, the *running* associated with texts like William Melvin Kelley's *dem* and Morrison's *Sula* feature the separation from an imposed cultural narrative or constraining mythology. Eventually, the protagonists' environments dictate that they not only shift from common ways but also that they literally move away and embark on their own journeys.

Just as the journey motif creates opportunities for personal development, it also acts as an acknowledgment of the incessant struggle for self-autonomy. Novelists have come to speak about the generation gap and the passing of, or the rejection of, the torch (read: cultural memory) to generations impacted by postmodern change. The portrayal of open-ended journeys in a narrative allows readers to focus on a protagonist's often harried movement from one unique environment or worldview to another. Suffice it to say, when such movement takes place, it is neither seamless nor linear. And that particular character bears the trace of ideological markers identifiable at several sites. The representation of journeys undertaken by male and female characters is a reflection of the intersecting thematic interests in late-twentieth-century works by black authors. Writers like Gloria Naylor, Alice Walker, and Colson Whitehead tend to portray their protagonists with equanimity in terms of character complexity. Like Morrison, these authors take on culturally weighted issues of authenticity and race consciousness, as well. The journey theme brings to the forefront not only the search for meaning and wholeness in the post–civil rights era but also the straining of attachments and the vulnerability that come with such pursuits.

While the journey motif stretches throughout early texts in African American literature, it has undergone nuanced complexity since the 1970s.

Slave narratives adopted the theme, featuring harrowing treks from slavery into freedom. Protest novels depicted withdrawal from the urban city that did not make good on its promises of opportunity, while some more recent fiction has deployed the symbolic retreat into prelapsarian communities. In general, mid-twentieth-century narratives mirror the frustration that fueled black social movements at the time. However, postmodernist writers pursue very real shifts in thinking about coping with material and social deprivation. Ultimately, black writers seem to be recasting the journey motif to realize the need for inner exploration, be it legitimized by a given social movement or otherwise. In addition, as writers reckon with the complexities of vulnerability and decenteredness, the journey motif gets put to extended use. It ends up underscoring the need to rework one's relationship to his or her cultural reality.

In the late twentieth century, postmodernism has lent credence to the authority of individual assumptions and truth-seeking in fiction. Loren Quall's *Dark Language: Post-Rebellion Fiction* uses the term *post-rebellion* to identify the nature of recent black writing, which seeks to provide an insightful reading experience as well as an understanding of material reality in black life after the civil rights movement. Quall describes this fictional rhetoric as based on nostalgia and critical memory. Critical memory "implies a continuous arrival at turning points and decisive change, which is usually attended by considerable risk, peril, or suspense and always seems imminent" (15). This drive resonates with Henri Lefebvre's description of space, which rejects the notion of space as a site of passive social relations (*The Production of Space* 11, 142). Lefebvre views space as something enmeshed in an inexorable power struggle. One has to muster the capability to both construct and defend a given space. In African American literature, protagonists can only establish and maintain the parameters of their ambitions, provided they contend with the gatekeepers of their respective cultural tradition.

While black novelists continue to lead us down a path away from burdensome traditions, African American life during the late twentieth century compels new strategies for enduring an age of rapid societal fragmentation. The political vanguards that once fought to keep the plight of black Americans at the forefront find themselves eroding. In "Black Strivings in a Twilight Civilization," Cornel West has remarked on the havoc wreaked by "imperial corporations as public life deteriorates due to class polarization, racial balkanization, and especially a predatory market culture" (115). Even as the political context in this era becomes more partisan, and so, too impotent to handle social decay, still some will speak out about the marginalization of urban black America. For West, in the post–civil rights era, black strivings will continue to move against the grain, marshaling a radical politics that can survive black America's escalating political crises.

Given contemporary social realities, the need to inflexibly tether oneself to past cultural traditions becomes fraught. Indeed, a postmodern self-awareness does not comport with upholding conventions but with flouting them. As a result of civil rights struggles, the minority cultural production about which Andreas Huyssen writes in *After the Great Divide: Modernism, Mass Culture, Postmodernism* "added a whole new dimension to the critique of high modernism and to the emergence of alternative forms of culture" (198). When we consult black women's writing, in particular, readers find that "women's art, literature, and criticism are an important part of the postmodern culture of the 1970s and 1980s and indeed a measure of the vitality and energy of that culture" (199). Significantly, African American literature illustrates that the inclusion of blacks into full citizenship brought about alternatives, disruptions even, to past allegiances.

In the post–civil rights era, African Americans are revising social expectations. With the expansion of the black middle class and the critical force of black popular culture, marginalized groups have shifted toward autonomy and individual desire. Yet, while group solidarity is no longer a foregone conclusion, a sense of collectivity has not eroded completely. Tommie Shelby's *We Who Are Dark: The Philosophical Foundations of Black Solidarity* salvages the crux of nationalist solidarity, arguing against collective identity and in favor of difference and what he calls "collective control." As Shelby points out, the former "is not a necessary condition for cultivating effective bonds among African Americans, and in fact . . . attempting to forge one would be self-defeating" (11). His liberatory project revises the struggle against racial disparity in the post–civil rights era. I share Shelby's sense that blacks could preserve distinct identities around race, class, and gender—which suggests that new cultural truths can be unveiled and preserved. Further, cultural truths can be appreciated collectively and for their value to a given individual. In sum, the exploitation and sense of alienation rife in American life necessitates a commitment to varied cultural ways of knowing.

Black literary criticism has accounted for the retooling of black traditions and understandings in this age. It has done so in a way that facilitates the critiquing and reframing of cherished traditions. In one example, Doreen Massey's essay "Double Articulation: A Place in the World" discusses the inevitable differences in the conception of any given place: an individual's relationship to a place cannot be deemed more legitimate that another's sense of that place. Even though Massey argues that there can be no single truth about a place, she does not dismiss the reality that traditions may be attached to particular locales. Rather, she calls for anti-essentialism in the way writers and critics think about cultural identity and place. As Massey sees it, tradition does not "have to be merely closed and self-serving: it too can recognize a past [and present] openness" (119). Massey's argument about the characterization of place is relevant to fictional settings. The way a character views long-held traditions or narratives often depends upon his or her attachment to them, and that sense of attachment is usually linked to certain settings. At a time when close-knit black communities are withering and dispersing, writers have come to see the challenging of ingrained ways of knowing as crucial to the maintenance (or advancement) of social ties, not their erosion.

Morrison's Historiography and Modernity

Over time, the study of Morrison's use of history has expanded to include her insight on social movements. In her nonfiction work *Remember: The Journey to School Integration*, Morrison captures the struggle of black Americans pursuing the desegregation of public schools. According to Karen Stein, Morrison examines "differing approaches to black identity during the Civil Rights Movement" (3). Madhu Dubey's *Black Women Novelists in the Nationalist Aesthetic* names Morrison's *Sula* as a work that "embodies a radically new black femininity that upsets all the oppositions (between past and present, individual and community, absence and presence) that structure Black Aesthetic Discourse" (51). Bridging an encounter between critical race theory and African American literary studies, Richard Schur's "Locating *Paradise* in the Post–Civil Rights Era: Toni Morrison and Critical

Race Theory"[2] reads Morrison's *Paradise* as a discussion of the civil rights legacy and the possibility of judicial reform in the twenty-first century.

Some explorations of Morrison's oeuvre tend to view it as beholden to a modernist perspective. Paul Gilroy's *The Black Atlantic: Modernity and Double Consciousness* and W. Lawrence Hogue's *Race, Modernity, Postmodernity: A History of People of Color Since the 1960s* have both examined the modern dimensions of Morrison's work. The constellation of arguments has suggested that Morrison interrogates modern black life and imagines a confrontation between Anglocentric ideas and black diasporic truths. The main reading seems to be that Morrison concerns herself with the experiences of black Americans before the onslaught of American modernization. Justine Tally's *The Story of Jazz: Toni Morrison's Dialogic Imagination,* and Yogita Goyal's *Romance, Diaspora, and Black Atlantic Literature,* critique both the modern *and* postmodern dimensions of Morrison's fiction. Undoubtedly, Morrison's work highlights a host of dialogic moments across music, tradition, and folklore. These moments, as they appear in Morrison's fiction, embody countercultural disruptions of mainstream structures. Filled with cultural and historical elements, Morrison's narratives often reclaim alternative mythologies and find certain cultural practices insoluble with the social imperatives of the present-day world.

Novels like *Beloved, Jazz,* and *Paradise* (all historical novels) receive the most critical attention concerning postmodernism. My view of Morrison's *Tar Baby* is that, unlike the aforementioned novels, it depicts postmodern American reality and undoes the modern tendency to cast individualism as a reckless endeavor. In particular, Morrison creates embattled characters so as to signal their influence in shifting entrenched values and practices. In this way, *Tar Baby* challenges the modern social order that appears in a number of Morrison's other works with a sense of postmodern nuance and complexity.[3]

Tar Baby champions the individual's process of gaining self-awareness. In this context, Morrison offers a perspective on the post–civil rights era through the neglected tensions held over from previous decades of sociopolitical upheaval. These tensions surface within familial, southern agrarian, and upper-class contexts. The novel disseminates many truths (or constructs for understanding the world) to protagonists for the purpose of demonstrating the ways in which acknowledging a diversity of subjectivity can lead one beyond the knee-jerk appropriation of traditional value systems. In a postmodern culture, protagonists must journey toward amenable paths in life despite the pull of obligatory norms, relationships, and practices.

Inasmuch as the journey motif signifies new prospects and a stepping away from the familiar, it also contains an element of instability. In an interview with Nellie McKay, Morrison suggests that the problems Jadine and Son face in *Tar Baby*, while irritated by gender roles, have more to do with achieving some semblance of stability. In particular, "they had a problem about what work to do, when and where to do it, and where to live. Those things hinged on what they felt about who they were, and what their responsibilities were in being black" ("An Interview with Toni Morrison" 422). Focused on the implications of Jadine's and Son's relationship, Morrison's novel addresses the extraneous pressures they face in society. The post–civil rights era, though marked by substantive life chances, comes pre-packaged with compromised issues of choice and trajectory that loop back into virtually all of Jadine's and Son's endeavors.

Uncertain Journeys and Prospects

In *Tar Baby*, Jadine's journeys unfold in the mainstream spaces of Europe and New York. At twenty-five, Jadine experiences an existential crisis that leaves her stricken with feelings of inauthenticity and vulnerability as a black American woman living abroad. In Paris, the sight of a stunning, dark-skinned woman in a yellow dress shakes Jadine to her core and causes her to experience a sublime moment.[4] In the words of the text, "Just a quick snatch of breath before that woman's woman—that mother/sister/she; that unphotographable beauty—took it all away" (46). Afterward, "the woman's insulting gesture [*spitting toward Jadine*] had derailed her—shaken her out of proportion to incident" (47). In response, Jadine returns home to see her family in Dominique and to sort through myriad challenges she faced in Paris. She leaves behind a promising modeling career and her white Parisian fiancé, Ryk, because he cannot understand her need to be conscious of her racial self. Though familiar with art and photography, Jadine found that she could not visually absorb the sight of the woman in yellow in a way that both grasped the sublimity of the moment and maintained the substance of her own black experience. It is this unnerving moment that epitomizes the kind of exploitation present in Europe, which ratchets up the pressure on Jadine's very sense of self.

Here, mainstream exploitation is very much about the ability of the modeling and magazine industries to other Jadine—to riddle her with doubt about her racial self and to compromise her identity in the most subtle ways—all while regaling her with laurels. In one sense, Jadine becomes vulnerable to the ploys of *Vogue* and *Elle* in Europe. We see this in her thoughts about having her picture on a magazine cover and passing her oral exams. Although Jadine acknowledges the airbrushed unreality of the cover on which "they gave what they believed was a nineteen-year-old face the eyes and mouth of a woman of three decades," her initial reaction to the black woman in yellow was to disparage her body image according to the biases and narrow assumptions about beauty held by an industry fully invested in appearance over reality: "Under her long canary yellow dress Jadine knew there was too much hip, too much bust. The agency would laugh her out of the lobby, so why was she [Jadine] and everybody else in the store transfixed." Tellingly, Jadine herself is somewhat uncomfortable with the misguided standard she uses to judge the woman. She cannot grasp "[w]hy she had wanted that woman to like and respect her. It had certainly taken the zing out of the magazine cover as well as her degree" (47).

The sway of mainstream European culture also inhabits Jadine's life at the level of her subconscious. Even after Jadine leaves Europe, she is struck by a disturbing dream of women's hats that shame and repel her. She awakens from the dream, attempting to stop "looking for the center of the fear" (44) that welled up in her in Paris. Unfortunately, as much as Jadine desires to end this taxing search, she continues to pursue this vaporous sense of fear, and this becomes a journey that never really takes her inward. Jadine's time in Europe has artificially centered her. In other words, her success as a fashion model and a student pursuing an advanced degree has brought her happiness, but it is a hollow, fleeting happiness that requires her to avail herself of a life of raucous men in "Yugoslavian touring cars with Bordeaux Blanc and sandwiches" (44). The modeling industry seems to circumscribe her life, exploiting the allure of her racialized beauty and the assumptions that attend it, to the point that it becomes just as stitched and designed as some ornate fabric. Everything, in terms of relationship, education, and opportunity seems to be in place for Jadine, but the Faustian bargain that mainstream magazines like *Vogue* and *Elle* impose is the sacrificing of one's core self. In fact, Jadine's sense of self is left stagnant while her body is surrounded by "all the people she loved and some she did not" in celebration of her accomplishments. The ability of European agencies to render Jadine in a figurative maze experiment, groping for the exit, could go uninterrupted—except that, when confronted with the life-altering decision to marry Ryk, she has a moment of honesty with herself in which she separates the expat-fashion-industry-molded Jadine from the Jadine that is inaccessible to her fiancé and friends in Paris. As Jadine explains it, "what will happen when he finds out that I hate ear hoops, that I don't have to straighten my hair, that Mingus puts me to sleep, that sometimes I want to get out of my skin and be only the person inside—not American—not black—just me?" (48).

Contemplating her next career move after she returns home, Jadine has to contend with the cloud of indecision plaguing her. Morrison suggests that Jadine's time abroad had the effect not only of co-opting her talent for a Eurocentric cultural agenda but also of stymieing her journey toward more instinctive artistic/intellectual undertakings. This cultural agenda becomes apparent in her studies at the Sorbonne, the oldest university in Paris. As an art history major, Jadine is exposed to some of Europe's greatest classical art, taught to admire its genius, and lectured on the intricacies of various pieces and aesthetics. It is not until Jadine is in Dominique that she becomes ambivalent about the usefulness of her education: "Too many art history courses, she thought, had made her not perceptive but simpleminded. She saw planes and angles and missed character. Like the vision in yellow—she should have known that bitch would be the kind to spit at somebody . . ." (158). At another point, Jadine thinks to herself that "she was lucky to know it, to know the difference between the fine and the mediocre. So she'd put that instinct to work and studied art history— there she was never wrong" (182). While the domain of the university afforded Jadine room in which to bask in intellectual endeavors, the world outside has slowly become an enigma to her. Jadine has to lean on her cultivated instincts and sharpened intuition, which are the byproducts of being raised, at least partially, in a black American ethos. Morrison seems to suggest that this ethos is uniquely threatened in a European context that wields the intellectual sector as well as the modeling industry to seduce young and gifted blacks like Jadine who are driven by their passions.

Illustrating the postmodern flow of late capitalism, hedonism, and cultural difference, New York City is a mainstream space par excellence. Late in the novel, Jadine and Son move there to begin their fledgling love affair. On the one hand, New York's dynamism awakens innovation and desire in Jadine. On the other hand, Son diagnoses the monotony of life for blacks in New York as a grievous and painful experience. According to Son, women sitting behind desks in large corporations are starved for meaning. The men display queer identities implicitly because of the absence of race men. Even the performances of black actors and actresses on television seem to lack substance, "without irony or defiance or genuine amusement. Now all he heard were shrieks of satisfaction" (216). Son, who feels "confronted with a whole new race of people he was once familiar with" (217), nearly succumbs to the allure of the city and the overwhelming preoccupation with upward mobility.

Fast-paced and intoxicating, New York exploits Jadine's desire to win in both her relationship and her career. For her, "if ever there was a black woman's town, New York was it" (222). While the city offers education, modeling, and more high-life opportunities for Jadine, the darker side is that the social undercurrent there seems to impose insidious distraction on Jadine and Son and to ultimately grind their relationship to a halt. Morrison marks their entire stint in New York with distraction: "Son and Jadine hadn't the foggiest notion that spring was on its way. Vaguely aware of such things when they were apart, together they could not concentrate on the given world. They reinvented it, remembered it through the other" (230). In addition, the superficial friendships Jadine makes along the way prove fleeting and unproductive. Rapidly, the "efficiency and know-it-all sass" she revels in begin to unravel along with her projections about quality opportunities in New York. First, Jadine's ability to make a living diminishes, and, at twenty-five, she is passed over by modeling agencies because they do not see her as young and vibrant: "In Europe, they liked older looking black models but in the U.S. the look was twelve" (267). In addition, Jadine fails at her mission to modernize (or civilize) Son. At one point, they take a brief trip to Eloe, but, feeling isolated and miserable, Jadine returns to

New York. When Son finally returns, the two argue constantly and their relationship becomes increasingly violent.

In one sense, the city itself dominates the minds of Jadine and Son. Essentially, they argue about the degree to which they are willing to bear the oppressive weight of the culture of the city. This form of almost psychic exploitation is most relevant to Jadine, who embraces the loaded proposition of living in the city. New York seems to insist that those who reside there contend with the burden to "make it," relying on the most self-sacrificial and, at times, self-defeating efforts. Jadine finds herself floundering, pondering business ideas, imposing the goal of a college education on Son, and filling out applications to teach at local colleges: "The modeling things was going bust fast—she'd make all she could as fast as she could since it was seven times what teaching would bring" (267). Ultimately, Morrison compels Jadine to wrestle with the following question: "Culture-bearing black woman, whose culture are you bearing?" (269). Perhaps Son best defines the "culture" that Jadine bears and wields, and which works to undermine her goals. Son views Jadine as a "model of industry and planning." This cynical description is discerning because it articulates the mainstream sleight of hand to which Jadine is subject. It also suggests that, even though Jadine embodies New York attributes, it does not follow that she is in any position to be productive. Instead, the implication is that Jadine becomes more of a metaphorical reproduction of the city's character than an example of someone en route to thriving in city life, amid the kinds of multifaceted problems Jadine faces.

Jane Jacobs, in *The Death and Life of Great American Cities*, offers context relevant to *Tar Baby*'s New York. She describes the ethos of modern cities as detrimental to people. The city's inhabitants see the illusion of diversity in the touting of ethnic communities and city centers. In the city, the vast development represents a false cultural pluralism, where decisions made by those in power outweigh the ideas of others. The detriment to most inhabitants comes by way of an unseen hierarchy that creates the veneer of substance through technology, luxury, and a fleeting sense of adventure. As Jacobs explains, a city coaxes its residents to embrace the financial apex of urbanization. However, urbanization disfavors minoritized others, who, while highly visible, experience the strongest sense of alienation.

The seedbed of group constraints most relevant to Jadine rest in the work-centered habitus of Sydney and Ondine Childs. Sydney's and Ondine's presence in the Street household informs the race and class dynamics there. The novel implies that Sydney comes from a long line of middle-class blacks, but we also learn that Sydney and Ondine adopt Jadine after the death of her father and mother. Beyond these morsels of information, the text never grants much access to Sydney's life before his post with the Street family; nor does it provide a window into Ondine's younger years. Readers do however catch a glimpse of their quiet, inchoate desires to leave the Street household and pursue a change of pace and place. Ondine dreams of "sliding into water, frightened that her heavy legs and swollen ankles will sink her. . . . [T]he dream dissolves and with it the anxiety" (61). The tentative and halting character of Ondine's dream conveys the security she associates with avoiding unknown waters, with toeing the working-class line undoubtedly passed to her by a black family that could claim very limited access to work options or imagine alternatives to clamping down on long-term employment, whether in the form of domestic work or industrial menial labor. Sydney's dream is in some ways more vivid, but it is also more forlorn: "He is in Baltimore now as usual and because it was always a red city in his mind—red brick, red sun, red necks and cardinals—his dream of it now was rust-colored. He had left that city to go to Philadelphia and there he became one of those industrious Philadelphia Negroes—the proudest people in the race. That was over fifty years ago, and still his most vivid dreams were the red rusty Baltimore of 1921" (61).

As much as Sydney hangs his subconscious hat on Baltimore, his adopted identity of Philadelphia Negro is the linchpin of his pride in being an industrious worker. The passage charts Sydney's journey for the reader, literally from one major city (witnessing an influx of African Americans during the Great Migration) to another and figuratively from one fount of cultural capital to another. While Sydney's and Ondine's driving force is economic stability, in some ways hard work itself seems to be the end all be all. By their very nature, these dreams are ephemeral, but their cultural, intellectual, and even spiritual investment in working with their hands is ingrained in their psyches.

Morrison articulates the work-centered narrative informing Sydney's and Ondine's politics when Jadine casually discusses her indefinite plans with them after leaving Paris. Jadine talks about starting her own business and, in the near future, living with them in their own home as a family, among other things. Their subtle reaction to Jadine's spiel is telling: "They smiled generously, but their eyes made her know they were happy to play store with her, but nothing would pull them away from the jobs they had had for thirty years or more" (49). This passage uncovers Sydney's and Ondine's tendency to not verbalize their opinions and assumption but to, unbeknownst to Jadine, tacitly expect her to understand their worldview. Having grown up in a different era, Sydney and Ondine would not see their silence as a kind of condescension. Yet they do not bother to challenge Jadine's insinuations with an alternative perspective because they are not seriously entertaining them. Jadine has to interpret nonverbal cues to gain an understanding of the cultural narrative to which they have committed themselves.

This silence represents a potent kind of group constraint for Jadine because the narrative of hard work and permanence is foundational to the lives of her aunt and uncle. While Jadine has not been constrained by this cultural logic from pursuing her dreams, she is certainly limited in the extent to which she can broker reciprocal communication with her relatives when it comes to change. On the one hand, it should be clear and understandable that Sydney and Ondine are set in their ways. On the other hand, Jadine's chance to experience what she sees as a normal family experience hinges on her ability to broach a penetrating conversation with them about the current arrangement and the possibility of reimagining it in a context independent of the Street family. Having grown up in an atmosphere in which her aunt and uncle decided not to saddle her with burdensome traditions and mores, Jadine becomes powerless in the face of a decades-old and enmeshed narrative to alter her familial circumstances. In essence, Ondine's commitment, which Sydney would second, to "a good and permanent job doing what she was good at for a boss who appreciated it; beautiful surroundings which included her own territory where she alone governed" (96) is what repels Jadine's disruptive ideas. In effect, Sydney and Ondine's working-class habitus serves to cordon off notions of radical change and flux that characterize Jadine's reality.

Significantly, when it comes to the quasi mother-daughter relationship between Ondine and Jadine, the work-centered narrative is most pronounced because nonverbal communication cannot suffice. Near the end of *Tar Baby*, Jadine feels the force of this narrative when Ondine breaks her silence around cultural tradition and becomes effusive about family matters. When Jadine decides to return to Paris, mentions choice, and asks Ondine to join her, Ondine replies: "Jadine, a girl has got to be a daughter first. She have to learn that. And if she never learns how to be a daughter, she can't never learn how to be a woman. . . . Now you didn't have a mother long enough to learn much about it, and I thought I was doing right by sending you to all them schools and so I never told you it and I should have" (281). This is the cultural lesson that Ondine has been demure and silent about all of Jadine's life. Morrison adds a level of gravitas to the war-of-words encounters between mother and daughter that Killens satirizes through Yoruba and Daphne. In doing so, Morrison raises the stakes on the knotty work of maintaining a family bond or reconciling strong beliefs. When Jadine finally hears the narrative that has inhibited her relationship with her aunt and uncle, in terms of closeness, she reacts defensively—reducing Ondine's words to a vulgar quid pro quo: "You worked for me and put up with me. Now it's my turn to do it for you, that's all you're saying." Here Morrison shows us the real nature of the damage that this cultural and generational wedge has done. Now that Ondine has made herself vulnerable through her revealing words, Jadine still cannot achieve a new depth of closeness with her aunt. In short, there are no doors opened via this difficult, if earnest, act of communication. If Jadine's response seems abrasive, notice that the narrative maintains its hold on Ondine even in the midst of her outpouring: "She [Ondine] reached out to touch her niece's hand, but something made her stop short or it." Perhaps the most unfortunate fact is that Ondine's tradition proves to be so dependent on work and responsibility to the point that it represses overt expressions of care and support. Either Jadine will insist upon reconciling her family notions with her aunt's or she will continue her uncertain journey toward a new incarnation of what it means to be both a daughter and a woman.

Throughout the novel, the mainstream exploitation that Son encounters can be linked to his time in the military and to modern society itself. Son at first appears without a family name or heritage. Dishonorably discharged during the Vietnam War and living as a fugitive from his criminal past (he inadvertently kills his wife, Cheyenne, in a fit of rage over her adultery), Son abandons ship and swims ashore to Valerian's private island. Questions regarding the significance of Son's character emerge in *Tar Baby*: How does Son's checkered background complicate his interactions? Why is he conflicted with and hostile toward socioeconomic mobility? Besides the legal repercussions, what exactly is he running from (or toward)?

When Morrison offers readers a brief portrait of Son's experience in Vietnam, she recalls the harrowing history of black men who, while fighting and dying for their country abroad, endured mistreatment at the hands of a racist society that saw even black soldiers as second-class citizens. In this sense, Vietnam is probably the most potent symbol of black exploitation at the hands of a mainstream institution that I have touched on in this book. Son describes his time in the theater of war as a situation in which only laughter could minimize the aura of expendability surrounding soldiers like himself. As Son puts it, "when trucks sank in mud and grenades exploded too soon or not at all, laughter was always there, almost always; but one day it ran out too, as unreliable as his fucked-up M-14. The silence in his throat where laughter or tears ought to be blew up in his head and he was stockaded, busted and, when he refused to re-up, discharged without honor or humor" (224). At another point, a quintessential image of Americana appears in the novel, which recalls for Son this unsettling period in his life and its implications for the capacity of nations to commit atrocities. Years removed from one of America's most unpopular conflicts, "when he thought of America, he thought of the tongue that the Mexican drew in Uncle Sam's mouth: a map of the U.S. as an ill-shaped tongue ringed by teeth and crammed with the corpses of children" (167). The disfigured image of the Uncle Sam poster suggests that Son can no longer buy into the "land of opportunity" narrative; his perception of an America that uses its people to perpetuate misery abroad and at home is much bleaker.

Concerning mainstream society, Son loathes the capitalist striving that pervades it. What nettles Son is society's capacity to cajole its inhabitants into a mocking vortex of endless pursuit and veiled sorrow. He could neither escape the vortex when he took odd jobs on ships sailing abroad nor when he and Jadine briefly lived in New York. Because of the ubiquity of a modernizing impulse, Son's journey toward some unencumbered, off-the-grid state of being fails. Even in the Caribbean, Son is met with the capitalist investment in real estate made possible by imported labor: "The end of the world, as it turned out, was nothing more than a collection of magnificent winter houses on Isle des Chevaliers" (9). This investment has altered Dominique by carving up its landforms and disturbing local geologies. Morrison writes, "The men had already folded the earth where there had been no fold and hollowed her where there had been no hollow, which explains what happened to the river." To get at Son's politics, we must look at his answer to a question Jadine poses when they are in New York: "What do you want out of life?" (169). To Son's thinking, the question implies how he will situate himself in the American rat race. However, after he reminisces about the first dime he ever earned from Frisco, an older man who worked in the gas field in Eloe, his replies with a loaded answer, "Something nice and simple and personal, you know?" (170). Son's spiel shows that the only adequate place he can imagine for his politics is a place of community, untrammeled by industry or permanence. But the only way for Son to rebuff exploitation en masse is to lead a life critical of the lack of attention to the simple and the personal in society.

For the most part Son wrestles with group constraints on two fronts. Having been homeless for nearly a decade after fleeing Eloe, Son "joined that great underclass of undocumented men" (166) and relinquished the need for a fixed identity. According to Morrison, "What distinguished them from other men (aside from their terror of Social Security cards and *cédula de identidad*) was their refusal to equate work with life and an inability to stay anywhere for long." Searching for some other way of being, Son forgoes a stable life, works as an unlicensed crewman on ships, and consorts with gamblers, gigolos, and part-time mercenaries. He also carries no official documentation because he imagines his life free of mainstream trappings. Added to that is Son's suspicion regarding the changes taking place in American culture, which he reads about in *Time* magazine and the international press. Ironically, though, even in the middle of the ocean among men like himself, somehow he comes across as tainted by mainstream impulses. For example, when Son, the Swede, and the Mexican decide to fish snapper from the bow of the ship, Son becomes frantic and overeager. Morrison writes, "if he was punching dying fish in anger, if he was pricked to fury by the outrageous claim of a snapper on its own life, stunned by its refusal to cooperate with his hook, to want, goddamn it, to surrender itself for his pleasure, then perhaps he was *cierto Americano* and it was time to go home" (167).

Notions of fraternity also make up the group constraints Son faces in *Tar Baby*. While he sees himself as a unilateral individual in many ways, Son cannot "give up the last thing left to him—fraternity" (168). He enjoys a sense of fraternity with the Swede and the Mexican, but his unwillingness to dispense with this elemental pleasure in life stems from his relationships in Eloe. When Son tells Jadine the entire story of his original dime, he talks about being hired by Frisco to clean fish. Son remarks, "Nothing I ever earned since was like that dime" (169). As he extols the simplicity of the whole process, Son reveals that the meaning he attached to his dime was rooted in his interaction and bonding with Frisco. In fact, Son does not mince words when he tells Jadine that Frisco, who later died tragically in a gas explosion, was a womanizer who mistreated his wife. Yet upon learning the news, Son "left town crying like a baby" (170). His nostalgic recollection suggests that his emotion has more to do with the fraternal bond and friendship that he will never again have with Frisco than with the death of a former boss.

In examining Son's conception of fraternity it becomes clear that it is not his own creation, but that it is rooted in the folkways of Eloe. Son returns to visit Eloe with Jadine when he learns that his father, Old Man, and three of his best friends, Drake, Soldier, and Ernie Paul, still reside there. Something Jadine notices is that Son and his friends seem to have their own language when they gather to catch up. Then, alongside his friends, Son visits a local night joint, decides to stay in Eloe a while longer, and promises to meet Jadine back in New York. Besides the cordial nature of their reunion, Jadine's conversation with Soldier captures just how fraternity gets defined in Eloe: "'Who's controlling it?' 'Controlling what?' 'The thing. The thing between you two. Who's in control?' 'Nobody. We're together. Nobody controls anybody,' she said. 'Good,' he said. 'That's real good. Son, he don't like control. Makes him, you know wildlike'" (255). This passage conveys the sense that Soldier's words, however presumptuous, have import not only for Son's relationship with Jadine but also Son's personal tendencies and blind spots when it comes to control. While there exists among Son and his ilk an unbreakable bond, it is not one built on controlling or guilting members of the group into staying fixed in a particular cultural context. The novel suggests that, in Eloe, fraternity is both profound and shallow, but, ironically, this is what enables it to constrain Son. He is free to leave the group, travel, drift, find himself, or run away from himself outside of Eloe, but his psyche has been seared with the ideal of "simple and personal" fraternity. This strains his ability to embrace either a life devoid of attachments or to invest in romantic relationships based on the complexities of love and partnership.

Toward the end of the novel, Son has a conversation with Gideon (who is also known as Yardman and does odd jobs for the Streets) about moving beyond "the man who prized fraternity" (205) to a man who might ask himself: "what was he doing thinking that Drake and Soldier and Ernie Paul were more precious than Catherine the Great's earrings . . ." (299). In this scene, Son recalls a playful and awkward exchange between himself and Jadine and weighs it against fraternity with his friends: "So he had changed, given up fraternity, or believed he had." This short-lived attempt comes to a halt when he becomes stunned (similar to Jadine's encounter with the woman in yellow) by the site of Alma Estée, a domestic worker in the Street household, wearing a red wig that "mocked and destroyed" her innocent face. When Alma Estée howled and resisted his attempt to remove the wig, "It was all mixed up. He did not know what to think or feel. The dizziness increased and played a middle ear drone in his head." This incident indicates that Son's first and second inclination is to grope toward fraternity. If not simply based on social familiarity, perhaps the next best thing for Son will be to create fraternity with Gideon through paternalistic means—using Alma Estée as a spur-of-the-moment project. While Son's patriarchal impulse here is based on genuine opposition to American accessories that have the power to define ideas about beauty overseas, it is shortsighted. Similarly, the volume of stock he puts into fraternity restricts his capacity to find another way to *be* in a complex world.

The Post–Civil Rights Domain: The Street Household

In *Tar Baby*, Morrison fashions a post–civil rights era devoid of overt political protest or the kind of racial vying for inclusion found in *The Intuitionist*. In one sense, Whitehead's novel wants to imagine a future world in which textured debates (the kind on display between Jadine, Son, and others) about black experience as something complex and not always in contention with mainstream elements would be commonplace. Implications for the post–civil rights era play out in the tenor of cultural and ideological battles among African Americans that can be read as holdovers from the 1950s and 1960s. The spirit of this political reality exists as backdrop in *Tar Baby*. In this context, Morrison's protagonists must articulate new and more personal methods of resistance, at once made possible and compromised by integration, civil rights struggle, and nationalist philosophy.

Because Morrison's aesthetic moves lend themselves to a number of readings, Marc Bonner, in *The Aesthetics of Toni Morrison,* interprets her writing through the lens of Western philosophical practice. Prior to exploring Morrison's use of classical aesthetic concepts, Bonner comments on the tendency "to focus exclusively on the political, cultural, racial elements" (xiii) in her oeuvre. His analysis compels a conversation about the illuminating act of reading Morrison's impulse to portray distinct socialized experiences and "to strip away the illusions to show why African-American life remains to many an embattled existence, and to minister to a beleaguered population . . ." (xxiv). In particular, Morrison's post–civil rights context assists her in fleshing out some of the neglected or glossed-over cultural tensions from past eras.

A number of tensions whether in terms of culture, ideology, or family surface in the novel's Caribbean sites, namely, the island of Dominique and L'Arbe de la Croix, the Street estate. In many ways, the home in which Valerian has chosen to live out his retirement is a site of contestation. His authority as a wealthy white patriarch is subtly, but frequently, called into question. Valerian not only has strained relations with Margaret but also with Ondine and Sydney. As denizens of the post–civil rights generation, when Jadine and Son come into the picture, they become catalysts for the hashing out of unaddressed sociocultural problems.

One post–civil rights concern in the novel has to do with the ways Jadine, as an adopted child, constructs her racial identity in the Street household. An independent thinker, Jadine is unsure about her surroundings, life choices, and family ties. Moreover, she struggles to accept her life as a departure from her aunt and uncle's domestic-worker status. As someone whose tastes and lifestyle do not subscribe to an essentialist notion of black womanhood, Morrison tasks Jadine with working through a racial identity crisis. Jadine begins this process of coming to grips with her identity after seeing a striking, dark-skinned woman in a yellow dress. After the encounter, Jadine not only questions the posh world of international modeling but also her place of privilege in the home of a wealthy white man. For Jadine, the tension at first revolves around validating her lived experience as authentically black. But this becomes a vexed endeavor, particularly because of her involvement with Son, who holds uncompromising, and near fundamentalist, views about race.

In one instance, Son asks Jadine a profane question about her time in Europe. A struggle ensues between the two of them, and, when Jadine warns Son what will happen if he rapes her, he taunts her: "Why you little white girls always think somebody's trying to rape you?" (121). The question enrages Jadine: "I am going to kill you. For that alone. Just for that. For pulling that black-woman-white-woman shit on me. Never mind the rest" (121). Working through a crisis of confidence centered on moving through the world as a black woman (brought on not only by the opportunities given to her but also the unfortunate circumstances surrounding her childhood), Jadine defuses Son's comments by deeming him uncivilized.

Jadine further questions Son's racial politics by appropriating Sydney's initial reaction to Son slipping into the house unnoticed: "Sydney was right. He should have shot you on the spot. But no. A white man thought you were a human being and should be treated like one" (121). In this passage, Jadine dehumanizes Son in a way that pits the tenor of his blackness against Sydney's. Interestingly, the novel mentions that Jadine has not seen a black man with whom she could associate southern black culture in ten years, and her New York entourage includes effete, apolitical black men who stand in stark contrast to Son. Her friends concern themselves with "making it" more than with racial consciousness. To be sure, Jadine's perspective on Son grows out of a context most identifiable with the post–civil rights era—an era in which she cannot place him. Son exists as an anachronism from an age of de jure racial exclusion and wholesale discrimination against blacks.

A second racialized encounter occurs between Jadine and Son, but this one happens after they have become lovers. In this situation, Son uses knowledge of Jadine's engagement to a white Frenchman both to demean and to cast her as a mammy figure thwarted at every turn from making choices that do not center on caring for whites or their children. Son says, "People don't mix races; they abandon them or pick them. But I want to tell you something; if you have a white man's baby, you have *chosen* to be just another mammy . . ." (270). This time Jadine does not respond in kind but rather denigrates him with subtlety and then, with little fanfare, decides to leave him. For Jadine, "Aloneness tasted good and even at a table set for four she was grateful to be far away from his original-dime ways, his white-folks-black-folks primitivism. How could she make a life with a cultural throwback, she asked herself, and answered No way" (275). Embracing the post–civil rights era as a time of bringing broader views of black life into focus, Jadine decides to lean on her education and comprehend the world as she understands it, to learn how to be the kind of woman she has been all her adult life. In short, she refuses to measure up to notions of black womanhood represented by the women of Eloe to whom the children are shunted off or by Ondine who prides herself on enduring years of domestic work. The post–civil rights era affords Jadine a vantage point that eclipses self-sacrifice and sidesteps repressive traditions.

Sydney broaches an interesting post–civil rights debate when he deploys class and respectability politics. When Son appears at L'Arbe de la Croix, Sydney reels from the shock of holding a pistol to the head of a stranger and then is taken aback when Valerian asks him to show Son to a guest room. At the outset, Sydney regards Son's social status as inferior to his own. Even Ondine reinforces the idea that "The man upstairs wasn't a Negro—meaning one of them. He was a stranger" (102). In this way, they pathologize Son as a racial and social other, someone far removed from their cultural sphere. When Son later explains why he hid inside their home for a time without revealing himself, Sydney declares, "I know you but you don't know me. I am a Phil-a-delphia Negro mentioned in the book of the very same name. My people owned drugstores and taught school while yours were still cutting their faces open so as to be able to tell one of you from the other. And if you looking to lounge here and live off the fat of the land, and if you think I'm going to wait on you, think twice!" (163).

Interestingly enough, Sydney signifies on W. E. B. Du Bois's *The Philadelphia Negro* (1899), a sociological text in which Du Bois himself places little emphasis on the ways in which working-class and poor blacks negotiate class hierarchies and varied social contexts. Readers can neither situate Son into the primitive barbarism Sydney ascribes to him, nor can they assign to him the sophistication of Philadelphia Negroes. In fact, though identified as southern, Morrison does not fix Son's background or character geographically. Instead, she makes him adaptive to various environments and contexts. What makes the struggle over class in the post–civil rights era unique, as evidenced in the novel, is that the conversation has moved beyond black access to upward mobility to the complexities of class identifiers like ostensibly respectable behavior. Because Son does not hold himself to a particular mode of decorum, Sydney deems him the type of black person whose fate is to identify with the unwashed masses of a black underclass.

Amid class tension, Morrison brings issues of parity to the forefront as Son comes to understand Sydney and Ondine—and vice-versa. At one point, Son visits Sydney and Ondine's apartment in the rear of L'Arbe de la Croix to apologize. He explains that he does not own any identification and will leave when Valerian secures papers for him. Then Son plays the role of remorseful reprobate to win over Sydney. He calls him "Mr. Childs" and feigns appreciation for Valerian's largess. But ultimately Son asserts himself as equal to both the black and the white residents of the Street home at Christmas dinner. At dinner, he openly questions Valerian's bias in firing Gideon and Marie "Thérèse" Foucault for stealing apples. Further, to Valerian's chagrin, Son refuses to leave when he orders him to do so, and, instead, triggers an airing of unspoken grievances (and grudges) from Sydney and Ondine. The site of the Christmas dinner controversy is similar to the Long Island cotillion depicted in *The Cotillion* where white debutantes and their escorts assert their privilege to debauch the evening into a melee. Class comportment and posh behavior get cast aside as the reality of racial diversity among the white bourgeoisie devolves into the oppressive ingratiating of white liberals, the predictable microaggressions aimed at Yoruba, and a brazen invitation for Lumumba to fulfill racist sexual fantasies.

The urge prevalent in WASP culture to run roughshod over minoritized others in *The Cotillion* is checkmated before it starts in *Tar Baby*. Son's critique proves to be the kind that could not be adequately unearthed during previous eras, in which racial hierarchy was so entrenched. A poor and admittedly homeless black man not only declaring himself to be on a level playing field with the black middle class and with privileged whites but also having the audacity to find nothing untoward in taking such a stance would have found his position precarious at best. Son's ability to communicate across cultural experiences fuels his actions. While on the island, he becomes familiar with the abiding folklore, the perspectives of its Haitian immigrants, and the strivings of its indigenous inhabitants. Son's post–civil rights perspective does not so much represent the defiance of either Sydney or Valerian as it conveys his awareness that neither of them is outside the orbit of the hard-won progress made by the disenfranchised and downtrodden.

Spotlighting the privilege enjoyed by white women and the continued sidelining of black women, Morrison addresses a post–civil rights tension held over from a time devoid of equal opportunity for blacks. As everyone reacts to Son's brazenness during Christmas dinner, Ondine finds herself wrestling with a moral dilemma. Most acutely, she harbors a deep distrust of Valerian's wife, Margaret, even though commonalities exist between them. For instance, Margaret married Valerian at the age of seventeen. Ondine also became a young wife and entered the Street household at twenty-three. Though at first cautious of each other, the two found a mutual interest in the "Search for Tomorrow" radio soap opera. However, Valerian reinstalled the dividing line by admonishing Margaret that "she should guide the servants, not consort with them" (59). In the midst of her ensuing isolation, Margaret abuses their son Michael. Ondine's knowledge of the abuse has loomed over her fragile relationship with Margaret for years.

Ultimately, Ondine decides to challenge Margaret's impunity because she comes to view her own silence as a kind of acquiescence, as a hindrance to her own autonomy in light of shifting social tides in the Street household. To Ondine, it is her duty to explode the mythical status of pure white womanhood bestowed upon Margaret by Valerian. While Valerian is a key player in this saga, Ondine and Margaret misdirect their anger toward each other. During Christmas dinner: "The real target, who would not be riled until now when she got fed up with the name-calling and shot her water glass across the table. 'Don't you come near me!' Margaret shouted, but Ondine did and with the back of her hand slapped Margaret across the face" (208). When Ondine lashes out at Margaret over her child abuse, she is retaliating against a system of racial backlash that denies her the right to enjoy, and to outright own, the comforts and privilege for which she has worked. True, Ondine has resided in the lavish Street manor, but she has done so as a subordinate, not as an equal. This repressive hierarchal system, even in the post–civil rights era, paints a dividing line between a black maid and a white wife who has done little more than inhabit the role of trophy wife.

By voicing past anxiety, Ondine releases the burden she has endured for years. Suppressing her moral instincts, Ondine protected her family and employment by not revealing Margaret's abuse. Now, Ondine discloses to everyone that she was the sole person to come to Michael's rescue. During the scuffle, Margaret speaks her pain, thanks Ondine, and begs her forgiveness. But this time Ondine rejects the burden of forgiving Margaret and responds with an imperative: "You forgive you. Don't ask for more" (241). In spite of their uncertain futures, Ondine finds agency in serving herself—in relieving herself of the burdens imposed upon her by the Streets.

Although Ondine chooses to continue working for the Streets, she does so in a different frame of mind under the aegis of a post–civil rights era outlook that literally destabilizes patriarchy (Valerian has a stroke after hearing the news) and that opens the door for discussion between Ondine and Sydney about the toll their labor has taken on them. Jadine and Son help to create the conditions for Ondine's paradigmatic shift. Generationally removed from a time overshadowed by racial proscription, Jadine and Son inhabit a world where they find the freedom and mobility to critique the society that affords them tortuous journeys toward self-determination. Apprehending life in a way that their older counterparts cannot, their critical energy spreads through L'Arbe de la Croix and enables Ondine in particular to muster the willingness to overtly resist the repressive system in place. Perhaps in keeping with the times, to a certain extent Ondine opens the door to new subjectivities that can reign even in an atmosphere which marginalizes opposing and contentious points of view.

Gender and Will

In *Tar Baby*, Morrison highlights barriers to gender equity. As it concerns women in the novel, many occupy marginal roles as menial laborers and caregivers. Others never gain access to a platform from which to voice their realities. For example, Margaret's wishes have been subordinated to Valerian's; Ondine serves as Valerian's maid; Gideon and Thérèse are fired for stealing apples; and Alma Estée along with the multiple Marys mentioned in the novel exist in a kind of exploitive anonymity. In this context, Jadine comes to act as a kind of Everywoman, articulating the complacencies and anxieties of women. Maneuvering through multiple social contexts grants Jadine the opportunity not only to speak her truth but also to perhaps expound upon the truths of other women with whom she has shared confidences. However, Morrison does not impose this task on Jadine. Instead, throughout the novel Jadine works to avoid absorbing the perceptions of other women. For instance, Jadine's gaze *others* the black woman in yellow without regard to what lessons about self-identity she might learn from her in that moment. In Eloe, it galls Jadine to spend time with the rural women there "who looked at her with outright admiration . . ." (250). She can only bring herself to communicate with Soldier's wife Ellen for ten minutes and feels vulnerable and exposed in the company of Rosa (Son's aunt). Lastly, Jadine disrespects Ondine by refusing to entertain messages about womanhood from the very woman who raised her.

In regard to Jadine's interactions with male characters, Morrison links gender issues to attempts by men to either deny the strength of Jadine's will or to rein it in. Along with the disturbing physical violence that mars Jadine's and Son's brief relationship, Son does a kind of violence to Jadine's penchant for survival. When Son and Jadine move to New York, Son thinks, "But underneath her efficiency and know-it-all sass were wind chimes. Nine rectangles of crystal, rain bowed in the light. Fragile pieces of glass tinkling as long as the breeze was gentle. But in more vigorous weather the thread that held it together would snap" (221). Despite the sexist assertion from Son that he would have to essentially protect Jadine from the weather (read: life's headwinds), the same thinking that allows him to project his anxieties onto her is present earlier in the novel when he stares at her sleeping body for hours, prior to anyone learning he was squatting in the house. Son attempted to "insert his own dreams into her so she would not wake or stir or turn over on her stomach but would lie still and dream steadily the dreams he wanted her to have . . ." (119). Though many of Son's anxieties have been externalized and have gone unspoken, when they emerge, Jadine subordinates them with pragmatism and a sense of confidence in her capabilities. Even when Son disparages her education because it was funded by Valerian, and because "whatever you learned in those colleges that didn't include me ain't shit" (264), she contrasts his retreat from modern life with her ample preparation for it: "I was being educated, I was working, I was making something out of my life. I was learning how to make it in *this* world. The one we live in, not the one in your head." Ultimately, Jadine distances herself from Son's mingling of anxiety and insult with the resolve to confront a menacing world and all its contradictions.

Even as sexist and retrogressive narratives challenge Jadine, her convictions enable her to repel such notions. To delineate one narrative, I offer a surface reading of Soldier's dialogue with Jadine about control. While Soldier's assumptions about control ("Who's controlling it?") contrast with Jadine's pragmatic ideas about relationships, he rehearses an interesting binary. To his essentialist thinking, either Son will dominate their relationship or she will. While Jadine could dismiss his questions as narrow-minded and fatuous, the realization that she cannot easily describe her and Son's relationship unsettles her. She finds her own hard-fought notions in competition with Eloe's southern bias toward a balance of power that favors men. In light of this bias, Jadine becomes well aware she cannot assume that Son shares her fluid sense of how a relationship might offer a level playing field for both of them. Jadine's encounter with Soldier is more than an innocuous, if provocative, question; rather, he is articulating for Jadine a notion of masculinity that consistently angles for control and despises sharing power in any partnership outside of one based on fraternity with like-minded males. In short, Soldier's message is that Son's past behavior will dictate his current and future behavior. Rather than dismiss Soldier's judgment outright, Jadine listens. In a final encounter with Son, she realized that Soldier's admonition had played itself out in their relationship. Admitting her efforts to persuade Son to improve his life, Jadine changes course and offers an aphorism, which takes a wider perspective on their relationship to each other and to society. Jadine tells Son, "There is nothing any of us can do about the past but make our own lives better. . . . That is the only revenge, for us to get over. *Way* over" (271).

In contrast to the swirl of masculine notions in Eloe, with which Son identifies, Jadine's convictions about black womanhood clash with the cultural lore of Dominique. Gideon recounts one of the island's timeworn folk narratives. Three hundred years ago, enslaved people (all men) aboard a sinking French vessel turned blind the moment they saw the island of Dominique. Seeing with the eyes of their minds, the men swam ashore along with the surviving horses and inhabited the island hills. According to Gideon, to this day "They ride those horses all over the hills. They learned to ride through the rain avoiding all sorts of trees and things. They race each other, and for sport they sleep with the swamp women in Sein de Veilles. Just before a storm you can hear them screwing way over here" (152–53).

Aside from the gender politics at play in Gideon's recounting, Jadine becomes familiar with the story by hearing it from one of Valerian's neighbors. Though she finds the idea that the blind race may still inhabit the island intriguing, Jadine cannot visualize one hundred blind men on horseback. She does however experience a chance encounter with the swamp women of whom Gideon speaks: "The women hanging from the trees. . . . [K]nowing their steady consistency, their pace of glaciers, their permanent embrace, they wondered at the girl's [Jadine's] desperate struggle down below to be free, to be something other than they were" (183). Accidentally, sinking into a mudhole in the Sein de Veilles swamp, Morrison couches Jadine's struggle in fighting terms that reflect an inward battle. In another instance, during her final night in Eloe, the night women "were all out to get her, tie her, bind her" in an attempt to lay claim to her in a dreamlike encounter (262). Accosting and tormenting her, Jadine believes that the night women want to choke out her sense of autonomy. Still, as a matter of sheer determination and stubbornness, she gives up "being the helpless victim of a dream" that she did not choose. Jadine stops fighting the night women and decides to live beholden to her own story, which, incipient though it may be, extends deep roots into her psyche.

Self-Renewal through Introspection

Tar Baby complicates the selfhood of its characters by disseminating a plethora of perspectives and convictions about life. As Anna Yeatman puts it in *Postmodern Revisionings of the Political*, "those of us who are attempting to work with, and out of, postmodern perspectives [must come to realize:] Acceptance of the reality of the postmodern condition means a relinquishing of a nostalgic holding on to modern(ist) standards of reflection and critique" (3). Enriching her perspective on African American experiences, Morrison takes a reflexive approach in the novel, which allows for an interrogation of the many truths that circulate in a postmodern moment. Ultimately, both the interplay of many meaningful convictions and truths about life and the contestation inspired by these ideas offers characters and opportunity for self-renewal and postmodern growth. Self-renewal is premised on the capacity to engage in postmodern introspection as well as to affirm one's suppositions and choices in the midst of disorientation and uncertainty.

One of the ways Morrison disseminates several perspectives and different ways of comprehending the world is through Valerian's son Michael, who holds postmodern views about connectedness. Though Michael has not visited in years (he is present in the novel only through flashback), Margaret naively expects him to come during the holidays. Meanwhile, Valerian scoffs about their son's eclectic lifestyle: "A band manager, shepherd, poet-in-residence, film producer, lifeguard ought to study law, the more environmental the better. An advantage really, since he's certainly had enough environments to choose from" (27–28). Even as Valerian describes Michael in postmodern terms, as occupying many subject positions, he interprets Michael's life as escapist because he lives an agrarian life, demonstrates solidarity with minority cultures, and embraces frugality. In addition, he has moved from anthropological work with several Native American tribes to numerous careers, but, despite criticism, his ideas have a lingering effect on members of the Street household. Ridiculing what he believes to be Michael's feelings about racial progress, Valerian opines, "I think he wanted me to string cowrie beads or sell Afro combs. The system was all fucked up he said and only a return to handicraft and barter could change it. That welfare mothers could do crafts, pottery, clothing in their homes, like the lace-makers of Belgium and *voila!* Dignity and no more welfare" (73). Even in his absence Morrison allows Michael's intellectual meanderings to become the catalyst for the eruption of deeply held opinions and beliefs.

Discussions of Michael's worldview are unavoidably fragmented. He is not the only character whose experiences are abbreviated in some way, but Morrison especially links the potency of his intellectual musings to the fragmentation inherent in post–civil rights society. While Michael's inability to focus on one cause or to fit one mold gets criticized, his wide-ranging interests are an oblique reflection of the profound grasping for meaning and wholeness in which each character, at some level, is engaged. Ultimately, the fragmentation dispersed throughout *Tar Baby*, which readers both experience and endure, signifies on the unavoidable shifts in social and cultural ground underneath the feet of the characters. Morrison's argument seems to be that the addressing of unheeded issues in the post–civil rights era creates an environment in which one's sense of wholeness is always weakening and eroding, making way for new ways of being.

Michael's views stir up convictions about black solidarity. For instance, when Valerian learns that Jadine is thinking about opening a retail business, he becomes concerned that Sydney and Ondine might leave his employment and join Jadine's venture. Valerian's and Margaret's biases are on display in their opposition to the very implications of black solidarity in their home. Ironically, Margaret and Valerian also judge the lack of racial solidarity they see among their workers. Margaret herself pushes Jadine toward "blackening up or universaling out . . ." (64), further muddling her racial consciousness. After he welcomes Son as a guest, Valerian has feelings of "[d]isappointment nudging contempt for the outrage Jade, Sydney, and Ondine exhibited in defending property and personnel that did not belong to them from a black man who was one of their own" (145). Whereas Valerian does not entertain any extensive conversation about his own racial bias, his thoughts imply that he views the blacks who reside in his home as on an equal social footing (as equally marginalized) with Son and the black islanders outside his home.

By having even Sydney and Ondine scrutinize Michael's ideas about race, Morrison opens the door for their postmodern introspection. Sydney and Ondine both utilize the uncritical thoughts and biased views circulating to build the sociocritical framework they need to question their subordination. Sydney labeled Michael a spoiled child because he does not focus on a single direction in life and Ondine deemed him a nuisance, hoping he would "stop coming in my kitchen to liberate me every minute" (36). However, while Michael's criticisms are paternalistic in nature—presuming that Sydney and Ondine could instantaneously make the privileged leap from working class to financial independence—in their current disorienting moment (brought on by Jadine and Son), it not in their interest to dismiss outright the issues Michael raises. The Christmas dinner fiasco provides the perfect inciting incident to compel them to spend time mulling over some of the matters Michael mentioned years ago. And the novel suggests that doing so may eventually redound to their advantage.

In a conversation not many days removed from Christmas dinner, Sydney and Ondine both acknowledge in their own way the aura of increasing knowledge and opportunity for black Americans characterizing the post–civil rights era: "It's more different for them than it was for us. There's a whole bunch of stuff they can do that we never knew nothing about. And a whole bunch they don't know nothing about,' he said" (283). The recognition of difference is significant because it comes on the heels of a heated exchange of ideas between Ondine and Jadine. Therefore, Jadine's opinions become one more set of ideas for them to personally reckon with. Further into the conversation, Ondine reminds Sydney, "This is not your property. . . ." Sydney replies, "No. but it's my home. If this ain't my home, then nothing is but the grave'" (284). This claiming of the Street home as his own is itself a postmodern notion. On his way to the greenhouse to bring Valerian lunch, Sydney begins seeing the place anew: "He noticed that the bricks that edged the courtyard were popping up out of the ground, leaning every which way. . . . 'This place dislocates everything,'" he says. At this point, Sydney and Ondine both feel a sense of dislocation even though they are literally occupying the same space.

Centralizing concerns about several inequities, Sydney and Ondine have a much-needed conversation about their future, their relationship with the Streets, and the prospect of having to fend for themselves economically as they age. For the first time, they consider their meager finances and their ability to find work should they leave the Streets' employment. The end result is their decision to be unself-conscious about their present and future. Even as they discuss death, a sense of renewal creeps in: "'I think we're going to have to bury ourselves, Sydney.' 'Well, in that case the shroud may as well be comfy.'" The anxiety around getting old that weighs on them early in the novel has diminished. If they are to survive in a time when "Old black people must be a worrisome thing to the young ones these days" (283), then they will have to remain open to further introspection regarding ideas that may alter even their newfound perceptions.

It is a fascinating turn of events that, as the two chat inside the greenhouse, Sydney offers Valerian the most postmodern way of rationalizing his muted feelings about leaving the island: "No reason to be anywhere . . ." (286). In the novel, Michael's postmodern philosophy calls for a rethinking of the capitalist system in which Valerian operates. His notions, however, do not offer a feasible alternative, prompting Valerian to decry them as "handicraft and barter." Morrison uses Michael's opinions on capitalism to create a much broader context around the impact of postmodern socioeconomic shifts. We witness the decline of industrial manufacturing as one facet of extensive economic disruption through Valerian, whose past life was spent as a candy businessman in Philadelphia. Valerian's departure from the candy industry brings several factors into focus. After his father's death, Valerian inherited the Street Brothers Candy Company at age seven. Then he immediately went under the tutelage of his uncles. Determined to retire before he became too "sentimental and not professional" (51), Valerian sold the candy factory to a conglomerate when he realized Michael would not take over. At sixty-eight he retired, but Morrison directs our attention to what Valerian considered his uncles' sentimental ways to understand his moves afterward.

Though Valerian describes his uncles' decision to sell Valerians (the candy named after Valerian) to a sizable black population in the South as sentimental, a racial animus exists in their practices, namely the exploitation of black labor. Not only do they make the product from the leftover "syrup sludge" of their number-one brand Teddy Boys, but also they plan to manufacture "Valerians in Mississippi where beet sugar was almost free and the labor too" (51). While Valerian thinks his retirement allows him to escape their ways, he himself seeks a paternalistic attachment to the black and minority inhabitants in Dominique, several of whom work for him.

Valerian purchases his home, L'Arbe de la Croix, and surrounds himself with a diversity that operates solely for the sake of his comfort. His home was designed by a Mexican architect and built by Haitian workers. He employs a Filipino boatman, an Algerian dentist, a mulatto landscaper, and Ondine and Sydney work as maid and butler. Morrison describes Valerian in methodical terms: "[H]e checked catalogs, brochures and entered into ringing correspondence with nurseries from Tokyo to Newburg, New York. He read only mail these days, having given up books because the language in them had changed so much—stained with rivulets of disorder and meaninglessness. He loved the greenhouse and the island, but not his neighbors" (14). Valerian wants relaxation and peace away from outsiders and the concerns he left behind on the U.S. mainland. The problem is that he attempts to avoid what he can neither control nor limit the scope of, namely encounters with the island's racial others and the postmodern sensibilities that have made their way to his home. Though inaccessible to him, Michael's philosophy would serve Valerian well in his effort to find perspective in the disorienting blow of learning that Michael suffered abuse at the hands of his wife.

In what accrues to the novel's sense of the postmodern, Valerian questions his state of being: "This is not life. This is some other thing. It comforted him a bit, knowing that whatever this was it was not life. He achieved a kind of blank, whited-out, no-feeling-at-all that he hoped would sustain him until the blood tears came. Until his heart, revivified, pumped its way along for a single purpose: to spill out his eyes throughout the millennia he would have to live" (234–35). In an interesting paradox, the passage suggests that Valerian's approach proves to be much more escapist than Michael's. The life that Valerian can no longer come to grips with had afforded him the privilege to divest the family business, marry a much younger beauty queen, and buy a private island on which to retire. In order to truly have avoided the so-called "sentimentality" of his uncles, Valerian could have embraced a social realm outside the purview of capitalism, been less methodical, and allowed exposure to the cultural difference surrounding him to aid him in introspection. Self-renewal, for Valerian, would be the achievement of a broad-minded worldview that might enable him to reach out to Michael, at some point over the years, on Michael's own terms.

Jadine's remembered experiences with Michael and her critique of his ideological leanings get to the heart of the identity concerns that precipitate her introspection. While Michael gets socialized in a world that privileges appearances over reality (Margaret abuses Michael right under Valerian's nose), the multiple epistemologies to which he later exposes himself represent a moving away from the capitalist legacy of his parents: "He was a poet, presumably, and a Socialist, so social awkwardness wouldn't trouble him the way it would have his father" (91). Through his solidarity with marginalized cultures, Michael dispenses with any simplistic notion of home. According to Jadine, Michael becomes a "cultural orphan" making "loving treks from ghetto to reservation to barrio to migrant farm . . ." (145). Significantly, Michael's and Jadine's quarrels represent the starting point of her misgivings about who she is as a black individual. Their debates over cultural matters also helped influence her arc toward personal truth and self-renewal and away from the need for validation. However, Jadine's ideas about race diverge from Michael's blinkered paternalism: "Actually, we didn't talk; we quarreled. About why I was studying art history at that snotty school instead of—I don't know what. Organizing or something. He said I was abandoning my history. My people. . . . But he did make me want me to apologize for what I was doing, what I felt" (74–75).

Jadine's process of rethinking her perceptions of family, career, and disabusing herself of the expectations she attaches to both is all-encompassing. Jadine is very much Yoruba Lovejoy's twenty-five-year-old doppelgänger. Similarly, Yoruba, who bore the weight of her mother's Brooklyn-high-society desires for her, felt the steady force of her father's practicality; and the tug of her feelings for Lumumba works to tread through the outsized influence of the voices in her life. When she returns to Dominique, Jadine does so, in part, to parse the many cultural perspectives and convictions that are espoused on the island. Balking at essentialist views on race, at home and abroad, Jadine dismisses any idea of either transcending race or owning it as some totalizing narrative. Instead, she comes to embrace her cultural convictions through the slippery prospect of dispensing with racial consciousness.

Numerous ideas about race, culture, and gender flow on Dominique by virtue of its culturally variegated makeup, particularly via folk tradition. However, because *Tar Baby* so thoroughly genders the folklore of Isle des Chevaliers—the story of the blind race of horse riders and swamp women—it offers little hope that Jadine will quell her feelings of inauthenticity and vulnerability through island lore. Cultural repositories in their own right, Thérèse and Gideon possess an organic understanding of the history of Dominique, but this epistemology becomes lost in translation when decoded for American tourists and other outsiders. It does not follow, then, that a connection to the island's mythic history will offer a guide to Jadine, who is contending with her past, present, and future.

One journey begins and another ends for Jadine when she rejects the need for discovering anything not already within her. In the interest of self-renewal, she gives up looking for "the center of the fear" that plagues her from the beginning of the novel. Instead, Jadine embraces her own complicated reality, where her conviction resides in her will to champion the prospect of an uncertain future. A postmodern subject, she neither requires a stabilizing narrative nor a clearly delineated attachment to the Streets, Sydney and Ondine, or Son. In some ways, Jadine appropriates the play-it-as-it-comes paradigm that Son began the novel with, and this cognitive reframe has immediate implications. In fact, the more Jadine engages in postmodern introspection, the more Morrison dissolves her social and familial attachments.

To isolate how this process unfolds, it is useful to revisit Jadine's tense conversation with Ondine. After the Christmas catastrophe, Jadine asks Ondine about the extent to which her and Sydney's relationship with the Streets has deteriorated. Despite the status of their situation, Jadine stands firm in her decision to leave everything behind and return to Paris. Morrison complicates Jadine's transgressive behavior here by pitting it against Ondine's beliefs about self-sacrifice. Ondine, who had effectively adopted and cared for Jadine, takes a mother's pride in her success. However, Ondine has assumed for years that Jadine would one day respond in kind and care for her and Sydney.

During their exchange, Ondine admonishes Jadine about the reciprocity of helping herself through others. According to Ondine, "What I want from you is what I want for you. I don't want you to care about me for my sake. I want you to care about me for yours'" (281). Nimble in her dialogue, Ondine's words articulate a generational way of conceptualizing family responsibility. But Jadine, very much a product of the post–civil rights era, can distance herself from obligations rooted in self-sacrificial notions. She acknowledges Ondine's convictions in their exchange but also inserts her own: "Your way is one, I guess it is, but it's not my way. I don't want to be . . . like you. Wait. Don't look at me like that. I'm being honest with you now and you have to listen! I don't want to learn how to be the kind of woman you're talking about because I don't want to be that kind of woman" (282). In this revealing moment, Jadine does not discount Ondine's truth. Instead, their dialogue signals Jadine's turn toward finding a personal sense of belonging by reclaiming an orphan identity and abandoning divisive conceptions of womanhood. Jadine comes to accept her own truth about the ambiguous path she will follow in life. In her mind, she has not rebelled against Ondine and Sydney's tenets but has chosen her own path and will not allow it to be seen as deviant. But nowhere in the novel does Jadine's reclamation completely free her from the ambivalence of her decision to return overseas. At best, she arrives at a place of fragile agency.

Given that Jadine frees herself from the will of others and declines to impose her will on others, she can enact a postmodern agenda removed from outmoded notions of traditional stability. In resituating Jadine as neither dissident nor obligated saver-of-the-downtrodden, but as a subject-in-transit, Morrison imbues her decision to leave the island with meaning. Jadine repurposes Ondine's argument as she entertains "[n]o more dreams of safety. No more. Perhaps that was the thing—the thing Ondine was saying. A grown woman did not need safety or its dreams. She was the safety she longed for" (290). At the end of the novel, Jadine spurns her previous expectations of returning home to the security of accommodating loved ones. Finding safety in herself, she neither fears the uncertainty of a fashion career nor a high-profile engagement, nor does she desire the solace of an island paradise.

Jadine's flight to Paris functions as a flight into the undefinable substance of lived reality, into fragmentation, not wholeness. As Jadine's plane leaves the tarmac, the novel describes her mindscape as the "stretch of fresh wings, the blinding anticipation and herself, there, airborne, suspended, open, trusting, frightened, determined, vulnerable—girlish, even, for an entire second and then another and another" (291). Jadine's achievement of self-renewal neither alleviates all her concerns nor diminishes her critical awareness—but it does poise her to endure life's headwinds and tailwinds. L'Arbe de La Croix had the effect of suppressing individual desires, making them incompatible with other circulating narratives and agendas. Jadine now has the space to think reflexively and imagine alternatives to Valerian's hierarchy and Ondine's impositions. Jadine's sensibilities fall in direct contrast to the unscrupulous norms of the Street household, which are passed off as universal givens.

The implications behind the flight are that Jadine has moved on from dreams of success, but there is an inherent contradiction in her decision to leave: "She had run away from New York City with the same speed she had run toward it" (288). Another quote records her perspective when she boards the plane. Jadine decides to "go back to Paris and begin at Go. Let loose the dogs, tangle with the woman in yellow—with her and with all the night women who had *looked* at her" (290). This passage is about relinquishing a false sense of control and either battling her demons or allowing them to roam unbound. The "dogs" are a reference to the volatility of New York; the woman in yellow is responsible for unsettling her racial sense of self, and the night women are perceptible hallucinations that accost Jadine in her dreams while in Eloe. While she has embarked on a postmodern path that embraces flux, Jadine's conspicuous manners on the plane seem to suggest that Paris, replete with as much uncertainty as New York, somehow holds more promise for the attainment of success. In particular, I am referring to the care with which she treats her sealskin coat while on the plane, folding it and resting it in the seat next to her. This coat, given to her by her former fiancé, becomes a type of armor for Jadine, which suggests she is not completely disabusing herself of the tenuous, if false, sense of shelter that had rendered her vulnerable. Without thoroughly shedding her deep-seated social and cultural assumptions (and equipping new ones), Jadine will be unprepared to weather the postmodern storms of alienation and disorientation that she will encounter in Paris.

Questions about the self tend to swirl around Son throughout *Tar Baby*. For example, when he jumps ship, he is looking for self-renewal, but what he stumbles upon is a confrontation with the self, with the assumptions and the beliefs he has heretofore held. As a squatter and guest, Son critiques the Street household from within and, in doing so, elicits outrage. Nonetheless, Morrison ties Son's unmaking process to his identification with those subordinated by social status outside the home. Ihab Hassan reads this process as a result of the influence of postmodern social phenomena, which reaches even the most hardened fugitives from modernity. In short, in a postmodern context, one's selfhood is always in question. In his unmaking, Son conceives of a symbiotic relationship with Gideon while staying with the Streets. As he watches Gideon working in the yard through a window, remembrances of his former life in Eloe move him to tears. Though surrounded by wealth, Son not only chooses to remain untainted by it but, also, this moment leads to his decision to oppose even the slightest whiff of upper-class bias in the Street home. While Valerian's servants reinforce his own authority, Son takes from the experience with the hierarchical structure at L'Arbe de la Croix the desire to live in the world differently. Throughout his nomadic journeys, Son's unpretentious disposition has not only granted him distance from privilege and power but also "Some other way of being in the world that he felt leaving him when he stood in the white towel watching Yardman's—Gideon's—back. But something had come loose in him, like the ball that looped around the roulette wheel, carried as much by its own weight as by the force of the wheel" (166). This passage highlights a point of renewal for Son in which he discards any norms or knowledge beyond what he feels viscerally. This approach serves him well with the Streets and in his relationship with Jadine, but if falters in New York when Son foregoes introspection.

In *Tar Baby*, Son operates as a knower—a strong, impassioned character, who through the vicissitudes of America's postmodern turn *and* his own choices (driving his car into his wife's bedroom, subsequent fugitive existence, and undocumented crewman status) develops germane wit and wisdom. Son unsettles, provokes, and quickens the anger of those around him, calling attention to the eight-hundred-pound gorillas of repression in the room, though not actually studying others' perceptions. Interestingly, a fear of otherness surfaces with his appearance at L'Arbe de la Croix. When Son greets Sydney at the dinner table, for the first time in his career, he drops a salad bowl and "barely made it to civility" (92). After Jadine calls Son uncivilized and inhuman, he grabs her fragrant body and says, "I smell you too" (122). Lastly, Son shatters Margaret's pride when he laughs at her irrational fear that he wants to rape her. Son's targets seem to be those who assume authority over him to some extent. And when those in authority ignore the views of the marginalized, Son voices their opinions and elevates their insight over and against advantaged perspectives. One such case is the deafening silence around race and class in the Street home, which Son packages in his rebuke of Valerian at Christmas dinner. Still, defending the most vulnerable does not inoculate him from past ordeals that thrust him into this space and time—and that still plague him. Adopting a postmodern approach does not mean that Son would need to process his past pain in any therapeutic sense, but it does mean that he could no longer run (or journey) away from it. Son's mission is to embrace the dizzying and disorienting substance of his past.

In the midst of Son's attempted unmaking of his erstwhile self, the postmodern hangs over his return stateside. Even before he travels to New York, Son begins to confront conformist pressures and to rethink his approach to life: "There was a future. A reason for hauling ass in the morning. No more moment to moment play-it-as-it-comes existence. That stomach required planning. Thinking through a move long before it was made" (219). Not only are these thoughts conflicted from the start, but they are short-lived. Not long after arriving in New York, Son clamps down on his opposition to futurity and, disillusioned by the crass materialism he sees, he comes to see the city as shallow and inadequate.

Morrison's message is clear regarding Son's unfortunate predicament. In order to achieve meaningful self-renewal, Son would need to locate some viable modus operandi within himself and within the complicated contexts of his life. Unfortunately, after a dispiriting breakup with Jadine, in his desperation Son returns to Dominique and chooses the mawkish sense of fraternity he relies on throughout the narrative, in lieu of introspection. He embraces Gideon's blind-horsemen narrative as the solution to his feelings of decenteredness. But to follow postmodern inclinations, an individual must understand truth and convictions as by-products of disparate and diverse experiences—and not always universally applicable. Son ends up blindly approaching the mythical hills of Isle des Chevaliers and running into the dark void: "the trees stepped back a bit as if to make the way easier for a certain kind of man" (306). At the end of the novel, Son's attempt to escape the chaotic present and retrieve a mythic past prevents him from actualizing his postmodern impulses.

In *Tar Baby*, Morrison's take on the post–civil rights era comes out of a dynamic in which characters, exposed to myriad perspectives and opinions (cultural, social, spiritual, or otherwise), engage in postmodern introspection and find self-renewal in their convictions. This dynamic contrasts with the tendency of individuals to retreat to personal truths during altercations when the viewpoints of others do not jibe with their own—or when they cannot square an opposing view with their perception of the world and their role within it. While Morrison's characters are no exception to this knee-jerk reaction, several of them at least strike out on unfamiliar life paths to explore larger notions. To one's benefit or detriment, such journeys take a toll, and, as individuals attempt to find themselves in the social and cultural throes of the post–civil rights age, self-renewal becomes crucial. As Jadine and Son leave behind uncertain pasts for uncertain futures, they upset the apple cart of family and friends, but what validates their journeys is the intentional embracing of life's contradictions and constants.

Morrison concerns herself with the recognition of different notions of personal truth and with different life choices. She presents "unsanctioned" life choices as acts of transgressive behavior for which one is marginalized by those closest to him or her. Son is cast aside by modern society for his crime and flouting of norms while Jadine is reproved and disregarded by her surrogate parents for daring to live for herself. Nevertheless, the kinds of choices *Tar Baby* spotlights embrace the social flux of postmodern culture. In other words, Morrison sets her characters on a course to master their own destinies, at once scrambling for control of their own lives while in need of stabilizing support. Ultimately, *Tar Baby* displays a range of critical inquiry where it concerns dodging repressing narratives and maneuvering through society.

The journey narrative in postmodern African American fiction is informed by the recourse of individuals to work out critically their own convictions about life. While the critical weight that the journey narrative carries appears to lessen as theories of postmodernism speak of cultural malaise and alienation, fictionalized black experiences are still a rich and critical fount. As sociological discourse begins to look at the African American literary canon, the portrayal of this kind of truth-claiming about self-renewal in postmodern society becomes a compelling path for writers to follow. Morrison's *Tar Baby* facilitates a cultural, political, and social convergence in which new perspectives are subject to emerge—truths yet bearing traces of group heritage but amenable to the individual psyche. It is the recognition of disparate assumptions and beliefs that fuels journeys toward introspection. Ultimately, Morrison distills issues of family obligation and societal change in a way that epitomizes the response of African American literature to post–civil rights era tensions. Moreover, in capturing the postmodern, *Tar Baby* opens conceptual windows through which to see a plurality of convictions as a complement to the exploration of black individuals.

African American literary portrayals of black social movements culminate in a sense of the contentious influence of a postmodern perspective. The authors in this study seem to suggest that conditions on the ground have been shaped by struggles at both ends of the group/mainstream American spectrum. The group narratives that hold sway over ambitious individuals cannot confine them forever. They clamber for a chance to take advantage of opportunities that seem innocuous but are racialized, gendered, and politicized. Unfortunately, mainstream opportunities are shaped by exploitive agendas designed with the goal in mind of wresting power away from upwardly mobile blacks and retaining it. Even so, the resistance theaters of integration, civil rights struggle, nationalism, and post–civil rights politics unearth and set the stage for a cultural politics attuned to compromised conditions. In short order, the postmodern emerges—this sensibility borne out of socioeconomic upheavals, fragmentations, and feelings of alienation. The authors seem to be saying that postmodern flux and instability are preferable to the modern stagnation and halting progress that has been represented across African American literature for far too long.

CONCLUSION

In her 1990 essay "Postmodern Blackness," bell hooks discusses the importance of black writers and critics leveraging the ideas of postmodernism to theorize about historical black experience. hooks is critical of exclusionary theories of postmodernism, which neglect insights from black cultural production on issues like master narratives, difference, and decenteredness. Comprehending the late twentieth century as a significant cultural moment, hooks writes: "To some extent ruptures, surfaces, contextuality, and a host of other happenings create gaps that make space for oppositional practices which no longer require intellectuals to be confined to narrow, separate spheres with no meaningful connection to the world of every day" (31). For hooks, postmodernists could conceptualize around marginalized writers and sociocultural concerns that have become particularly vexed since the sixties. While she is, in many ways, calling for an anti-essentialist critique of identity, which would serve to expand narrow notions of blackness, hooks also connects the dots between past black freedom struggles and the overdetermined circumstances in which black Americans find themselves today. In short, "Postmodern Blackness" helped set the tone for the need to theorize postmodern imaginaries and cultural politics that are germane to the lives of black individuals.

My discussion has turned on drawing attention to the cultural and social circumstances hooks frames. Specifically, I have highlighted both the constraining nature of group narratives and the prevailing exploitations in mainstream institutions that contour black life. Navigating this new terrain and maneuvering around its obstacles require that ambitious black individuals, who are intent on climbing the socioeconomic ladder, find strategic and nuanced ways to operate. These nuanced ways exist in the sphere of postmodern cultural politics, where one's chief aim becomes to divest self-defeating assumptions and fully engage the ethos of vulnerability, uncertainty, fragmentation, and exploitation that looms large in American society. Moreover, the possibility of achieving autonomy through postmodern politics hinges on one's capacity to accept ambivalence and ambiguity as features of our current reality.

The exploration of black social movements (including their contextual influence and lasting implications) in African American literature is significant because it offers a valuable corrective to dominant theories that *other* black historical experience. This literary project is also valuable because it continues the work of fleshing out the complexities of postmodern black cultural politics. Black writers have created an aesthetic discourse on black postmodernism that circumvents theory and, therefore, can be situated in outside intellectual spaces. Some of the latest debates about African American literature want to periodize away its sense of being a collective undertaking. While the very idea of a monolithic black experience has been thrown into crisis by legal reforms and socioeconomic shifts, one contradiction is that many creative writers still claim an investment in racial particularity. Ultimately, just as black writers have done retrospective exploration, our current historical moment necessitates critical thinking about the experience of living in the fraught world created by civil rights struggles.

In a cultural studies context, one thought has been that we are experiencing a post-racial moment in America, in which race can no longer be seen as the primary determining factor in one's success. In addition, assumptions about an age of post-blackness permeate today's intellectual discussions. Touré's *Who's Afraid of Post-blackness? What It Means to Be Black Now* argues that the possibilities for an individual to forge his or her own sense of black identity in this era are infinite. Rather than limit the breadth of blackness to collective notions, Touré views blackness as a vast and diverse, yet accessible, cultural legacy. Regarding post-blackness, Wahneema Lubiano has said, "One of the things I associate with what people are calling post-Black is the determination not to have history weigh on our individual shoulders as something that's only and always serious, right" (qtd. in Touré 59). At a time when black intellectuals are trying to account for the racialized logic baked into the contemporary era, having a framework through which to examine cultural phenomena becomes critical.

The post-racial narrative is too naive in its suggestion that the weakening of wholesale racism—in certain contexts—heralds a moment of transcendence for all minorities. This mantra operates under a simplistic conception of transcendence, which posits total overcoming as the only meaningful progress. The concept of post-blackness may be slightly more practical in that it signals new possibility in racial interplay, fragmented black experience, the withering of monolithic conceptions of identity. However, a postmodern perspective understands blackness as an atmospheric, which is why finding a place outside the orbit of blackness for black people is such a vexed undertaking. Whereas popular culture offers a space for this sort of maneuvering, in reality this kind of social positioning does not go uncontested by black men and women. Not even literature is willing to imagine a space devoid of the in-group social pressures that come with blackness. The group narratives and other self-selecting habits that were adopted and infused with fidelity over generations of racism have imbued blackness with resolve, albeit a splintered, uncertain, and complex resolve.

That said, in order for postmodernism to maintain its critical clout in the twenty-first century, black writers and critics must bring this inquiry to bear on the lived reality and cultural speculations (post-race, post-black) of black people. To do so, intellectuals will have to expose the modern underpinnings of these notions and observe and critique twenty-first-century social conditions. Michael Thomas's *Man Gone Down* is a recent example of a postmodern novel that makes such observations and addresses the social and cultural issues I have highlighted. Reminiscent of Ralph Ellison's unnamed protagonist in *Invisible Man,* Thomas's narrator accounts for constraining group narratives and exploitation in mainstream spaces through his experiences as an educated black man and a worker. Although the narrator grows up in an abusive home, his mother's ambition is for him to become educated—a path he sets out to follow by earning a scholarship to Harvard. The mother's resolve also shows up in her patronage of a black-owned superette in lieu of an Italian corner store, which seeds an awareness of race and the potential unequal treatment in the narrator, who is eyeballed by whites years later (seemingly out of both curiosity and suspicion) when he shops at swank markets. Exploitation in academia and in the freelance economy is not hard to come by for the narrator, who works irregular construction jobs and is a former English graduate student and lecturer. In a timely and significant move, Thomas mines the post-black era for its implications and impact on racial individualism. As with *Man Gone Down*, the degree to which recent African American novels function as a discourse on postmodern cultural politics has to do with writers' nuanced assessments of black lived reality.

If black men and women are to navigate the compromised conditions surrounding them, they will have to grasp the reality that postmodern black cultural politics are woven into the fabric of American society. Moreover, if we are to make this cultural resource intelligible to blacks inhabiting social worlds of dislocation and disorientation, then elevating the historical insights of African American literature is an apt place to start. bell hooks underscores the value of a postmodern perspective, which maps out the constraints and exploitations facing ordinary black individuals: "knowledge, especially that which enhances daily life and strengthens our capacity to survive, can be shared" (30).

NOTES

Introduction

1. As it concerns black politics in the late 1960s, civil rights struggles and nationalism involved a complex conditioning for African American and minority communities, which produced social transformations. However, Michael Omi and Howard Winant in *Racial Formation in the United States* have read the 1960s and 1970s as "a period of racial upsurge, failed consolidation, and reaction which . . . demonstrated the centrality of race in shaping American politics and culture" (5). They explore Harold Cruse's theories of cultural nationalism, which criticized the civil rights movement for proffering a liberal agenda of policy demands and lacking a cultural component. Cruse favored "the development of a culturally-based radical perspective" (41) and "stressed the importance of 'cultures of resistance' in unifying and promoting collective identity among the oppressed" (42).

2. For information on the seventies' impact on America, the sixties' interpretation of America, and an overview of the countercultural movements that held sway in the seventies, see Bruce Schulman's *The Seventies* and Edward Berkowitz's *Something Happened: A Political and Cultural Overview of the Seventies*.

3. McGowan "insist[s] that significant individual differences are possible and can be preserved only within a social whole that *recognizes* such differences and contains norms and institutions empowered to protect them" (15). As McGowan explains, freedom belongs to the individual and, if an open future can exist, it can only do so to the extent that human diversity and creativity are given liberty.

4. See Cornel West's "Postmodernity and Afro-America" (168–70) and bell hooks's "Postmodern Blackness" (24–29).

5. See Phillip Harper's *Framing the Margins* (12–13), Madhu Dubey's *Signs and Cities* (40), and W. Lawrence Hogue's *Race, Modernity, Postmodernity* (16–25) and *The African American Male, Writing and Difference* (18–19).

6. According to John N. Duvall, "History is unquestionably one of the most contentious areas of debate among those concerned with postmodernism" ("Troping History" 1). While Duvall critiques Jameson's and Hutcheon's accounts of history in postmodernism for preferring high-cultural artifacts and drawing from architectural history to discuss aesthetic production, respectively, he does see their views as a "useful starting point for thinking about contemporary representation" (20).

7. While it is true that theoretical tropes and concepts generally register some sort of sociocultural complement (usually charting aesthetic, intellectual, and political epochs), Mike Featherstone has remarked that, "[w]hen terminology shifts, it is possible to see this reanimating process as a strategic move in the field of academic and intellectual cultural production. . . . A new generation of scholars can confine a previous one to history and make them appear outdated if they succeed in imposing a new, allegedly superior set of concepts" (148).

8. In *Yearning,* bell hooks remarks that the "overall impact of postmodernism is that many other groups now share with black folks a sense of deep alienation, despair, uncertainty, loss of a sense of grounding even if it is not informed by shared circumstance" (27). Similarly, Phillip Brian Harper investigates texts "predating the heyday of postmodernist culture and thus indicating the degree to which social marginality diverges from postmodernism, even when it apparently approximates and coincides with it" (*Framing the Margins* 19). One of the novels Harper discusses is Ralph Ellison's *Invisible Man,* which is an important precursor to the postmodern works in this study—in that it features near-endless unraveling, resistance, questioning, ambivalence, and renewal in its critiques of nationalist movements, communist ideology, and cultural revolt.

9. See Aldon Nielsen's *Black Chant* (4–37) and Andreas Huyssen's *After the Great Divide* (191–94).

10. bell hooks discusses this concept in her chapter titled "The Politics of Radical Black Subjectivity" in *Yearning.*

Chapter One

1. For instance, Hogue's *The African American Male* looks at the emergence of traditions that have been excluded from the pre-1960s uplift narratives and the 1970s–80s black aesthetic canons. Hogue suggests, "What is emerging is a polycentric reading of African American literature, allowing us to talk about differences within that literature" (50).q

2. For instance, see Isiah Lavender's *Race in American Science Fiction,* in which he suggests that Whitehead's ethnoscapes examine race and physical structure (165); Frankie Bailey's *African American Mystery Writers* looks at the ways Whitehead roots his geographical spaces in historically black conceptions of morality and social identity (108); Steven Belleto's *No Accident, Comrade* pegs *The Intuitionist* as an allegory of the relationship between individuals, state authority, and society (33, 80).

3. The notion of a future city that "will possess untold arms and a thousand eyes, mutability itself, constructed of as-yet unconjured plastics. It will float, fly, fall, have not need of steel

armature, have a liquid spine, no spine at all" (198) in *The Intuitionist* instantiates an example of the ontological play Brian McHale associates with postmodernist fiction. For McHale, the ontological dominant governs postmodernist fiction as it draws from the fantastic.

4. Pompey's story scene is an allusion to Richard Wright's *Black Boy*. See Saundra Liggins's "The Urban Gothic Vision of Colson Whitehead's *The Intuitionist*," 359–69.

5. Antonio Gramsci's "Hegemony" fleshes out his concept of social power with the notion of hegemony. Gramsci is concerned with how and why the elite maintain power over the dominated without force. For Gramsci, while the consent of the dominated comes through socialization and education, he finds consent bound up in the relationship between intellectuals and the world of production. Gramsci understands the "intellectual [and cultural] strata and their degree of connection with a fundamental social group, and to establish a gradation of their functions and of the superstructures from the bottom to the top" (673).

6. Qtd. in Hakutani and Butler, *The City in African American Literature*, 10–11.

7. In Cornel West's 1990 essay "The New Cultural Politics of Difference," cultural politics hinges upon the demystification of institutional power structures. Therefore, West calls for a move from "homogeneous communalism," which thrives in sameness (28). In the late twentieth century, there is a sense that people must challenge the status quo, lest our current dilemmas escalate. In that respect, the new cultural politics of difference faces challenges in subverting the concentrated power we see portrayed in *The Intuitionist* with the elevator industry.

8. In *Black Feminist Thought*, Patricia Hill Collins writes that "Black women's persistence is fostered by the strong belief that to be Black and female is worthy of respect" (120). Whitehead has Lila Mae's own social development reflect this sentiment. Her nurturing comes from the influence of strong black women like Fanny Briggs, a brave enslaved African in the novel who teaches herself to read and whose name graces a municipal building.

9. Whitehead signifies on the words of Jim Trueblood's character in Ralph Ellison's *Invisible Man* regarding Trueblood's ability to escape punishment for the crime of incest. In a similar vein, Fulton wants to move unfettered by race in the elevator world, which he implies through an extended metaphor about elevators.

10. Jeanne Rosier Smith's *Writing Tricksters* sees the "trickster, who embodies a divided, fluid, shifting identity, as a mythic trope for the postmodern" (16).

Chapter Two

1. In *Black Feminist Cultural Criticism,* Jacqueline Bobo considers the creativity of black women and emphasizes the merits of analyzing the artistic output of black women in academe, according to its historical and political dimensions and other criteria. Stanlie M. James, Frances Smith Foster, and Beverly Guy-Sheftall, the editors of *Still Brave,* pay homage to the development and significance of black women's studies. Born of much intellectual and social striving, the program challenges "disciplines such as history, art history, sociology, and literary studies to acknowledge and seriously address the intersectionality of identity" (xxiii).

2. Through the positing of a cultural spirit, the establishment of a historically symbolic grammar of folk cultural terms, the articulation of a return to communal consciousness and

language, and the affirmation of a folk cultural and spiritual matrix that resists the interests of domination, Walker's fiction resonates broadly. Marjorie Pryse and Hortense J. Spillers's *Conjuring*, Debra King's *Deep Talk*, Houston Baker's *Workings of the Spirit*, and Susan Willis's *Specifying* all explore Walker's spirit motif in some manner.

3. Walker coins this term, which she sees as more germane to the challenges black women face (as distinguished from white feminist perspectives), in her collection *In Search of Our Mother's Gardens* and describes it as "referring to outrageous, audacious, courageous or willful behavior" and "Commitment to survival and wholeness of entire people, male *and* female" (xi).

4. See "The Self in Bloom: Alice Walker's Meridian" 168.

5. "A Matter of Focus: Men in the Margins of Alice Walker's Fiction," by Erna Kelly, gives insight into Walker's penchant for othering her male characters and making them brutal and self-indulgent. Kelly sees Walker moving away from this trend in *Meridian* and entertaining wholeness and healing for all.

6. Lois Holzman and John R. Moss, the editors of *Postmodern Psychologies*, draw a distinction between reflexivity and critical reflection, the former having more to do with a contemplative effort and interiority, and the latter "an active rebellious practice that drives the individual into action as he or she identifies the exercise of power that pins him or her into place and the fault lines for the production of spaces of resistance" (42).

7. Deborah McDowell argues that Walker engages the tensions of black womanhood and self-discovery. Walker explores "universal concerns about individual autonomy, self-reliance, and self-realization. In addition, she weaves these issues into her Bildungsroman in a way that allows the title character of *Meridian* to achieve wholeness in the face of fragmentation" ("The Self In Bloom" 168).

Chapter Three

1. The phrase "law-and-order" is a reference to the conservative political ideology espoused by Richard Nixon in his 1968 Republican presidential nomination speech and, subsequently, in his approach to criminal justice as president.

2. Andreas Huyssen in "The Search for Tradition: Avant-garde and Postmodernism in the 1970s" paints a picture of 1970s culture in the United States as fighting "tradition, and this revolt took place at a time of political and social turmoil" (*After the Great Divide* 223).

3. See Daryl Dickson-Carr, *African American Satire* (143–46); William L. Van Deburg, *New Day in Babylon* (96, 273); Alan Wald, *Trinity of Passion* (62); and Sasha Torres, ed., *Living Color* (70).

4. Chantal Mouffe highlights the ideological politics operative in the concept of tradition in postmodern culture: "Tradition allows us to think our own insertion into historicity, the fact that we are constructed as subjects through a series of already existing discourses, and that it is through this tradition which forms us that the world is given to us and all political action made possible" ("Radical Democracy" 39).

5. As it concerns black church politics, Charles Eric Lincoln's and Lawrence H. Mamiya's 1990 study *The Black Church in the African American Experience* remarks on a political proposition: "As the primary social and cultural institution, the Black Church is deeply embedded in black culture in general so that the sphere of politics in the African American community cannot be easily separated from it" (234).

Chapter Four

1. See *The Complete Tales of Uncle Remus* by Joel Chandler Harris for the commonly referenced text of the tar baby story. For further cultural and historical contextualization of the tale, see *African American Folktales: Stories from Black Traditions in the New World* by Roger Abrahams.

2. The designation "Post–Civil Rights Era" largely refers to the time since the passing of the Civil Rights Act of 1964.

3. John Duvall's *The Identifying Fictions of Toni Morrison* cites her complex representation of blackness and questioning of subjectivity (15, 17). Linden Peach, in his *Toni Morrison*, points out the intersection between black cultural legacy and moral responsibility (2, 6). Lastly, Thomas Hove's essay "Toni Morrison" looks at Morrison's attention to the construction of meaning among marginalized populations.

4. Cribbing from this concept from Immanuel Kant, Lyotard's *The Postmodern Condition* describes the sublime. For Lyotard, "We can conceive the infinitely great, the infinitely powerful, but every presentation of an object destined to 'make visible' this absolute greatness or power appears to us painfully inadequate" (78).

WORKS CITED

Abrahams, Roger. *African American Folktales: Stories from Black Traditions in the New World*. New York: Pantheon, 1999. Print.

Anderson, Perry. *The Origins of Postmodernity*. New York: Verso, 2002. Print.

Andrews, Marcellus. *The Political Economy of Hope and Fear: Capitalism and the Black Condition in America*. New York: New York University Press, 1999. Print.

Bailey, Frankie Y. *African American Mystery Writers: A Historical and Thematic Study*. Jefferson, N.C.: McFarland, 2008. Print.

Baker, Houston, Jr. *Workings of the Spirit: The Poetics of Afro-American Women's Writing*. Chicago: University of Chicago Press, 1991. Print.

Bakhtin, Mikhail. "Rabelais and His World." *Literary Theory: An Anthology*. Ed. Julie Rivkin and Michael Ryan. Oxford, U.K.: Blackwell, 1998. 686–92. Print.

Bambara, Toni Cade. *The Salt Eaters*. New York: Vintage Books, 1980. Print.

Banner-Haley, Charles T. *The Fruits of Integration: Black Middle-Class Ideology and Culture, 1960–1990*. Jackson: University Press of Mississippi, 1994. Print.

Barry, Andrew. *Political Machines: Governing a Technological Society*. New York: Athlone Press, 2001. Print.

Bates, Gerri. *Alice Walker: A Critical Companion*. Westport, Conn.: Greenwood Press, 2005. Print.

Battle, Juan, and Sandra L. Burns, eds. *Black Sexualities: Probing Powers, Passions, Practices, and Policies*. New Brunswick, N.J.: Rutgers University Press, 2010. Print.

Bell, Bernard. *The Contemporary African American Novel: Its Folk Roots and Modern Literary Branches*. Amherst: University of Massachusetts Press, 2004. Print.

Belleto, Steven. *No Accident, Comrade: Chance and Design in Cold War American Narratives*. New York: Oxford University Press, 2012. Print.

Berkowitz, Edward. D. *Something Happened: A Political and Cultural Overview of the Seventies*. New York: Columbia University Press, 2006. Print.

Binder, Amy. "Friend and Foe: Boundary Work and Collective Identity in the Afrocentric and Multicultural Curriculum Movements in American Public Education." *The Cultural Territories of Race: Black and White Boundaries*. Ed. Michele Lamont. Chicago: University of Chicago Press, 1999. 221–48. Print.

Bobo, Jacqueline, ed. *Black Feminist Cultural Criticism*. Malden, Mass.: Blackwell, 2001. Print.

Booker, Peter. *New York Fictions: Modernity, Postmodernity, the New Modern*. New York. Longman, 1996. Print.

Butler, Robert. *Contemporary African American Fiction: The Open Journey*. Plainsboro, N.J.: Associated University Presses, 1998. Print.

Byerman, Keith. *Remembering the Past in Contemporary African American Fiction*. Chapel Hill: University of North Carolina Press, 2005. Print.

Byrd, Rudolph P. "I Know What the Earth Says": Interview with William R. Ferris from *Southern Cultures* (2004). *The World Has Changed: Conservations with Alice Walker*. New York: New Press, 2010. 225–38. Print.

Carby, Hazel. "The Multicultural Wars." *Black Popular Culture*. Ed. Gina Dent. Seattle: Bay Press, 1992. 187–99. Print.

———. *Reconstructing Womanhood, Reconstructing Feminism: Writings on Black Women*. New York: Routledge, 1996. Print.

Christian, Barbara. *Black Feminist Criticism: Perspectives on Black Women Writers*. New York: Pergamon Press, 1985. Print.

———. *Everyday Use: Alice Walker*. New Brunswick, N.J.: Rutgers University Press, 1994. Print.

———, et al. *New Black Feminist Criticism 1985–2000*. Urbana: University of Illinois Press, 2007. Print.

Clay, William. "The Congressional Black Caucus Revolution." *The Politics of Race: African Americans and the Political System*. Ed. Theodore Reuter. New York: M. E. Sharpe, Inc., 1995. 199–211. Print.

Cochran, Carroll David. *The Color of Freedom: Race and Contemporary American Liberalism*. Albany: State University of New York Press, 1999. Print.

Collins, Patricia Hill. *Black Feminist Thought: Knowledge, Consciousness, and the Politics of Empowerment*. New York: Routledge, 2000. Print.

Cruse, Harold. *The Crisis of the Negro Intellectual: A Historical Analysis of the Failure of Black Leadership*. New York: New York Review of Books, 2005. Print.

Davis, Angela. "Black Nationalism: The Sixties and the Nineties." *Black Popular Culture*. Ed. Gina Dent. Seattle: Bay Press, 1992. 317–24. Print.

Dawson, Michael C. *Behind the Mule: Race and Class in African-American Politics.* Princeton, N.J.: Princeton University Press, 1994. Print.

———. "A Black Counterpublic? Economic Earthquakes, Racial Agendas(s), and Black Politics." *The Black Public Sphere Collective: A Public Culture Book.* Ed. Black Public Sphere Collective. Chicago: University of Chicago Press, 1995. 199–228. Print.

DeKoven, Marianne. *Utopia Limited: The Sixties and the Emergence of the Postmodern.* Durham, N.C.: Duke University Press, 2004. Print.

Dery, Mark. "Black to the Future: Interview with Samuel R. Delany, Greg Tate, and Tricia Rose." *Flame Wars: The Discourse of Cyberculture.* Ed. Mark Dery. Durham, N.C.: Duke University Press, 1994. 179–222. Print.

Dickson-Carr, Daryl. *African American Satire: The Sacredly Profane Novel.* Columbia: University of Missouri Press, 2001. Print.

Dixon, Melvin. *Ride Out the Wilderness: Geography and Identity in Afro-American Literature.* Champaign: University of Illinois Press, 1987. Print.

Dubey, Madhu. *Black Women Novelists in the Nationalist Aesthetic.* Bloomington: Indiana University Press, 1994. Print.

———. *Signs and Cities: Black Literary Postmodernism.* Chicago: University of Chicago Press, 2003. Print.

———. "South to a Very Old Place; Toni Morrison's Song of Solomon." *Mastering Western Texts: Essays on Literature and Society for A. N. Kaul.* Ed. Sambuda Sen. Delhi: Permanent Black, 2003. 71–90. Print.

Duvall, John N. *The Identifying Fictions of Toni Morrison: Modernist Authenticity and Postmodern Blackness.* New York: Palgrave, 2000. Print.

———. "Troping History: Modernist Residue in Jameson's Pastiche and Hutcheon's Parody." *Productive Postmodernism: Consuming Histories and Cultural Studies.* Ed. John N. Duvall. Albany: State University of New York, 2002. 1–22. Print.

Eisner, Allen Marc. *The American Political Economy: Institutional Evolution of Market and State.* New York: Routledge, 2011. Print.

Ellison, Ralph. *Invisible Man.* New York: Knopf, 2010. Print.

Emanuel, James. "Blackness Can: A Quest for Aesthetics." *The Black Aesthetic.* Ed. Addison Gayle Jr. Garden City, N.Y.: Doubleday, 1971. 195. Print.

Ewen, Stuart. *All Consuming Images: The Politics of Style in Contemporary Culture.* New York: Basic Books, 1988. Print.

Featherstone, Mike. *Consumer Culture and Postmodernism.* London: Sage Publications, 1991. Print.

Fendrich, James. *Ideal Citizens: The Legacy of the Civil Rights Movement.* Albany: State University of New York Press, 1993. Print.

Fokkema, Douwe Wessel. *Literary History, Modernism, and Postmodernism*. Amsterdam: J. Benjamins, 1984. Print.

Freedman, Carl. *Conversations with Samuel R. Delany*. Jackson: University Press of Mississippi, 2009. Print.

Gates, Henry Louis, Jr. *Loose Canons: Notes on the Culture Wars*. New York: Oxford University Press, 1992. Print.

Gilroy, Paul. *The Black Atlantic: Modernity and Double Consciousness*. Cambridge, Mass.: Harvard University Press, 1993. Print.

Gilyard, Keith. *Liberation Memories: The Rhetoric and Poetics of John Oliver Killens*. Detroit: Wayne State University Press, 2003. Print.

Goyal, Yogita. *Romance, Diaspora, and Black Atlantic Literature*. New York: Cambridge University Press, 2010. Print.

Graff, Gerald. "The Myth of the Postmodernist Breakthrough." *The Novel Today: Contemporary Writers on Modern Fiction*. Ed. Malcolm Bradbury. Manchester, U.K.: Manchester University Press, 1977. Print.

Graham, Lawrence Otis. *Our Kind of People: Inside America's Black Upper Class*. New York: HarperCollins, 1999. Print.

Gramsci, Antonio. "Hegemony." *Literary Theory: An Anthology*. Ed. Julie Rivkin and Michael Ryan. Oxford, U.K.: Blackwell, 1998. 673. Print.

Griffin, Farah Jasmine. *"Who Set You Flowin'?" The African-American Migration Narrative*. New York: Oxford University Press, 1995.

Gupta, Suman. *Globalization and Literature*. Cambridge, U.K.: Polity, 2009. Print.

Gysin, Fritz. "From Modernism to Postmodernism: Black Literature at the Crossroads." *The Cambridge Companion to the African American Novel*. Ed. Maryemma Graham. New York: Cambridge University Press, 2004. 139–55. Print.

Habermas, Jurgen. "Modernity—An Incomplete Project." *Postmodernism: A Reader*. Ed. Thomas Docherty. Oxford: Cambridge University Press, 1993. 98–109. Print.

Hakutani, Yoshinobu, and Robert Butler. *The City in African American Literature*. Cranbury, N.J.: Associated University Presses, 1995. Print.

Harper, Phillip Brian. "Extra-special Effects: Televisual Representation and the Claims of 'The Black Experience.'" *Living Color*, ed. Sasha Torres. 62–81.

———. *Framing the Margins: The Social Logic of Postmodern Culture*. New York: Oxford University Press, 1994. Print.

Harris, Joel Chandler. *The Complete Tales of Uncle Remus*. Boston: Houghton Mifflin, 2002. Print.

Harrison, Faye. *Outsider Within: Reworking Anthropology in the Global Age*. Champaign: University of Illinois Press, 2008. Print.

Harvey, David. *The Condition of Postmodernity: An Inquiry into the Origins of Cultural Change*. Oxford, U.K.: Blackwell, 1990. Print.

Hassan, Ihab. *The Dismemberment of Orpheus: Toward a Postmodern Literature.* 2nd ed. Madison: University of Wisconsin Press, 1992. Print.

Henderson, Mae, and E. Patrick Johnson. *Black Queer Studies: A Critical Anthology.* Durham, N.C.: Duke University Press, 2007. Print.

Hibbs, Douglas A. Jr. *The American Political Economy: Macroeconomics and Electoral Politics in the United States.* Cambridge, Mass.: Harvard University Press, 1987. Print.

Hoffman, Gerhard. *From Modernism to Postmodernism: Concepts and Strategies of Postmodern American Fiction.* New York: Rodopi B.V., 2005. Print.

Hogue, W. Lawrence. *The African American Male, Writing and Difference: A Polycentric Approach to African American Literature, Criticism, and History.* Albany: State University of New York Press, 2003. Print.

———. *Discourse and the Other: The Production of the Afro-American Text.* Durham, N.C.: Duke University Press, 1986. Print.

———. *Race, Modernity, Postmodernity: A History of People of Color Since the 1960s.* Albany: State University of New York Press, 1996. Print.

Holloway, Karla F. C. *Moorings & Metaphors: Figures of Culture and Gender in Black Women's Literature.* New Brunswick, N.J.: Rutgers University Press, 1992. Print.

Holt, Thomas C. "Afterword: Mapping the Black Public Sphere." *The Black Public Sphere Collective: A Public Culture Book.* Ed. Black Public Sphere Collective. Chicago: University of Chicago Press, 1995. 325–28. Print.

Holzman, Lois, and John R. Moss, eds. *Postmodern Psychologies, Societal Practice and Political Life.* New York: Routledge, 2000. Print.

hooks, bell. "The Chitlin Circuit: On Black Community." *Yearning,* 33–40. Print.

———. "Dialectically Down with the Critical Program." *Black Popular Culture.* Ed. Gina Dent. Seattle: Bay Press, 1992. 48–55. Print.

———. "The Politics of Radical Black Subjectivity." *Yearning,* 15–22. Print.

———. "Postmodern Blackness." *Yearning,* 23–32. Print.

———. *Where We Stand: Class Matters.* New York: Routledge, 2000. Print.

———. *Yearning: Race, Gender, and Cultural Politics.* Boston: South End Press, 1990. Print.

———, and Cornel West. *Breaking Bread: Insurgent Black Intellectual Life.* Boston: South End Press, 1991. Print.

Hove, Thomas. "Toni Morrison." *Postmodernism: The Key Figures.* Ed. Hans Burtens and Joseph Natoli. Malden, Mass.: Blackwell Publishers, 2002. 254–60. Print.

Hutcheon, Linda. *A Poetics of Postmodernism: History, Theory, Fiction.* New York: Routledge, 2000. Print.

Huyssen, Andreas. *After the Great Divide: Modernism, Mass Culture, Postmodernism.* Bloomington: Indiana University Press, 1986. Print.

Jackson, Lawrence. *The Indignant Generation: A Narrative History of African American Writers and Critics, 1934–1960*. Princeton: Princeton University Press, 2011. Print.

Jackson, Sandra, and Julie E. Moody-Freeman. *The Black Imagination, Science Fiction, Futurism and the Speculative*. New York: Peter Lang, 2011. Print.

Jacobs, Jane. *The Death and Life of Great American Cities*. New York: Modern Library, 1993. Print.

James, Stanlie Myrise, and Abena P. A. Busia, eds. *Theorizing Black Feminisms: The Visionary Pragmatism of Black Women*. New York. Routledge, 1993. Print.

——, Frances Smith Foster, and Beverly Guy-Sheftall, eds. *Still Brave: The Evolution of Black Women's Studies*. New York: Feminist Press, 2009. Print.

Jameson, Fredric. *Postmodernism: Or, the Cultural Logic of Late Capitalism*. Durham, N.C.: Duke University Press, 1991. Print.

Jarrett, Gene Andrew. *Deans and Truants: Race and Realism in African American Literature*. Philadelphia: University of Pennsylvania Press, 2007. Print.

——. *Representing the Race: A New Political History of African American Literature*. New York: New York University Press, 2011. Print.

——. "What Is Jim Crow?" *PMLA* 128.2 (2013): 388–90. Electronic.

Johnson, Charles. "The End of the Black American Narrative." *American Scholar,* 1 June 2008. Web. Accessed 5 March 2017.

Johnston, John. "*The Intuitionist* and *Pattern Recognition*: A Response to Lauren Berlant." *American Literary History* 20.4 (2008): 861–69. Electronic.

Joyce, Joyce Ann. *Warriors, Conjurers and Priests: Defining African-Centered Literary Criticism*. Chicago: Third World Press, 1994. Print.

Kariel, Henry. *The Desperate Politics of Postmodernism*. Amherst: University of Massachusetts Press, 1989. Print.

Katz, Tamar. "City Memory, City History: Urban Nostalgia, *The Colossus of New York,* and Late Twentieth-Century Historical Fiction." *Contemporary Literature* 51.4 (2012): 810–51. Electronic.

Kelley, Robin D. G. *Race Rebels: Culture, Politics, and the Black Working Class*. New York: Free Press, 1996. Print.

Kelley, William Melvin. *dem*. Minneapolis: Coffee House Press, 2000. Print.

Kelly, Erna. "A Matter of Focus: Men in the Margins of Alice Walker's Fiction." *Critical Essays on Alice Walker*. Ed. Ikenna Dieke. Westport, Conn.: Greenwood Press, 1999. Print.

Killens, John Oliver. *And Then We Heard Thunder*. New York: Knopf, 1962. Print.

——. *The Cotillion: Or, One Good Bull Is Half the Herd*. Minneapolis: Coffee House Press, 2002. Print.

——. *Youngblood*. New York: Trident Press, 1954. Print.

King, Debra Walker. *Deep Talk: Reading African American Literary Names*. Charlottesville: University Press of Virginia, 1998. Print.

Klotman, Phyllis. *Another Man Gone: The Black Runner in Afro-American Literature*. Port Washington, N.Y.: Kennikat Press, 1977. Print.

Laclau, Ernesto, and Chantal Mouffe. "Hegemony and Radical Democracy." *Hegemony and Socialist Strategy: Towards a Radical Democratic Politics*. Ed. Ernesto Laclau and Chantal Mouffe. New York. Verso, 2001. Print.

Landry, Bart. *The New Black Middle Class*. Berkeley: University of California Press, 1987. Print.

Lavender, Isiah. *Race in American Science Fiction*. Bloomington: Indiana University Press, 2011. Print.

Lefebvre, Henri. *The Production of Space*. Cambridge, U.K.: Blackwell, 1991. Print.

Lehman, Paul R. "The Development of the Black Psyche in the Writings of John Oliver Killens, 1916–1987." *Black Studies* 22 (2003): 131. Print.

Leonard, Elisabeth. "Race and Ethnicity in Science Fiction." *The Cambridge Companion to Science Fiction*. Ed. Edward James and Farah Mendlesohn. New York: Cambridge University Press, 2003. 253–63. Print.

Liggett, Helen. *Urban Encounters*. Minneapolis: University of Minnesota Press, 2003. Print.

Liggins, Saundra. "The Urban Gothic Vision of Colson Whitehead's *The Intuitionist*." *African American Review* 40.2 (2006): 359–69.

Lincoln, C. Eric, and Lawrence H. Mamiya. *The Black Church in the African American Experience*. Durham, N.C.: Duke University Press, 1990.

Lubiano, Wahneema. "Shuckin' Off the African-American Native Other: What's 'Po-Mo' Got to Do With It?" *Cultural Critique* 18 (1991): 149–86. Online.

Lyotard, Jean-François. *The Postmodern Condition: A Report on Knowledge*. Minneapolis: University of Minnesota Press, 1984. Print.

Macleod, Ken. "Politics and Science Fiction." *The Cambridge Companion to Science Fiction*. Ed. Edward James and Farah Mendlesohn. New York: Cambridge University Press, 2003. 230–40. Print.

Marable, Manning. *Beyond Black and White: Transforming African-American Politics*. London: Verso, 2009. [AU: 1995 in text] Print.

———, and Leith Mullings. "The Divided Mind of Black America: Race, Ideology and Politics in the Post–Civil Rights Era." *Race and Class* 36 (1994): 61–72. Electronic.

Massey, Doreen. "Double Articulation: A Place in the World." *Displacements: Cultural Identities in Question*. Ed. Angelika Bammer. Bloomington: Indiana University Press, 1994. 110–124. Print.

———. *Space, Place, and Gender.* Minneapolis: University of Minnesota Press, 1994. Print.

McDowell, Deborah. *"The Changing Same": Black Women's Literature, Criticism, and Theory.* Bloomington: Indiana University Press, 1995. Print.

———. "The Self In Bloom: Walker's *Meridian.*" *Alice Walker: Critical Perspectives Past and Present.* Ed. Henry Louis Gates and Anthony Appiah. New York: Amistad Press, 1993. Print.

McGowan, John. *Postmodernism and Its Critics.* Ithaca, N.Y.: Cornell University Press, 1991. Print.

McHale, Brian. *Postmodernist Fiction.* New York. Routledge, 1987. Print.

McKay, Nellie. "An Interview with Toni Morrison." *Contemporary Literature* 24.4 (1983): 413–29. Print.

McRobbie, Angela. *Postmodernism and Popular Culture.* New York: Routledge, 1994. Print.

Mercer, Kobena. *Welcome to the Jungle: New Positions in Black Cultural Studies.* New York: Routledge, 1994. Print.

Miller, Laura. "Going Up." *Salon,* 12 Jan. 1999, www.salon.com/1999/01/12/cov_si_12 int/. Accessed 30 October 2017.

Morrison, Toni. *Beloved.* New York: Knopf, 1987. Print.

———. *Jazz.* New York: Knopf, 1992. Print.

———. *Paradise.* New York: Knopf, 1998. Print.

———. *Remember: The Journey to School Integration.* Boston: Houghton Mifflin Co., 2004. Print.

———. *Sula.* New York: Vintage International, 2004. Print.

———. *Tar Baby.* New York: First Vintage International Books, 2004. [AU: 1981 in text] Print.

Mosley, Walter. "Black to the Future" *New York Times.* 1999: [AU: Need full date] 32–34. Print.

Mouffe, Chantal. "Radical Democracy: Modern or Postmodern?" *Universal Abandon? The Politics of Postmodernism.* Ed. Andrew Ross. Minneapolis: University of Minnesota Press, 1989. 31–45. Print.

Murray, Roland. "How the Conjure-Man Gets Busy: Cultural Nationalism, Masculinity, and Performativity." *Yale Journal of Criticism* 18.2 (2005): 299–321. Electronic.

Nadel, Alan. "Reading the Body: Alice Walker's *Meridian* and the Archeology of Self." *Modern Fiction Studies* 34.1 (1988): 55–68. Electronic. 25 April 2012.

Nelson, Alondra. "Future Texts." *Social Text* 20.2 (2002): 1–15. Electronic.

New, Michael. "'Nothing But A Man': Racial Identity and Musical Production in John Henry Days." *New Essays on the African American Novel: From Hurston and*

Ellison to Morrison and Whitehead. Ed. Lovalerie King and Linda F. Selzer. New York: Palgrave Macmillan, 2001. 241–58. Print.

Nicholson, Linda J. "Social Criticism without Philosophy: An Encounter between Feminism and Postmodernism." *Feminism/Postmodernism.* Ed. Linda Nicholson. New York: Routledge, 1990. 19–38. Print.

Nielsen, Aldon Lynn. *Black Chant: Languages of African-American Postmodernism.* Cambridge, U.K.: Cambridge University Press, 1997. Print.

Norman, Brian. *Neo-segregation Narratives: Jim Crow in Post–Civil Rights American Literature.* Athens: University of Georgia Press, 2010. Print.

Omi, Michael, and Howard Winant. *Racial Formation in the United States: From the 1960s to the 1980s.* New York: Routledge, 1986. Print.

Ongiri, Amy Abugo. *Spectacular Blackness: The Cultural Politics of the Black Power Movement and the Search for a Black Aesthetic.* Charlottesville: University of Virginia Press, 2010.

Page, Phillip. *Reclaiming Community in Contemporary African American Fiction.* Jackson: University Press of Mississippi, 1999. Print.

Pauley, Garth. *The Modern Presidency and Civil Rights: Rhetoric on Race from Roosevelt to Nixon.* College Station: Texas A&M University Press, 2001. Print.

Peach, Linden. *Toni Morrison.* New York: St. Martin's Press, 2000. Print.

Pifer, Lynn. "Coming to Voice in Alice Walker's *Meridian*: Speaking Out for the Revolution." *African American Review* 26.1 (1992): 77–88. Electronic.

Pinkney, Alphonso. *The Myth of Black Progress.* New York: Cambridge University Press, 1984. Print.

Prince, Valerie Sweeney. *Burnin' Down the House: Home in African American Literature.* New York: Columbia University Press, 2005. Print.

Pryse, Marjorie, and Hortense J. Spillers, eds. *Conjuring: Black Women, Fiction, and Literary Tradition.* Bloomington. Indiana University Press, 1985. Print.

Quall, Lauren L. *Dark Language: Post-rebellion Fiction: The Continued Journey of African American Literature.* Lanham, Md.: University Press of America, 2009. Print.

Ramsey, William. "An End of Southern History: The Down-Home Quest of Toni Morrison and Colson Whitehead." *African American Review* 41.4 (2007): 769–85. Electronic.

Reed, Adolph. *Stirrings in the Jug: Black Politics in the Post-Segregation Era.* Minneapolis: University of Minnesota Press, 1999. Print.

Reed, Ishmael. *Mumbo Jumbo.* Garden City, N.Y.: Doubleday, 1972. Print.

Reed, Thomas Vernon. *The Art of Protest: Culture and Activism from the Civil Rights Movement to the Streets of Seattle.* Minneapolis: University of Minnesota Press, 2005. Print.

Ross, Marlon, and Xiomara Santamarina. "What Was African American Literature?" *PMLA* 128.2 (2013): 386–408. Electronic.

Rueter, Theodore. *The Politics of Race: African Americans and the Political System.* New York: M. E. Sharpe, Inc. Print.

Schulman, Bruce J. *The Seventies: The Great Shift in American Culture, Society, and Politics.* New York: Free Press, 2001. Print.

Schur, Richard. "Locating Paradise in the Post-Civil Rights Era: Toni Morrison and Critical Race Theory." *Contemporary Literature* 45.2 (2004): 276–99. Electronic.

Selzer, Linda. "New Eclecticism: An Interview with Colson Whitehead." *Callaloo* 31.2 (2008): 393–401. Electronic.

Shelby, Tommie. *We Who Are Dark: The Philosophical Foundations of Black Solidarity.* Cambridge, Mass.: Harvard University Press, 2005. Print.

Skrentny, John. *The Minority Rights Revolution.* Cambridge, Mass.: Harvard University Press, 2002. Print.

Smethurst, James. "The Black Arts Movement." *A Companion to African American Literature.* Malden, Mass.: Blackwell, 2010. 302–14. Print.

Smith, Jeanne Rosier. *Writing Tricksters: Mythic Gambols in American Ethnic Literature.* Los Angeles: University of California Press, 1997. Print.

Smith, Valerie. *Self-Discovery and Authority in Afro-American Narrative.* Cambridge, Mass.: Harvard University Press, 1987. Print.

Standley, Anne. "The Role of Black Women in the Civil Rights Movement." *Women in the Civil Rights Movement: Trailblazers and Torchbearers 1941–1965.* Ed. Vicki L. Crawford et al. Bloomington: Indiana University Press, 1990. 183–202. Print.

Stein, Karen. *Reading, Learning, Teaching Toni Morrison.* New York: Peter Lang, 2009. Print.

Stephanson, Anders. "Regarding Postmodernism—A Conversation with Fredric Jameson." *Universal Abandon? The Politics of Postmodernism.* Ed. Andrew Ross. Minneapolis: University of Minnesota Press, 1989. 3–30. Print.

Tally, Justine. *The Story of Jazz: Toni Morrison Dialogic Imagination.* Hamburg: Lit, 2001. Print.

Tate, Claudia. "Interview with Claudia Tate from Black Women Writers at Work (1983)." *The World Has Changed: Conversations with Alice Walker.* Ed. Rudolph Byrd. New York: New Press, 2010. Print.

———. *Psychoanalysis and Black Novels: Desire and the Protocols of Race.* New York: Oxford University Press, 1998. Print.

Thomas, Kendall. "Ain't Nothin' Like the Real Thing." *Representing Black Men.* Ed. Marcellus Blount and George P. Cunningham. New York: Routledge, 1996. 55–72. Print.

Thomas, Michael. *Man Gone Down: A Novel.* New York: Grove Press, 2007. Print.

Thomas, Sheree R. *Dark Matter: A Century of Speculative Fiction from the African Diaspora*. New York: Warner, 2001. Print.

Torres, Sasha, ed. *Living Color: Race and Television in the United States*. Durham, N.C.: Duke University Press, 1998.

Touré. *Who's Afraid of Post-blackness? What It Means to Be Black Now*. New York: Free Press, 2012. Print.

Tucker, Jeffrey Allen. "African American Science Fiction." *A Companion to African American Literature*. Ed. Gene Andrew Jarrett. Malden, Mass.: Blackwell, 2010. 360–75. Print.

Van Deburg, William L. *New Day in Babylon: The Black Power Movement and American Culture, 1965–1975*. Chicago: University of Chicago Press, 1992. Print.

Wald, Alan. *Trinity of Passion: The Literary Left and the Antifascist Crusade*. Chapel Hill: University of North Carolina Press, 2007.

Walker, Alice. *Color Purple*. New York: Washington Square Press, 1983. Print.

———. *In Search of Our Mothers' Gardens: Womanist Prose by Alice Walker*. New York: Harcourt Brace Jovanovich, 1986. Print.

———. *Meridian*. New York: Harcourt Brace Jovanovich, 1976. Print.

———. *The Temple of My Familiar*. New York: Harcourt Brass Jovanovich, 1989. Print.

Walton, Hanes, Jr. *African American Power and Politics: The Political Context Variable*. New York: Columbia University Press, 1997. Print.

Warren, Kenneth W. *What Was African American Literature?* Cambridge, Mass.: Harvard University Press, 2011. Print.

Washington, Robert. *The Ideologies of African American Literature: From the Harlem Renaissance to the Black Nationalist Revolt*. Lanham, Md.: Rowman and Littlefield, Inc., 2001. Print.

Watkins, Craig S. "Black Youth and the Ironies of Capitalism." *Representing: Hip Hop Culture and the Production of Black Cinema*. Chicago: University of Chicago Press, 1998. 50–76. Print.

Weir, Margaret. "From Equal Opportunity to the New Social Contract: Race and the Politics of the American Underclass." *Racism, the City, and the State*, Ed. Malcolm Cross and Michael Keith. New York: Routledge, 1993. 93–107. Print.

Welch, Sharon. "An Ethic of Solidarity and Difference." *Postmodernism, Feminism, and Cultural Politics: Redrawing Educational Boundaries*. Ed. Henry Giroux. Albany: State University of New York Press, 1991. Print.

West, Cornel. "Black Culture and Postmodernism." *A Postmodern Reader*. Ed. Joseph Natoli and Linda Hutcheon. Albany: State University of New York Press, 1993. 390–97. Print.

———. "Black Strivings in a Twilight Civilization." *The Cornel West Reader*. New York: Basic Books, 1999. 87–118. Print.

———. "The New Cultural Politics of Difference." *Out There: Marginalization and Contemporary Cultures.* Ed. Russell Ferguson et al. Cambridge, Mass.: MIT Press, 1992. 19–36. Print.

———. "Postmodernity and Afro-America." *Prophetic Fragments: Illuminations of the Crisis in American Religion and Culture.* Trenton, N.J.: Eerdmans, 1988. 168–70. Print.

———. and Henry Louis Gates, Jr. *The Future of the Race.* New York: A. A. Knopf, 1996. Print.

White, Evelyn C. *Alice Walker: A Life.* New York. W. W. Norton & Co., 2004. Print.

Whitehead, Colson. *The Colossus of New York: A City in Thirteen Parts.* New York: Doubleday, 2003. Print.

———. *The Intuitionist.* New York. Anchor Books, 1999. Print.

———. *John Henry Days: A Novel.* New York: Doubleday, 2001. Print.

Willentz, Gay. *Binding Cultures: Black Women in Africa and the Diaspora.* Bloomington. Indiana University Press, 1992. Print.

Willis, Susan. *Specifying: Black Women Writing the American Experience.* Madison: University of Wisconsin Press, 1987. Print.

Winant, Howard. "Postmodern Racial Politics in the United States: Difference and Inequality." *The Politics of Race: African Americans and the Political System.* Ed. Theodore Reuter. New York: M. E. Sharpe, Inc., 1995. 55–70. Print.

Winchell, Donna. *Alice Walker.* New York. Twayne Publishers, 1992. Print.

Yeatman, Anna. *Postmodern Revisionings of the Political.* New York. Routledge, 1994. Print.

INDEX

capitalism, 15, 89–90, 114, 173; industrial, 54, 63; late, 65, 72, 83, 151

Carby, Hazel, 71–72

Christian, Barbara, 20, 72

City in African American Literature, The (Hakutani and R. Butler), 45

"City Memory, City History" (Katz), 33

Cochran, David, 11–12

Collins, Patricia Hill, 20, 189n8

Color Purple, The (Walker), 71

"Coming to Voice in Alice Walker's *Meridian:* Speaking Out for the Revolution" (Pifer), 92

communities, black, 8, 135, 187n1; challenges of 19–20; social commitment in, 73–74

Condition of Postmodernity, The: An Inquiry into the Origins of Cultural Change (Harvey), 66

Contemporary African American Fiction: The Open Journey (R. Butler), 142

Cotillion, The (Killens), characters in: Ann Brasswork in, 105; Ben Ali Lumumba in, 22, 101; Beverly Brap-bap in, 124–25, 128–29, 133, 134; Billy "Bad Mouth" Williams in, 120; Black and Beautiful Burlesque (BBB) in, 123; Brenda Brasswork in, 118; Café Uptown Society in, 111; Daphne Lovejoy in, 102, 113, 119, 120, 125–27; Daphne Lovejoy and the Brooklyn Memorial Episcopal Cathedral in, 123–24; Father Madison Mayfair in, 123, 124; Father Thatcher in, 123; Femme Fatales in, 102, 104, 105, 124, 128–29, 133; group constraints on Lumumba in, 114–15; Johnny Carson and Jomo Mamadou Zero the Third episode in, 103; Kool Krazy Kats (KKK) in, 111; Lumumba in, 114–15, 122–23, 129–30, 136; Lumumba at the Grand Cotillion in, 119, 133, 163; Lumumba's inclination toward "acting" black in, 115; Lumumba's participation in bourgeois activities in, 118–19; Lumum-

ba's postmodern aesthetic in, 132–33; Lumumba as a purveyor of culture in, 116–17; Lumumba and Yoruba and the exploitation embodied in the Femme Fatales debutante process, 117–18; Matthew Lovejoy in, 115, 120–21, 133; Mr. Shyler in, 115–16; Phil Potts in, 125–26; Way-Out Restaurant in, 111–12; Yoruba Lovejoy in, 22, 118, 125–27, 129–30, 136; Yoruba at the Grand Cotillion and the activation of the postmodern in, 130–31; Yoruba's search for self-identity in, 112–13, 130

Cotillion, The (Killens), themes in, 5, 10, 101–2; black nationalism and black nationalist discourse, 101, 120–25; black socialization, 123; black solidarity, 122–23; black subjectivity, 108; class-driven politics, 111–19; commodification of blackness, 116; the cotillion metaphor and the debutante process, 104; critical focus of on class, 109; critique of Anglocentric education, 122; critique of class stratification and division, 22, 134–35; cultural nationalism and black cultural production, 109, 124–25; the folly of black middle-class imitators of white people, 109–10; gender and its ramifications, 125–27; open-ended structure of, 102–3; polemics, 108–11; rejection of totalizing narratives, 131–32; resistance to consensus, 127–35; satirical design of the text, 110; satirizing of constitutional protections, 104–5; trickster motif, 119, 138

countermodernity, 17

critical and cultural paradigms, African American, 18–23

Cruse, Harold, 187n1

culture: cultural difference, 151; cultural heritage, 20; folk cultural spirit, 189–90n2. *See also* black culture; literary culture, African American

Hutcheon, Linda, 13–14, 108; on the "insider-outsider" position, 132; view of the postmodern, 91

Huyssen, Andreas, 145

Ideal Citizens: The Legacy of the Civil Rights Movement (Friedrich), 73

identity: collective notions of, 20; generalization of black identity, 108; monolithic identity formations, 21; as a process, 19–20

Ideologies of African American Literature, The: From the Harlem Renaissance to the Black Nationalist Revolt (Washington), 73

Intuitionist, The (Whitehead), characters in, 5; Arbergast in, 27; Ben Urich in, 28–29, 42, 60; Chuck Gould in, 26, 46, 53; confrontation of Lila Mae and Pompey in, 37–40; Elisha Graves Otis in, 25; Frank Chancre in, 28, 36, 38, 45, 60; Frederick Gorse in, 27; Grady, Jr. in, 50; Holt in, 37–38; James Fulton in, 21, 25, 43–44; James Fulton as Lila Mae's quasi-mentor in, 54–55; James Fulton's transformation in, 55–56; Jim and John in, 47–48; Lila Mae in, 21, 24–25, 37, 43–44, 52, 53, 56–57, 85; Lila Mae's co-opting of the othering process in, 62; Lila Mae's critique of Empiricism in, 45–46; Lila Mae's cultural narrative in, 35–36; Lila Mae's decision to attend the Institute for Vertical Transport, 35; Lila Mae's dismissive view of Pompey in, 40, 53; Lila Mae's fixation on Fulton's genius, 28–29; Lila Mae's range of worldviews in, 57–61; Marie Claire Rogers in, 51, 56–57, 60; Mr. Reed in, 37, 48–49, 52, 57; Ms. Parker in, 34; Oliver Lever in, 28, 36, 38, 52; Pompey in, 34, 37–40, 43–44, 189n4; Pompey's rant in, 38; Professor McKean and the "Dilemma of the Phantom Passenger" in, 27–28; Raymond Coombs in, 40–43, 43–44

Intuitionist, The (Whitehead), themes in: the concept of "interminable progress," 34–35; on the constriction of discourse by higher education, 27–28; critique of ambition, 53–54, 61; the cultural narrative of diligence, 35–36; the exploitation of Lila Mae, 36–37, 41–42, 48–49; the "integration metropolis," 43–49; Intuitionists versus Empiricists, 25, 27, 46; the northern city and integration, 44–45; the notion of owning/ownership, 38–39; the postmodern unraveling of cultural notions, 52–63; significant postmodern elements of, 25–26; tokenism, identity formation, and the threat of co-optation facing black workers, 24; trickster motif, 41, 55; the trope of the detective with superior deductive reasoning, 28–29; vacillating tone of, 26; women and the politics of roles, 49–52

Invisible Man (Ellison), 184, 188n8; Jim Trueblood in, 189n9

Jacobs, Jane, 152

Jameson, Fredric, 13

Jarrett, Gene Andrew, 6, 29, 73

Jazz (Morrison), 147

Jim Crow, 6–10

John Henry Days (Whitehead), 33

Johnson, Charles, 8

Johnson, E. Patrick, 20–21

Johnston, John, 52

Jones, Gayl, 106

Journal of Blacks in Higher Education, 108–9

Joyce, Joyce Ann, 108

Kariel, Henry, 99

Katz, Tamar, 33

Kelly, Erna, 190n5

Killens, John Oliver, 5

King, Debra Walker, 70

Klotman Phyllis, 142–43

Lefebvre, Henri, 144
liberalism, post–civil rights, 107
literary culture, African American, 106–7
literature, African American, 6–13, 31,
47, 70, 144, 145, 188n1; and the African
American culture-work narrative, 106;
exploration of black social movements
in, 183; historical insights of, 185; the
journey motif in, 189, postmodern, 15,
17–18, 144; and the post-racial moment
in America, 183–84 sociopolitical value
of, 73; trickster motifs in, 41, 55, 119, 138,
189n10
"Locating *Paradise* in the Post-Civil Rights
Era: Toni Morrison and Critical Race
Theory" (Schur), 146–47
Lubiano, Wahneema, 13; on post-blackness,
183–84; on static constructions, 14
Lyotard, Jean François, 12, 127–28; on the
sublime, 191n4

Man Gone Down (M. Thomas), 184–85
Marable, Manning, 107
Marshall, Paule, 70
Massey, Doreen, 146
McDowell, Deborah, 71
McGowan, John, 12; on freedom, 187n3
McHale, Brian, 103–4, 188–89n3
McRobbie, Angela, 113
Mercer, Kobena, 20
Meridian (Walker), characters in: Anne (not
Anne-Marion Coles) in, 84; Anne-Marion
Coles in, 65, 76, 76–78, 89–90, 94;
Anne-Marion's loathing of capitalism
in, 90; Fast Mary in, 88; Louvine in, 88;
"Marlene O'Shay" circus exhibit in, 88,
93; Meridian Hill in, 22, 64–65, 67–68,
99, 136; Meridian's bizarre illness in,
93–94; Meridian's encounter with Lynne
Rabinowitz in, 94–95; Meridian's exis-
tential crisis in, 83; Meridian's politics
in, 77–78; Meridian's postmodern prac-

tice in, 91, 97; Meridian's priorities in,
90; Meridian's restless questioning in,
91–100; Meridian's spirituality in, 96–97;
Meridian's transformations in, 85; Miss
Winter in, 88–89; Tommy Odds in, 81;
Truman Held in, 65, 67–68, 78–81, 92,
93, 99, 136; Truman Held and Lynne Rabinowitz in, 81–83; Truman's hedonism in,
80, 99; Wile Chile in, 88
Meridian (Walker), themes in, 5, 9, 10,
21–22; black cultural politics, 100; black
struggle and lived reality, 75–83; the complexities of sacrifice, 95–96; the ethos of
black struggle, 76–77; the impact of the
civil rights movement on budding revolutionaries, 83–87; importance of Saxon
College, 75–76; interrogation of the alienating nature of the civil rights movement,
71, 91–92, 98; "Pilgrimage" chapter in
and the limits of political influence, 68–
69; as a postmodernist novel, 65–66, 98–
100; the psychology behind revolutionary
practice, 98–99; "The Recurring Dream"
chapter of, 67–68; reflections on the
decade of the 1960s, 97–98; southern patriarchal ethos, 88; subversion of power,
66–67; tensions of postmodern critical
reflection among movement activists,
94–95; use of transitions, 67–68; women
and the civil rights movement, 87–90
"*Meridian*: Alice Walker's Critique of Revolution" (Stein), 74
*Modern Presidency and Civil Rights, The:
Rhetoric on Race from Roosevelt to Nixon*
(Pauley), 73
modernity/modernism: contribution of
racial others to, 28; high modernism,
145; late modernity, 17; urban modernity,
51–52
Morrison, Toni, 5, 9, 70, 87, 143; aesthetics
of, 160; historiography and modernity in
her work, 146–48

Mulling, Leigh, 107
multiculturalism, 107
Mumbo Jumbo (I. Reed), 6
Murray, Rolland, 110
"Myth of the Postmodernist Breakthrough"
(Graff), 115

Nadel, Alan, 83
nationalism, black, 101, 107, 109, 120–25;
legacy of, 110–11
nationalism, cultural, 112, 187n1; and black
cultural production, 124–25
Naylor, Gloria, 70, 87, 143
Nelson, Alondra, 30, 31
*Neo-segregation Narratives: Jim Crow in
Post-Civil Rights American Literature* (Norman), 32
Norman, Brian, 32
novelists, African American, 2–3; and the
discourse on postmodern black culture,
3–4; women novelists, 20

Omi, Michael, 187n1
Ongiri, Amy, 107–8
oppositional gaze, the, 12
Origins of Postmodernity, The (Anderson),
12–13

Paradise (Morrison), 147
patriarchy, 19, 35, 165
Pauley, Garth, 73
Philadelphia Negro, The (Du Bois), 162
Pifer, Lynn, 92
*Political Machines: Governing a Technological
Society* (Barry), 61
politics: American, 12; black church politics, 191n5; black cultural politics, 11–12,
15, 100; critique of politics that marginalize the functions of individuals in social
contexts, 17–18; ideological politics operative in the concept of tradition, 190n4;
postmodern cultural politics, 64
post-blackness, 183–84

post-Marxism, 17
"Postmodern Blackness" (hooks), 182
*Postmodern Condition, The: A Report on
Knowledge* (Lyotard), 127, 191n4
Postmodern Revisionings of the Political (Yeatman), 168
postmodernism, 2–4, 91, 144; and the demystification of class stratification, 4–5;
and history, 188n6; the interrogative posture and postmodern cultural politics, 4;
postmodern defamilarization, 19. *See also*
feminism, postmodern; postmodernism,
black
postmodernism, black, 5, 184; gender and
sexuality issues within, 20–21; and historical insight, 13–18
Postmodernism and Its Critics (McGowan), 12
Postmodernism and Popular Culture (McRobbie), 113
Postmodernist Fiction (McHale), 103–4
Pryse, Marjorie, 70
*Psychoanalysis and Black Novels: Desire and
Protocols of Race* (Tate), 69–70

Quall, Loren, 144

*Race, Modernity, Postmodernity: A History of
People of Color Since the 1960s* (Hogue),
42, 147
Racial Formation in the United States (Omi
and Winant), 187n1
Ramsey, William, 33
"Reading the Body: Alice Walker's *Meridian*
and the Archeology of Self" (Nadel), 83
*Reconstructing Womanhood, Reconstruct-
ing Feminism: Writings on Black Women*
(Carby), 71–72
Reed, Adolph, 11
Reed, Ishmael, 6, 31, 106
reflexivity/critical reflection, difference be-
tween, 190n6
Remember: The Journey to School Integration
(Morrison), 146